The Poetry of

Louise Glück

Daniel Morris

The Poetry of Louise Glück

A Thematic Introduction

University of Missouri Press
Columbia

University of Missouri Press, Columbia, Missouri 65211
Printed and bound in the United States of America

First paperback printing, 2020

Library of Congress Cataloging-in-Publication Data

Morris, Daniel, 1962–
The poetry of Louise Glück : a thematic introduction / Daniel Morris.
p. cm.
Summary: "Explores Glück's utilization of masks of characters from history, the Bible, and fairy tales, discussing the persistent themes and transitional tone of her poetry through close reading of her early work, Firstborn; through the book-length sequences Ararat, Meadowlands, and The Wild Iris; to her latest, including Vita Nova and Averno"—Provided by publisher.
Includes bibliographical references and index.
ISBN: 978-0-8262-1693-9 (hard cover : alk. paper)
ISBN: 978-0-8262-2238-1 (paperback : alk. paper)
1. Glück, Louise, 1943—Criticism and interpretation. I. Title.
PS3557.L8Z75 2006
811'.54—dc22

2006024591

∞™ This paper meets the requirements of the American National Standard for Permanence of Paper for Printed Library Materials, Z39.48, 1984.

Designer: Stephanie Foley
Typesetter: *foleydesign*
Typefaces: Baskerville and Vladimir Script

For Joy, Isaac, Aaron, and Hannah

Contents

Acknowledgments

I want to thank the several kind persons who read portions of this book in draft, tentative or final, or who encouraged me in other ways. At Purdue, Ann Astell and Wendy Stallard Flory deserve enormous credit for their close attention to style and substance throughout the manuscript. Alan Berger gave the project initial support. Ethan Goffman provided important editorial help. I am grateful to Louise Glück for generously allowing me to quote from her poems and essays. At the University of Missouri Press, I am grateful to two anonymous readers whose responses to my manuscript were filled with useful advice for revision. I cannot express enough gratitude to Clair Willcox, Jane Lago, and Beverly Jarrett for believing in the book and seeing it to press in such a timely fashion. Pippa Letsky did an extraordinary job copyediting the manuscript. My greatest debt, however, goes to my wife, Joy, and to our three blessings, Isaac, Aaron, and Hannah, who make every day special.

D.M.

List of Abbreviations

The following primary works by Louise Glück will appear in the text with an identifying abbreviation and page number.

AR	*Ararat*
AV	*Averno*
DF	*Descending Figure*
F	*Firstborn*
FFB	*The First Four Books of Poems: Firstborn, The House on Marshland, Descending Figure, The Triumph of Achilles*
HM	*The House on Marshland*
M	*Meadowlands*
PT	*Proofs & Theories: Essays on Poetry*
SA	*The Seven Ages*
TA	*The Triumph of Achilles*
WI	*The Wild Iris*
VN	*Vita Nova*

The Poetry of
Louise Glück

Introduction

Considered among America's foremost contemporary lyric poets, by many critics as well as ordinary readers, Louise Glück has identified with a variety of rhetorical styles other than the traditional lyric poem, which remains her forte. Her individual poems are best read in the context of a book-length collection of lyrics, spoken by competing voices in an open, dialogic relationship, or in a sequence that offers them a narrative dimension. Her poems range from the persona poem to blunt confessionalism to dialog to a kind of mock epic that, like Joyce's *Ulysses,* regards the author's life, however ironized, through a Homeric template. Because she composes her poetry from a mosaic of multicultural resources, Glück has appealed to critics representing diverse, often diametrically opposed communities of interpretation.

Championed by formalist critics such as Helen Vendler for writing lyrics "of high assertion . . . as from the Delphic tripod" that give "not a voice of social prophecy, but of spiritual prophecy—a tone that not many women had the courage to claim," Glück has nonetheless proved equally relevant to radical philosophical discussions that include intertextuality, French feminism, and Lacanian psychoanalytic theory. In the online journal *Postmodern Culture,* for example, Eric Selinger reads *Ararat* through the lens of Julia Kristeva's theory of love, as resting on a foundation of primary identification with the "imaginary father." In a reading of Glück's poem "All Hallows" (HM), on the other hand, Diane Bonds offers a feminist critique of Lacan's association of language acquisition with a woman's disavowal of the "presymbolic" communication that is said to exist between mother and unborn child. Bonds explores Glück's concern with the psychic cost involved in developing symbolic meanings in nature writings that switch registers from the literal to the figurative. In a dissertation from 2000, Margaret Ann Gordon associates Glück with ecofeminism, a poetics "grounded in the biological, psychological, and spiritual experience of being a woman—a daughter, a sister, a lover, and a mother—in late-twentieth-century America." We may dismiss these scholars as over-reaching, or deride them for trying to fit Glück's eclectic poems into fashionable paradigms. But we should consider it significant that Glück's work lends itself so well to readings that often come to differing conclusions about how, in her poetics, she addresses fundamental issues such as feminism, patriarchy, maternity, psychoanalysis, nature, and most of all, language, which in her case is a medium that pivots between candor and disguise.[1]

Critics and scholars may disagree on how to interpret her work, but it is becoming clear that Louise Elisabeth Glück is a major voice in contemporary American poetry. Born in New York City in 1943, and raised on Long Island, she has published eleven volumes of poetry ranging from ***Firstborn*** (1968) to ***Averno*** (2006), and an award-winning collection of essays ***Proofs & Theories*** (1994). A chancellor to the American Academy of Poets and judge of the Yale Younger Poets series, she has received virtually every national award for American poetry, including the Pulitzer Prize for ***The Wild Iris*** (1992), the National Book Critics Circle Award for ***The Triumph of Achilles*** (1985), and most recently, the Bollingen Prize for ***The Seven Ages.*** In August 2003, she was named to succeed Billy Collins as the twelfth poet laureate of the United States.

Awards, honorary degrees, and a position at Yale, all merely reflect the revered place she holds in contemporary American letters. Glück has been praised in literary journals and in newspaper reviews for more than thirty years. This present study, however, marks the first publication of a single-authored and comprehensive treatment of her persistent themes (desire, hunger, trauma, survival, commentary, autobiography, nature, spiritual witnessing), and a close reading of her major book-length sequences from the 1990s. These are ***Ararat, Meadowlands,*** and ***The Wild Iris,*** all highly ambitious, innovative, and complex attempts to analyze the authorial self via central metaphors more or less sustained through the entire volume. The present study also offers a chapter on ***The House on Marshland*** (1975), Glück's second book, which, through its revision of Romanticism and nature poetry, becomes a strong lead-in to the later book-length sequences.

Both a study in how poems may be read as a form of commentary on the meanings of great literature and myth as well as a revision of a poet's own

1. Helen Vendler, ***Soul Says: On Recent Poetry*** (Cambridge, Mass.: Harvard University Press, 1995), 16; Eric Selinger, "'It Meant I Loved': Louise Glück's ***Ararat,***" ***Postmodern Culture*** 3.3 (May 1993): 7; Diane S. Bonds, "Entering Language in Louise Glück's 'The House on Marshland': A Feminist Reading," ***Contemporary Literature*** 31.1 (1990): 58–75; Margaret Ann Gordon, "Reconceiving the Sacred: Louise Glück and Postmodern Spirituality" (Ph.D. diss., University of Mississippi, 2000).

prior writings, this book emphasizes Glück's irreverent attitude toward the canons of literature, scripture, and myth, an attitude through which she at once expresses herself and deflects her autobiographical impulse. This study demonstrates how the author creates personal narratives of public significance, using the masks of legendary characters from the Bible (Moses), from history (Joan of Arc), from myths of the origins of poetry as based in loss (Orpheus and Eurydice), and from fairy tales (Gretel). Her position as a mystic poet—with an ambivalent relationship to religious discourse that verges on Gnosticism as well as one that is in line with the ancient rabbinic tradition of reading scripture known as midrash—has not been previously discussed.[2]

Given Glück's ecumenical relationship to traditions, her mutable stylistics, and the fact that her career now stretches over five decades from 1968 to 2006 and over eleven volumes of poetry, the issue of how to divide and organize a comprehensive study of her work imposed both difficulties and some intriguing possibilities. The most straightforward of the possibilities would have been to interpret the overall trajectory of the poet's career, perhaps even book by book. Robert Hass, James Longenbach, Charles Berger, and Eric Selinger have in fact discussed her books as poetic sequences, so that each volume is interpreted to be greater than the sum of its lyric parts. They have shown how each book deals with traumatic incidents or life-cycle events, most often concerning the author's profoundly ambivalent relationship to other family members, to lovers, or to her natural surroundings.[3]

A book-by-book sketch of the author's oeuvre might read something like the following. The first book, ***Firstborn,*** represents the speaker in a gloomy, even diseased landscape ("The crocus spreads like cancer," in "Easter Season," FFB 46) in which she, through situations more nakedly autobiographical than in later volumes, responds to a world of brutal relationships with bitterness, disappointment, and disgust at how she is treated by lovers, doctors, and family

2. Only Liz Rosenberg's brief mention of the "unexpected Jewish humor of poet-as-philosopher," whose comedy is based on interrogating cultural pieties and tired myths, may begin to suggest something of Glück's flexible relationship to Jewish tradition and to the literary canon. Rosenberg quotes the following lines from "Winter Morning" (TA) to make her point: "Today, when I woke up, I asked myself / why did Christ die? Who knows / the meaning of such questions?" Liz Rosenberg, "Geckos, Porch Lights, and Sighing Gardens," *New York Times Book Review,* December 22, 1985, 22–23.

3. Robert Hass, dust jacket commentary, *Vita Nova;* James Longenbach, "Poetry in Review," *Yale Review* 84.4 (October 1996): 158–69; Charles Berger, "Poetry Chronicle: Amy Clampitt, Louise Glück, Mark Strand," and Selinger, "'It Meant I Loved.'"

members. A poem about an abortion, entitled "The Wound" (F), symbolizes the grim nature of the poet's world. In her first book, Glück's topics are morbid, but her style is pyrotechnical, at times over the top. Her elevated idiom, clotted syntax, internal rhyming and punning resemble the intense poetics of Hart Crane, or the early Robert Lowell of "The Quaker Graveyard in Nantucket." In "Early December in Croton-on-Hudson" (F), for example, she writes:

> Spiked sun. The Hudson's
> Whittled down by ice.
> I hear the bone dice
> Of blown gravel clicking. Bone-
> pale, the recent snow
> Fastens like fur to the river. (FFB 17)

Critics have generally considered *The House on Marshland* in both sound and sense to be the poet's breakthrough volume, in terms of the discovery of a distinctive voice. In the *New York Times* in 1975, Helen Vendler described the thirty-two-year-old poet as a "new species of poet."[4] If *Firstborn* is focused on abortion, broken love relationships, and a diseased landscape, then *The House on Marshland* is a book about maternity and a human world filled with life. Perhaps the fact that Glück's son, Noah, was born in 1973 influenced the author's focus. In spite of the emphasis on birth-giving and on imagery that critics have described as Edenlike, the number of poems dealing with harvests suggests the author's awareness of mortality, of the loss of innocence, as well as the exchange of lived reality for its reflection in the constructed realm of poetry.

Biblical creation myths—and the pain of consciousness that stems from the author's fear of desertion by husband, son, and sibling—are among the obsessive themes of *Descending Figure* (1980), as are poems of death and dying children. Perhaps because Glück herself was now the mother of a young child, her fears of losing that child became transformed into controversial lyrics such as "The Drowned Children" (DF), in which the author, rather matter-of-factly, describes the gradual process of the dissolution and silencing of the anonymous children (referred to only as "they") into an icy pond, metaphorized as a sinister (drowning) and yet maternal (lifting) figure that "lifts them in its manifold dark arms." It is "natural that they should drown," she writes in "The Drowned Children" (FFB 105). Besides this risky poem,

4. Helen Vendler, "Review of *The House on Marshland*," *New York Times Book Review*, April 6, 1975, 37.

in which a maternal figure either is imagined as indifferent to the loss of children or else is represented as herself the source of the children's suffocation through the personification of the icy pond, the volume also includes lyrics that call up memories of Glück's sister who died at birth. The poem "Descending Figure" (DF), as James Robinson has written, "is a child's view, in three parts, of a dead sister—a figure descending, a sick child in a painting in the Rijksmuseum, and the speaker's dead sister."[5]

The Triumph of Achilles is a pivotal work. It deals with typical lyric themes, such as taking the risk to love what one knows must be lost, but it is distinct from the prior three books in that it looks forward to Glück's repeated use of biblical and classical analogs to treat her primary themes in the three major narrative sequences from the 1990s: *Ararat* (1990), *The Wild Iris* (1992), and *Meadowlands* (1996). *The Triumph of Achilles* is pivotal because it marks Glück's first major attempt (in Vendler's phrase) to "give experience the permanent form of myth," without (as in Lowell) attempting to make the author's autobiographical experience itself mythic.[6] Not choosing a single mythic template through which to allow herself the analyst's detachment from experience that she associates with the psychoanalytic process, Glück tries on several of the masks that will play more expansive roles in her next three books.

Besides the title poem, other poems from *The Triumph of Achilles* that emphasize classical material include "The Reproach," an apostrophe to Eros; "Night Song," which Glück has herself read as a reflection upon the figures of Eros and Psyche (see "The Dreamer and the Watcher" [PT]); "The Mountain," which discusses the myth of Sisyphus; and "Mythic Fragment," which recalls Ovid's story of Apollo and Daphne, who, to avoid the "captivity / in praise" from the "stern god" who is also her suitor, turns for help to her father, the river god Peneus, who transforms her into "a tree forever" (FFB 165). As Vendler points out, since a myth such as that of Daphne and Apollo is already known to most readers, "interest consequently has to center almost entirely on interpretation and manner." In "Mythic Fragment," Vendler continues, Glück retells the myth as "a Freudian story, the tale of a girl too much in love with her father to accept a lover," and as "a modern story of virginity, revealing its roots in incestuous desire."[7] As Vendler's comments strongly suggest, *The Triumph of Achilles* turns to the mythic mode for

5. Helen Vendler, *The Music of What Happens: Poems, Poets, Critics* (Cambridge, Mass.: Harvard University Press, 1988), 438; James Robinson, "Louise Glück," in *Contemporary Poets,* 6th ed. (New York: St. James Press, 1996), 395.

6. Vendler, *Music of What Happens,* 437.

7. Ibid., 438, 439.

the detachment that allows Glück to explore components that would have likely been subjects for the analytic process she had undertaken years earlier. The impact of the daughter's ambivalent affection for, identification with, and mourning over the loss of the mythified father will become central motifs in both *Ararat* and *The Wild Iris.*

While the classical template connects *The Triumph of Achilles* to *Meadowlands,* other key poems engage with interpretations of major characters and narratives taken from the Bible. "Day Without Night" is a long poem in which Moses is imagined as an "entirely human baby."[8] "A Parable" discusses the life of King David. "Legend" proceeds, through the story of Joseph in Egypt, to discuss the life of Glück's paternal grandfather, a Hungarian immigrant who, once a "man of property," becomes a roller of cigars in a factory in New York City (FFB 209). "Winter Morning" is a poem about Jesus Christ.

Besides its biblical and classical subject matter, *The Triumph of Achilles* also explores themes that will unfold in later work. Glück expresses her ambivalence toward physical experience; her sense (as with Frost in "Birches") that the "Earth's the right place for love," coupled with her revulsion toward mutability.[9] This ambivalence toward human experience will become centralized in *The Wild Iris* and *The Seven Ages,* two of the author's most recent full-length volumes.

Glück's confrontation with the fragility and risk involved in allowing oneself to love what is passing, a motivating impulse in *Descending Figure* and *The Triumph of Achilles,* remains crucial. *Ararat* and *The Wild Iris* are major examples of her imagining lyrics as a book-length sequence, which provides a dialogic aspect to her writing not evident in the first four books. Glück had expressed her debt to Romanticism through her subjective exploration of nature in *The House on Marshland,* but she evokes the language of flowers to perform various speech acts in both *Ararat* and *The Wild Iris.* Both Glück's father and her elder sister who died at birth are invoked often in *Ararat.* Flowers become a language of mourning through which the distraught speaker attempts to commemorate her father, as well as to compete with her sister for ownership of nature as a meaningful system of symbolism. Writing about coming to terms with extreme feelings of grief after the loss of the beloved, Glück extends her range as an author by devoting lyrics to

8. Peter Stitt, review of "The Triumph of Achilles," in *Contemporary Literary Criticism Yearbook,* vol. 44, ed. Sharon K. Hall (Detroit: Gale Research, 1986), 215.

9. Robert Frost, "Birches," in Jahan Ramazani, Richard Ellmann, and Robert O'Clair, eds., *The Norton Anthology of Modern and Contemporary Poetry,* vol. 1, 3rd ed. (New York: Norton, 2003), 212.

alternative subjectivities, to examine how other family members have learned to cope with the major losses so affecting the main speaker.

Ararat revises depictions of nature from her first two books, but it is also a work of personal revision and stylistic transformation in how she inscribes nature. In effect tearing down the authorial personae of pyrotechnical stylism so evident in *Firstborn,* Glück's reticent tone of voice mirrors the speaker's emotional numbness to the point where the trauma of her father's death and the reexperiencing of her sister's death have become "written" into the texture of her work. The laconic tone also reflects her desire to replicate in speech a quality of silence and emotional unavailability she associates with her late father. The short lines, which often break in unexpected places, the skimpy forms and reserved manner of so many of the volume's poems resonate with the author's literary style: the sense that she is barely able to say anything at all. "A Fable" (AR) is one poem that works from a preexisting text, in this case the story of how King Solomon discovered the birth mother of a baby by threatening to cut it in half. This tactic of working from a previous text further allows her to work in concise symbolism, as the plot content is already known to the reader.

The Wild Iris recalls the nature lyrics from *The House on Marshland* as well as the mourning for the absent father of *Ararat.* The secular imagery and familial concerns of the earlier volumes, however, change here into a poignant confrontation with mortality, and a complex exploration into eschatological mysteries through an old-fashioned type of meditative verse that recalls the work of George Herbert and Wallace Stevens. The book, perhaps the author's most ambitious attempt to displace the monologue perspective of the traditional lyric form, is divided into categories, which include (1) the flowers speaking, (2) the voice of nature as a medium for the divine force, and (3) the voice of the authorial persona. In fourteen flower poems, flowers "speak to" the poet, at times describing their own situation (that is, what it is like to be a flower, to be in the ground, to be a bulb), at other times responding to the poet-gardener's anxieties, and often critiquing the poet. What the flower says may be considered an externalization of the poet's mood, attitude, misgiving, or concern. There are also "Voice of Nature" poems. As my colleague Wendy Stallard Flory put it in a handout for a presentation at Purdue University: "In these lyrics, a phenomenon of the natural world speaks as a medium for some 'divine' force, beyond the human."[10] A good example of this type of poem would be "Retreating Wind" (WI), in which

10. Wendy Stallard Flory, handout on *The Wild Iris,* for a course on American Women Poets, Purdue University, fall 2003.

the voice of divinity critiques the speaker—and humanity in general—for the frivolous, trifling nature of human endeavors, as well as for the unreasonable desire for immortality or rebirth. In this collection, there are several poems spoken in what seems to be the poet's own voice, on her relationship to her husband and son. There are also the "Hours" poems, several poems entitled "Matins" and several others entitled "Vespers," which constitute the structural backbone of the volume. These serve as "addresses" or "prayers" to this divine force. The supplicant offers her apostrophes to Yahweh, but *The Wild Iris* draws upon a mosaic of sources, both diverse and yet interrelated, such as Puritanism, Catholicism, Judaism, Romanticism, and Modernism.

Meadowlands extends Glück's use of a classical template to represent the concerns of a contemporary speaker, but now the relationship between the Homeric figures (in this case from *The Odyssey*) and members of a contemporary American family on the verge of splitting apart seems at once heartfelt and parodic. The volume suggests the degree of separation between the banalities of a stale suburban marriage with a philandering husband and the mythic strains of Homer's tale of longing and return. For all the obvious parody in *Meadowlands,* the resonances of the Homeric structure allow Glück to break out of the exploration of a single speaker's contemplative life and, by contrast, to represent a main plot line from many viewpoints. The polyvalent aspect of the text conforms to the emphasis on commentary in Glück's work as the characters interpret the words of other lyricists within the sequence as the primary vehicle toward their own identity formation. As was the case with biblical and natural personae in other books, *The Odyssey* becomes Glück's temporary forum to stage (as well as conceal) her evolving sense of self as a construct, subject to constant revision in and through a canonical proof text (one focused on Homer's foremost character of wandering and metamorphosis).

As Glück then writes about recovery from the trauma of divorce, a house fire, and relocation in *Vita Nova* (1999), she distinguishes between the "particular life" of human beings and the concept of "personhood." Only the term "personhood" may be conferred by the poet. A trace of an absence, "personhood" reconstructs "particular life" as an artifact. Poetry may confer the dignity of visibility in the form of "personhood," but Glück now critiques her prior lyric practice as having been another disaster notation.[11] She

11. It is "personhood" (a figure of image conservation and not of natural presence) that is within the power of the poet to design, through the verbal art that can inaugurate what Elaine Scarry calls the "mental practice of radiant ignition." Elaine Scarry, *Dreaming the Body* (New York: Farrar, Straus and Giroux, 1999), 83.

expresses reservations about her enactment of identity in such an impersonal form as language that nature, erotic desire, and the nuances of material existence disappear into the ethereal realm of abstraction. In poems from *Vita Nova* such as "Relic" and "Orfeo," which revisit one of the founding stories of male lyric ordination (the myth of Orpheus and Eurydice), Glück's speakers confront poetry's posthumous dimension. She interprets her lyric practice through an unforgiving calculus involving much loss and little gain. At the same time, she creates a "new life"—for poetry and, by extension, for the poet—beyond the registration of "personhood" by contextualizing "voice" in narrative form through the expansive frame of the book-length sequence. Taking the reader into account, she asserts the author's freedom to reposition herself in a psychological sense away from the epicenter of trauma.

As with Dante's *La Vita Nuova,* Glück lists "real grief" as the prerequisite to "songs of a high order" in *Vita Nova* ("Orfeo," 18). She also pursues a new direction that she will build upon in *The Seven Ages* by writing poetry with an enhanced attention toward the pleasures one derives from accepting a descent into ordinary life. In *The Seven Ages,* Glück writes from the perspective of age fifty in a personal register stripped of the mythic personae prevalent in earlier volumes. In several poems she recalls her antagonistic childhood with her sister during the long hot summers on Long Island. Playmates and companions "trapped inside" the parents' ideals of how little girls were supposed to look and behave, the sisters nonetheless felt "safe" inside the home—"a closed form" that provides an oasis from a world described as "violent" and "dangerous" (SA 19). "Rain in Summer," however, concludes with a typical Glück image: sisterhood interpreted as a zero-sum contest for survival and mastery:

> It was obvious to us two people couldn't
> prevail at the same time. My sister
> took my hand, reaching across the flowered cushions.
>
> Neither of us could see, yet,
> the cost of any of this.
> But she was frightened, she trusted me. (SA 36)

In other poems Glück recalls a failed love affair, carried on in part by a letter exchange—"Deep intimacy over great distance! / Keats to Fanny Brawne, Dante to Beatrice" (SA 24). In poems about childhood or life as a mature adult, the primary theme remains the speaker's attempt to go against her instincts to transcend the ordinary and to embrace life—what she calls in

"Birthday" the "partial, the shifting, the mutable / —all that the absolute excludes" (SA 21), while at the same time remaining painfully aware of the passage of time. In "Radium," a childhood memory poem, Glück foregrounds the passage of time as an element of real life beyond the control of a poet known for her wish to dictate circumstances through writing. The poem records a kind of vertiginous horror at time's whirlwind, but nonetheless ends on a comparatively upbeat note as the speaker admires how the cooking process (a product of time and heat and culinary skill) combines ingredients into a seamless combination of flavors that the poet describes as a "miracle":

> And then the fall was gone, the year was gone.
> We were changing, we were growing up. But
> it wasn't something you decided to do;
> it was something that happened, something
> you couldn't control.
>
> Time was passing. Time was carrying us
> faster and faster toward the door of the laboratory,
> and then beyond the door into the abyss, the darkness.
> My mother stirred the soup. The onions,
> by a miracle, became part of the potatoes. (SA 19)

In many poems from *Vita Nova* and *The Seven Ages,* Glück imagines her speaker taking part in the social exchanges and goings-on that constitute the mild kind of happiness many people take as life's daily joy. "Nest," "Ellsworth Avenue," "Lute Song," "Formaggio," and the concluding "Vita Nova," all signal that the author wishes to challenge her emphasis in the Orphic "Lute Song" on "personhood" as a textual self that requires the "pure soul rendered / detached, immortal, / through deflected narcissism" (VN 17) to signify symbolic accomplishment.

Glück is nothing if not a revisionary poet, as well as a visionary poet. Restless with creative stasis, she takes to heart Wallace Stevens's declaration about the work of modern poetry in "Notes toward a Supreme Fiction": "It Must Change."[12] And so, we see in her most recent work to date, *Averno,* a retraction of the hard-won truce it seemed she had made with nature, mortality, the body, and the pleasures of the quotidian in the comic, at times even light-hearted poems of *Vita Nova.* In a book that returns to what the poet Mark Strand calls her "starker, more direct" voice, Glück repudiates her brief

12. Wallace Stevens, "Notes toward a Supreme Fiction," *Stevens: Poems,* selected by Helen Vendler (New York: Knopf, 1993), 169.

flirtation with Romanticism as a movement that understood nature as a source of spiritual redemption.[13]

A descent into the ordinary is a theme of *Vita Nova,* but *Averno* then suggests that the poet's experience of pleasure at landing in the real world of Cambridge, Massachusetts, was short-lived and that a radical disconnection from the body has occurred. The laconic tone of *Averno* implies a speaker who feels altogether shut off from everyday human experience. She seems more acquainted with the cosmic silence of death than with the singing birds, harmonious winds, and human chatter characteristic of earthly life.

In *Averno* (the title refers to a crater lake outside Naples that, in myth, is said to be the portal to Hades), a key expression of just how disenchanted the poet has become with nature, and just how removed she feels from the realm of the body, can be found in "October," a long six-part lyric poem that was first published as a stand-alone chapbook in 2004. *Vita Nova* featured the friendly grocery clerks of the cheese shop along Ellsworth Avenue in Cambridge, but in the first stanza of "October," in the same city, "Frank" (presumably Bidart, the author's close friend, favored poet, and fellow Cambridge resident) has slipped "on the ice," in a scene described as "winter again" and "cold again," even as the poem's title leads us to expect lovely autumnal scenery. Not only has embodied experience now become vulnerable to the ravages of nature, as a fellow poet suffers the indignity and pain of slipping on ice, but the poet herself seems blocked from communicating with other human beings because of nature's interference. "I can't hear your voice / for the wind's cries, whistling over the bare ground." Now figuring nature as a malevolent adversary, rather than a restorative balm, the poet claims that she has been "silenced" by nature's "cries," and she turns her back on a sympathetic imagining of nature. "I no longer care / what sound it makes" (AV 5). In what may be read as the author's own projection of her dissociation with all living things, and her entrance into a realm of spiritual malaise, the earth itself, still described as "my friend," is also described as a female figure divorced from "the sun" (AV 15).

While it is true that Glück has represented herself and her poetry as being in opposition to the rhythms of nature in poems from *The House on Marshland* and *The Wild Iris,* the tone of these earlier expressions of antagonism between mind and matter often suggested the author felt her linguistic victories compensated for experiential loss. Not here. The idea that poetry could be interpreted as a form of companionship, a way of coming to terms with loneliness, is explicitly described as a thing of the past:

13. Mark Strand, *October* (New York: Sarabande Books, 2004), back cover.

I was young here. Riding
the subway with my small book
as though to defend myself against

this same world:

you are not alone,
the poem said,
in the dark tunnel. (AV 14)

Overwhelmed by the proximity to death, and convinced of her isolation from other human beings, the poet in "October" at times borders on silence altogether. The author no longer feels she can use poetry as a form of communication of her extreme depression to the outside world. "I am / at work, though I am silent" (AV 13). Understood as a spiritual exercise in the tradition of *The Wild Iris, Averno* is Glück's *via negativa,* her account of a Dark Night of the Soul akin to that written by St. John of the Cross.

From an autobiographical perspective, the book returns to the family drama enacted most fully in *Ararat,* but this time with an emphasis not on the relationship between the father and the daughter but between the mother and the daughter. Writing about life from the age of sixty, Glück nonetheless suggests that her attempts to please the mother in youth by following a traditional narrative pattern for a female of the mother's generation—falling in love, marrying, maintaining her looks, pleasing a man—continue to haunt the speaker's contemporary perspective as a woman entering later maturity. As in earlier volumes, Greek mythology informs her way of seeing personal experience, in this case with the myth of Persephone, Demeter, and Hades centralized, but recast, as a triangulated love story in which Persephone (Glück) is cast as nothing more than the "meat" upon which the overbearing and spiteful mother (Demeter) and male lover (Hades) compete for dominance.

The language in *Averno* is uniformly bleak, even apocalyptic, symbolically reflecting the state of the speaker's severe depression. Nature is either depicted in its wintry state, covered with ice or snow, or else has been charred and scorched by a catastrophic fire, as is the case in two poems that relate the story of a young farm girl who sets fire to a dry field, sending an entire rural homestead ablaze. In terms of the theme of commentary, Glück highlights the role of revision and interpretation of commonly known tales as a way of coming to know the self. She specifically discusses the theme of commentary in the poems dealing with the Persephone myth by offering two poems entitled "Persephone the Wanderer" with the initial poem cast as "the first version" of the myth, and the later poem described as "the second version" (AV 16, 73).

A book-to-book treatment such as the one sketched out above has the merits of a kind of clarity that only a chronological analysis can afford. But the truth is that the poet's questioning of "Why love what you will lose?" and her expression of the courage to continue to do so in the face of death, in part because "There is nothing else to love," is a characteristic of her entire oeuvre. What changes is Glück's increasingly comic tone of voice. Even so emotionally barren a poem as "October" (AV) contains moments of humor, as when the speaker mocks her own penchant for ventriloquizing nature: "*Come to me,* said the world. / This is not to say / it spoke in exact sentences / but that I perceived beauty in this manner" (AV 9). What also changes is her tilt toward an embrace of the pleasures of the quotidian—as well as her willingness to explore more extravagantly the kinds of masking of the autobiographical self through commentary poems she begins to play with, most notably in *The Triumph of Achilles.* As much as her poetry is a commentary on prior literatures, composed by other hands, her later work may also be read as a commentary on what she comes to see as the limitations of the voice and tone evident in her earlier works.

In a recent interview with Joanne Feit Diehl, Glück speaks in anxious terms about her fear of repeating past achievements, of failing to change her style, failing to "make it new" by broadening her emotional range through experiments with tone and voice:

> Pragmatically, at a certain point (around the time I began *Ararat*) I began to see that my work had rather stringently limited its tonal palate; it never, for example, sounded like my speech. [I realized] there might be interesting discoveries around the attempt to enlarge an existing range. I didn't, as I aged, develop a taste for comedy. Rather, I figured out how comic elements could be introduced . . . I liked the result; I felt, again, like an explorer.[14]

As much as this present study emphasizes her commentary on work by prior masters, Glück's comments on the shifting tones in her own work, and especially the introduction of what she calls "comic elements," suggest that she perceives her completed work as itself emanating from a prior master, another composed version of the authorial self that stands in need of revision, change, refashioning.

14. Joanne Feit Diehl, ed., *On Louise Glück: Change What You See* (Ann Arbor: University of Michigan Press, 2005), 184.

Instead of a straightforward chronological method, I have chosen a hybrid approach, in which I divide the book into two halves: Part I, "Thematic Keywords," and Part II, "A Poet of the Book." In the first part, I bring together poems and essays from throughout Glück's career that correspond to a mosaic of "keywords," themes or issues she has wrestled with throughout her long career: therapy, psychoanalysis, autobiography, desire, hunger, midrash commentary on both Old and New testaments, feminism, trauma, survival, and spiritual witnessing. These opening chapters, sometimes weaving two or more interrelated "keywords" into a single discussion, serve as a spectrum of critical views through which to perceive her entire poetry and poetics. In the second part, the chapters are devoted to Glück's major book-length sequences from the 1990s. *Ararat, Meadowlands,* and *The Wild Iris* are highly ambitious, innovative, and complex attempts to analyze the authorial self, via central metaphors more or less sustained throughout the entire volume. There is also a chapter on *The House on Marshland,* Glück's second book, which, through its revision of Romanticism and nature poetry, becomes a strong lead-in to *Ararat* and *The Wild Iris.*

Before subsequent chapters demonstrate how Glück transforms her autobiographical self into a fictional construct, made available to the interests of readers not sharing her "subject position" largely through her lyric commentaries on classical, biblical, Romantic, and modernist precursor texts, this study starts with a "keywords" chapter, which takes a psychobiographical approach to Glück's writings. Because so much of this study pivots around how the author bends her experience into a public form through relationship to proof texts, I believe it worthwhile to sketch out the contours of her biography. This helps us see how she transforms the facts of her experience into the illuminating distortions of her poems (at least to the extent she lets readers come to understand this personal narrative through her essays). Unlike many poets of her generation, she is not enamored of the published interview as a way to influence how her work is received by readers. In a preface to an interview with Joanne Feit Diehl, Glück states that she has resisted this form of personal disclosure because "I change my mind and preferences, often," and so the appearance of candor may be mistaken for fixed truths.[15] Even so, we can, especially with the help of the essay "Education of the Poet" in *Proofs & Theories,* begin to say a few things about how Glück, however subjectively, has imagined her childhood and

15. Ibid., 183.

early adulthood in ways she believes bear significantly on her subsequent literary personae.

The second chapter discusses how the twin terms of "desire" and "hunger" function in her poetics to express the author's perpetually inconclusive yearning to reach the beloved through words. Glück's account of desire in terms of family relationships compares to her relationship to the proof texts through which she forms her identity. Because the state of desire is by definition one of anticipation and not fulfillment, Glück's emphasis upon desire becomes a literary opportunity, a chance for her to engage in further lyric reflection upon an opened version of the literary canon, with poetry becoming a form of revision, a commentary on an incomplete text.

I then examine how she has invoked literary and religious traditions to make her own brand of unique poetry. A discussion of why I consider her an unconventional "Jewish" poet leads me in Chapter Three to concentrate on the keyword "midrash" through Glück's reading of the Hebrew Bible and Judaism. The penultimate "keywords" chapter, which treats the related issues of trauma and survival, addresses the way Glück has, in her recent volumes, charted a course in which her speaker acts out and potentially works through the psychological wounds that have characterized her registration of experience.

As helpful a lens as trauma studies has been for me in coming to terms with some of Glück's poetry, I conclude that trauma theorists' description of witnessing simply does not speak to the issue of "spiritual witnessing," or testimony that concerns a relationship to the ineffable, the divine. For this reason, the "keywords" section ends with a discussion of spiritual witnessing, as it takes place in Glück's poems dealing with the Christian Gospels and the life of Jesus. The Christian Gospels emphasize multiple interpretations of a central narrative event. They may be thought of as an extension of the Jewish commentary tradition, the belated interpretative revision of a prior text. I believe that Glück's fascination with the Jesus narrative marks an appropriate conclusion to Part I of my study of an author who develops her identity through interpretations of prior texts, interpretations that imply the incompleteness of both her literary project and the texts through which she develops her self.

Although the individual chapters that make up the second part, "A Poet of the Book," continue to treat Glück's poetry thematically by emphasizing "keywords" such as "nature" and "commentary," and although each chapter can be read as an essay that stands alone in its focus on one of Glück's major book-length achievements, I group these essays together under this title for three reasons. First, Glück has become a poet of the book quite literally, in that she has become increasingly interested in designing sequences in which the sum total of the individual poems equals more than the sum of the lyric parts. Second, Glück is a poet of the book in the sense that she is a bookish poet; she has written of "the scholar's inclination to meditation," if not her "taste for research" (PT xii). Glück's poetry is informed as much by her idiosyncratic and sometimes combative relationship to prior texts as it is to a recollection of her own lived experience. Third, Glück is a Jewish poet, and thus a poet of the Book, in the sense that Jews have frequently been described as a "People of the Book." Glück's frequent use of sacred and secular canonical texts as a starting point for her lyric meditations has much in common with the Jewish penchant for commentary and critique.

The second part of this study begins with chapters devoted to three volumes that all in their own way address the keywords "Romanticism" and "nature" poetry. Glück's poems are often set in a natural environment, but her nature poems in *The House on Marshland* should be understood as illustrations of (as Wordsworth scholar James Chandler put it) "second nature" poetry, that is, writing that collapses "such abstract oppositions as 'nature' and 'culture'" by including "the habits generated by social circumstance."[16] After showing Glück's debt toward and problems with Wordsworthian Romanticism, I connect her interest in nature writing to her main cultural work of mourning and prayer. To do so, I read sequences of poems from *Ararat* and *The Wild Iris* as pieces that also belong to a larger narrative patterning—in which Glück explores her speaker's inner journey, as she struggles to cope with love, creativity, loss, and death, by constructing and reconstructing her life into a voice that appears as part of a performance of the self in a text. This second part concludes (and the book, too) by bringing to the fore the extent to which a Hebraic approach can accommodate Glück's Hellenism. Chapter Eight relates the combination of high and low in *Meadowlands,* at least by analogy with the midrashic impulse to connect biblical narratives to contemporary events and daily application in the present.

Throughout this study, I have tried to develop a balanced course, one that would show how Glück's relationship to persistent themes has changed and evolved over time, but one that would also allow me to devote attention to her exploration of masks in single volumes as primary structuring devices. She has begun to imagine herself more as an author of books of poems than as a poet who collects selected lyrics into a book. I capitalize on the space allowed by this book-length forum to extend the analysis made by those critics who have focused only on each individual book when they address Glück

16. James K. Chandler, *Wordsworth's Second Nature: A Study of the Poetry and Politics* (Chicago: University of Chicago Press, 1984), 72.

as a narrative poet interested in sequences. In my "keyword" chapters, I treat her many books as a larger narrative sequence, a meta-text composed from the books of lyric sequences, written over thirty years, and revealing the shifting impressions of her imagination as a fluid construct, subject to constant change, deconstrual, and textual renewal. I read Glück's poetry against a general narrative pattern that shifts from the tones of anger, despair, and resentment (characteristic of *Firstborn*) toward a voice of resignation (in later works such as *Ararat*) and (in the latest volumes, *Vita Nova, The Seven Ages,* and *Averno*) toward an ambivalent embrace of embodied life as the aging speaker perceives her time on earth to be limited, and therefore especially precious. My chapter on trauma and survival addresses the way Glück has, in several of her most recent volumes, charted a course in which her speaker acts out and potentially works through the psychological wounds that have characterized her registration of experience in previous volumes.

Part I

Thematic Keywords

Chapter One

"Poems Are Autobiography"

Toward Imagining a Postconfessionalist's Biography

Since the late 1960s when the twenty-five-year-old author published *Firstborn,* her first collection of poems and one that yokes together two of her persistent themes (childbearing and language-bearing), a range of talented poets and critics have appreciated how Louise Glück combines lyrical and narrative strategies into a unique testimony.[1] Blurring the borders between modernist and contemporary styles, her poetry has been judged individualistic and universal, ordinary and oracular, momentary and mythic, tragic and comic. But just as scholars have disagreed about how to place her in regard to theories of language, they have also disagreed on where to place her in a history of twentieth-century poetics that has often been divided into personal and impersonal strains. In *Contemporary Poetry and Introspection* (1984), Alan Williamson observed that Glück has few peers in her synthesis of remote and confessional approaches to poetry. In an essay on "Autobiography and Vulnerability" (1995), William Doreski downplayed her relationship to High Modernism by emphasizing her debt to Robert Lowell's later work: "Glück's plaintive, evasive, revelatory language echoes Lowell's rejection of his own metaphorically armored early poems and acceptance of the plain speech of the psychological imperative that gave vent to his fear of madness."[2] So much for her relationship to modernist impersonality, at least according to Doreski.[3] In the context of academic, literary, historical, and critical

1. For an excellent survey of appreciations of Glück's work by poet-scholars such as Paul Breslin, Stephen Yenser, James Longenbach, and Linda Gregerson, see Diehl, *On Louise Glück*.
2. Alan Williamson, *Contemporary Poetry and Introspection* (Cambridge, Mass.: Harvard University Press, 1984); William Doreski, *The Modern Voice in American Poetry* (Gainesville: University Press of Florida, 1995), 150.
3. I personally can think of only Glück's friend and fellow Cambridge resident Frank

evaluations of authors that are based on identity politics, or on the "tribal" quality of poetry's various schools, movements, or camps, Glück's "subject position" in contemporary letters seems malleable enough to occupy multiple spaces and to appeal to different constituencies. Her work now appears in many of the competing literary anthologies that define what is significant about American poetry after 2000.

A telling connection exists between how Glück has shaped her biographical experience through a range of sacred and secular literatures and the perplexingly varied critical reception of her work. It is hard to think of another American poet since Elizabeth Bishop who has appealed to so wide an audience of critics, readers, and fellow poets—an audience whose members often hold such differing or even contradictory positions on why they believe Glück is worthy of respect as one of the handful of paradigmatic poets of the last few decades of the twentieth century. Glück's self-fashioning, like Bishop's, is in fact autobiographical, but, stylistically, we are persuaded to understand that her alter ego, the lyric persona that speaks many of her poems, is designed to be read as a construct, something made, hard won, achieved through a denial of life's rich ongoingness.

Unlike the allusiveness characteristic of modernists such as T. S. Eliot in *The Waste Land* (1922), Glück does not attempt to conceal the relevance of the proof text to the anguish and longing for connection with others that characterizes her representation of her personal life. Nor does she assume, as Robert Lowell did in *Life Studies* (1959), that the incidental details of her personal life are in and of themselves of great import to most readers. Nowhere does Glück do anything like declare without irony "I myself am hell," as Lowell does in "Skunk Hour," and expect readers to connect her personal suffering with that of Milton's Satan. As Bonnie Costello argues in her analysis of Glück's "Against Sincerity" (PT), an essay concerning John Berryman, Glück "attempts to define . . . an art involving the self and yet impersonal, negatively capable, or at least able to inhabit more than one perspective, to dramatize questions rather than project views."[4]

Glück's myth-making in books such as *Ararat, The Wild Iris,* and *Meadowlands,* which turn to biblical, natural, and classical analogs, allows the

---

Bidart (b. 1939), in "The War of Vassily Nijinsky" and "Ellen West" as rivalling her in the ability to integrate the modern dramatic monologue while still carrying on the legacy of lyric intensity found in *Life Studies* by Robert Lowell, the *Dream Songs* of John Berryman, *Heart's Needle* by W. D. Snodgrass, and *Ariel* by Sylvia Plath.

4. Robert Lowell, "Skunk Hour," in *Twentieth-Century American Poetry,* ed. Dana Gioia, David Mason, and Meg Schoerke (Boston: McGraw-Hill, 2004), 559; Bonnie Costello, "*Meadowlands*: Trustworthy Speakers," in Diehl, *On Louise Glück,* 51.

author to come to terms with her biographical experience in a way that is both removed from life's ongoingness and enriched and elevated through the parallel she makes with a proof text. In spite of (or because of) the sense of isolation and disconnectedness that comes through so many of her poems, Glück displays an ecumenical search for myths, metaphors, and narrative resources, in order to assuage this loneliness, to provide her with a sense of the community, albeit a literary one, that she is missing in her lived experience. By imagining the significance of her life story through fantasy with mythic, biblical, and folkloric materials, Glück does not so much attempt to escape from experience as she finds a means of giving shape to the documentary facts of her life, or what the poet has called "a proof that suffering can be made somehow to yield meaning."[5]

Lee Behlman has argued that contemporary Jewish American authors such as Nathan Englander, Michael Chabon, and Art Spiegelman have attempted to come to terms with their "second generation" version of the Holocaust experience through fantasy, folklore, and magical-realist devices. Their contrived and provisional relationship to myth and folklore, Behlman argues, suggests the impossibility of gaining direct access to the past, or any way of representing it, except through a medium that announces its own contrived and provisional nature. Like these other contemporary Jewish American authors, Glück suggests how much pleasure and value may be found in producing and reading versions of the self through acts of fantasy and projection.[6]

Besides being a source of imaginative release, the turn to myth allows Glück the necessary emotional distance to approach intimate, upsetting materials in a way that remains, for her, safely under control. A postconfessional autobiographer, she attempts to translate the meaning of her personal experience into a narrative of general consequence, by transforming liminal or trying episodes of her life into commonly known mythic structures that merge (or sometimes contrast) familial conflicts with the narrative canon. Perhaps Glück's most important contribution to postconfessional American poetry, since the mid 1970s, has been to find a way (through her idiosyncratic relationship to the proof texts) to negotiate a kind of middle ground between the ambitious but often forbidding strains of High Modernism (which attempted to tell what Pound called the "tale of the tribe" by regarding culture as a whole), on the one hand, and sensitivity to the distinctiveness of individual experience that was characteristic of the confessionalists, on the other.

5. Louise Glück, "Afterword: The Restorative Power of Art," in ibid., 190.

6. Lee Behlman, "The Escapist: Fantasy, Folklore, and the Pleasure of the Comic Book in Recent Jewish American Holocaust Fiction," *Shofar* 22.3 (Spring 2004): 56–71.

"Poems *are* autobiography, but divested of the trappings of chronology and comment, the metronomic alteration of anecdote and response," Glück wrote in her essay "The Best American Poetry 1993: Introduction" (PT 92). A poet known for her desire to achieve the frozen quality of aesthetic permanence through an emphasis on what Frank Bidart referred to as the "decisive finality of structure, the accent of fatality characteristic of her lines," in her writing Glück seeks to distinguish the often uncontrollable aspects of the psyche—and the mutability of the body—from the linguistic self or selves that are more under the artist's control.[7]

In creative tension with the chaotic aspects of the self that have caused her so much uneasiness, Glück continues: "If a poem remains so selectively amplified, so casual with fact, as to seem elusive, we must remember its agenda: not simply to record the actual but to continuously create the sensation of immersion in the actual" (PT 92). She is uninterested in the Lowellian project of encouraging readers to believe they were getting "the *real* Robert Lowell" when reading a book such as ***Life Studies***. But Glück does admit that the poet's "choices constitute a portrait" and that a poem offers "a highly specific portrait of an individual mind" through the poet's "choice of metaphors" and "recurring concerns."[8] Echoing Lowell's question "Yet why not say what happened?" in "Epilogue," Glück in "Summer Night" (SA) writes: "Why not? Why not? Why should my poems not imitate my life?" (SA 67).[9]

It is possible to connect, in a rough way, major episodes and recurrent autobiographical issues in the author's life with published information about her history. In her most autobiographical essay to date, "Education of the Poet" (PT), Glück recalls several aspects of her childhood and teenage years that are important to our interpretation of her poetics: the nature of her training as a reader and writer in early childhood, her battle with anorexia nervosa in her teens, and the seven years of psychoanalysis in which she learned to come to terms with her illness. Finally, she discusses her relationships with teachers of creative writing in her late teens and early twenties, which influenced her decision to follow in their footsteps by spending her professional (nonwriting) life as a teacher of writing for more than thirty years. Oddly, in this essay, Glück does not report on the impact of the death of an older sister shortly after the child was born, a subject

7. Frank Bidart, "Louise Glück," in Diehl, ***On Louise Glück,*** 23.

8. "Interviewed by Frederick Seidel," a 1961 ***Paris Review*** interview reprinted in ***Robert Lowell: A Collection of Critical Essays*** (Englewood, N.J.: Prentice Hall, 1968), 12–35. Glück is cited from "An Interview with Louise Glück," in Diehl, ***On Louise Glück,*** 183.

9. Robert Lowell, "Epilogue," in ***The Longman Anthology of Poetry,*** ed. Lynne McMahon and Averill Curdy (New York: Pearson Longman, 2006), 1291.

that will, along with the death of her father, become a dominant theme in *Ararat.* She does, however, discuss the sister who "died before I was born" in another essay, "Death and Absence" (PT). In this essay, Glück connects her anorexia to her traumatic reaction to her sister's death. She links an illness associated with self-abnegation to the survivor's guilt she experienced after her sister's death.

In "Education of the Poet" (PT), Glück recalls her childhood as that of a precocious child, during which her parents nourished her creative talents in writing and drawing.[10] But she also remembers the pressure her parents put on her to excel in everything she attempted. The eldest of two surviving sisters (Tereze, her younger sister, is a Manhattan banker), she was "encouraged in every gift. . . . If we hummed, we got music lessons. If we skipped, dance." Her mother (whom she describes as "the judge") would, later in the author's adolescence, read her poems, stories, and essays. "It was her approval I lived on" (PT 7). The desire of the budding author to seek maternal affection in the form of approval for her writing influenced the kind of sibling rivalries that animate the relationship between Glück and her living sister in much of *Ararat.*

By contrast her father, who "wanted to be a writer" (PT 6), is associated with the transmission of stories and myths that in part determined Glück's primary strategy for transforming the confessional type of poetry associated with a prior generation of authors such as Sylvia Plath, John Berryman, and Lowell into an autobiographical poetry detached from the author's natural experience through its mythic dimensions. "Before I was three, I was well grounded in the Greek myths, and the figures of those stories, together with certain images from the illustrations, became fundamental referents." With her characteristic wry humor, Glück mentions that her father's "particular favorite" was "the tale of St. Joan, with the final burning deleted" (PT 7). She adopts the persona of Joan in several poems throughout her career, in part to portray her desire for purity through a release of the spiritual self by starving the body, a practice connected in her mind with the aspiration to "glorious achievement" that was part of her father's interest in telling her the tale of Joan when Glück was a child (PT 7).

Glück describes a childhood informed by wide reading at an almost impossibly early age, in which she was encouraged to express herself through creative writing. But she also recalls her struggle to speak in a boisterous family where conversation verged on a form of competitive sport:

10. Louise Glück is the daughter of Daniel Glück, an executive who invented the X-acto knife, and Beatrice (Grosby) Glück.

> I was born into an environment in which the right of any family member to complete the sentence of another was assumed. Like most of the people in that family, I had a strong desire to speak, but that desire was regularly frustrated: my sentences were, in being cut off, radically changed—transformed, not paraphrased. (PT 5)

Glück's struggle to be heard—and especially for her words to be appreciated as valid by older family members—is writ large in the Bloomian contest for mastery with ancient, Romantic, and modern forebears in her poetry. In fact, Glück includes a paragraph in which she describes "Blake and Yeats and Keats and Eliot" as part of "my inheritance," next to her discussion concerning the value of writing as a way to meet her need to "finish my own sentences," the very struggle that she associates with her family's conversational style (PT 7).

In "Education of the Poet," Glück devotes much attention to her struggle with what she calls "the tragedy of anorexia." A primary subject of the long poem "Dedication to Hunger" (DF) as well as a kind of physical analog for her, at times austere, poetry that speaks to unfulfilled spiritual yearnings, Glück's focus on anorexia suggests that her illness and recovery were perhaps the most important experiences of her late adolescence and early adulthood in their impact on her life and her art (PT 11). Glück informs us that, "by the time [she] was sixteen," her anorexia had reached the point at which she could either die or try to live and seek help through psychoanalysis. "I realized that I had no control over this behavior at all. And I realized, logically, that to be 85, then 80, then 75 pounds was to be thin; I understood that at some point I was going to die. What I knew more vividly, more viscerally, was that I didn't want to die" (PT 11).

Reflecting in 1989 about herself as a morbidly ill high school senior seeking a psychoanalyst to help her deal with a condition that had spun out of control, and with a degree of humorous self-mockery that would become a characteristic feature of her mature autobiographical poetry, Glück comments on how unprecedented her request for an analyst was, living, as she did, in a family of upper-middle-class assimilated Jews in what she calls the "affluent suburbs" of Long Island. "I have no idea where the idea, the word, came from. Nor was there, in those days, any literature about anorexia—at least, I knew of none. If there had been, I'd have been stymied; to have a disease so common, so typical, would have obliged me to devise some entirely different gestures to prove my uniqueness" (PT 11).

Glück's strategy for coming to terms with her eating disorder as a sixteen-year-old girl led her into seven years of psychoanalysis. She credits the process not only with saving her life but also with teaching "me to think" (PT 12). Analysis, she notes,

> taught me to use my tendency to object to articulated ideas on my own ideas, taught me to use doubt, to examine my own speech for its evasions and excisions. It gave me an intellectual task capable of transforming paralysis—which is the extreme form of self-doubt—into insight. I was learning to use native detachment to make contact with myself, which is the point, I suppose, of dream analysis: what's utilized are objective images. I cultivated a capacity to study images and patterns of speech, to see, as objectively as possible, what ideas they embodied. (PT 12)

Freud suspected that what the person under analysis represses and so excludes from utterance in the psychoanalytic encounter is in fact the object of desire that, although unspoken, continues to haunt the patient. Silence, absence, what is unsaid, all become, for Glück, an essential element of the "language" of psychoanalysis.

Freud was sensitive to the relationship between the story a patient has to tell about experience and that patient's symptoms of mental suffering. In *Studies on Hysteria* (1895), he stated that he had realized, through his work on case histories, that the Freudian psychoanalyst is more like a critical analyst of a literary work than a neuroscientist. At times collaborative with and at other times in rivalry with poetry as a linguistic medium in touch with interior states of mind, Freudian psychoanalysis may be viewed as an interpretation of the patient's flawed poetry. Or the unfiltered dream work is brought to the session in hopes of finding an alternative poetic to shape the patient's language into meaning. Freud honored creative writing in his early essay on daydreaming, but the psychoanalyst Adam Phillips remarks that Freud understood his project less as a form of creative writing than as a form of literary interpretation. Equipped with its own poetics (for example, the language of repression, projection, mourning, defense mechanisms, and neurosis), the alternative discourse of psychoanalysis, Freud hoped, might translate the raw stuff of the patient's poetry—the nonsensical and associative dream work—into a meaningful utterance that is "bound to a project of knowledge" and thus in the service of producing mental health.[11]

In Glück's description of her psychoanalysis, she (like Phillips) imagines the analytic process as a crucial event in the transformation of herself into

11. Adam Phillips, *Promises, Promises: Essays on Literature and Psychoanalysis* (New York: Basic Books, 2001), 31.

the kind of analyst of her own language, including the silences and deletions of thought that, she realizes, "speak" to her evasions of her fundamental concerns. She affirms her wish to save her life through the act of composing a version of it, as a text, but also indicates that the type of writer she will become is informed by Freud's insights into the relationship between expression and repression. Her spare open-ended lyrics often point the reader to concentrate on what is not being said, on the gaps and silences in the lyric speaker's account of experience. "When I'm quiet, that's when the truth emerges," she says in "The Untrustworthy Speaker" (AR 34). Many of the points she makes about therapy—how it taught her to regard her own dream imagery and "patterns of speech" from a position of detachment, allowing her to come to know the "ideas they embodied" as if they were not personal to her—are uncannily reminiscent of her poetic style, which offers a similarly detached, almost disembodied, analysis of the self.

After her first year of therapy, she found "one other form" of "social interaction . . . open to me," which was the writing of poems and then discussing them with trusted teachers. To this end, she spent the next two years (1963–1965) studying with Leonie Adams and Stanley Kunitz at Columbia's School of General Education (from which she never graduated). Expressing "profound gratitude" and "a sense of indebtedness" to these teachers, Glück managed to suppress her "competitiveness" in dealing with works by other poets and instead to "serve others' poems in the same way, with the same ferocity, as I felt compelled to serve my own" (PT 16–17).

Glück dismisses the therapeutic function of poetry writing. Since she understands the self as it appears in the poem to be a construct, something made, not given, she recoils at the idea that writing about loss could be interpreted as a "catalyst for self-improvement," a way of healing the broken heart and wounded soul through a narrative "filled with markers like 'growth' and 'healing' and 'self-realization.'" This said, she does associate the shaping of poems with how analysis sheds light on areas of the analysand's experience that would otherwise remain dark and formless: "the artist, like the analyst, cultivates a disciplined refusal of self-deception, which is less a moral position than a pragmatic act, since the only possible advantage of suffering is that it may afford insight."[12]

Glück credits psychoanalysis—not creative writing workshops—with saving her life, as well as with casting her mind in a direction that would facilitate her art through objective scrutiny of her unspoken thoughts. She recalls,

12. Glück, "Afterword," 190–91.

however, being worried "in a conventional way" that, by becoming "so well, so whole," she would lose her ambition and "never write again." She reports the doctor assured her that "the world . . . will give you sorrow enough" (PT 12). The sorrows, pains, and major losses she has faced as an adult are normal, but the doctor's prognosis proved correct. Perhaps the most dramatic if not the most emotionally stunning episode of a major material loss in her adult life occurred in April 1980, when her house on an isolated country road in Vermont was destroyed by fire. In a 1985 essay, "The Dreamer and the Watcher," Glück recalls that, for an author who "was obsessed with loss" and who "had spent twenty years waiting to undergo the losses I knew to be inevitable" (PT 106), the devastation of the house and the loss of many possessions produced in its aftermath "a period of rare happiness—not ecstasy but another state, one more balanced, serene, attentive" (PT 100).

A period of "natural silence imposed by crisis" (PT 99) ended in June 1980, when she wrote thirteen poems "over a period of two weeks" (PT 100). One of these was "Mock Orange" (TA), a controversial and yet much anthologized poem expressing the female speaker's revulsion because sex with a man seemed a fiction of togetherness as well as a literal form of silencing the female with the covering male lips. By her next book she had found "a sense of direction, a sense of how I wanted to sound" (PT 100) and this resulted in *The Triumph of Achilles,* the National Book Critics Circle Award winner for poetry in 1985. For Glück, loss and lack in her personal and interpersonal experience have tended to precede episodes of major work. "On the subject of change, of loss," she declares, "we all attain to authority"; for her, such "authority" has taken literal form as her wish to record what she calls the "representative life" that had "somehow to be lived" (PT 106).

Less dramatic perhaps than the house fire but at least as devastating to her emotional well-being and thus at least as informative of her work have been Glück's divorces, which became primary subjects for her poetry. Currently living by herself on a quiet side street in Cambridge, Massachusetts, Glück is twice divorced. Her marriage to Charles Hertz Jr. in 1967 produced one son, Noah Benjamin, who is now a sommelier in San Francisco. Glück's second marriage was in 1977, to John Dranow, a prose writer and vice president of the New England Culinary Institute. While sexuality, failed relationships, family dynamics, and birth-giving are among Glück's main themes in her poetry throughout her career, the breakup of her second marriage seems to have most directly influenced two of Glück's books, *Meadowlands* (1996) and *Vita Nova* (1999). Loosely based on the story of Ulysses, Penelope, and Telemachus, *Meadowlands* interrogates a marriage coming apart. One theme of *Vita Nova* and *The Seven Ages* is life after divorce, expressed in a tone of hope for positive change. *Averno* (2006) covers similar ground, but the tone in the later work is much darker, more hopeless.

Book-length sequences of related lyric poems such as *Meadowlands* and *Vita Nova* are in some respects "about" the conclusion of Glück's marriage to John, and *Ararat,* which dealt with a family of three women in the aftermath of the death of a husband and father, is "about" Glück's autobiographical experience of mourning the death of her father, Daniel Glück. The lyric voice she construes in the poems from these volumes is, however, as much a fiction of the self as are her vocalizations of flowers, weeds, and God in *The Wild Iris.* Although Wendy Lesser is, in a tonal sense, correct to say that the directness of Glück's language suggests a kind of "self-centeredness," the authorial persona is as much a composition as are the monologues of Circe and Penelope in *Meadowlands.*[13] However intimate, the lyric speaker remains detached from the author's business of daily life even as she, in "Parable of the Dove," recalls her desire to refrain from thinking "I / am higher than they are" and so chooses to "walk among them, / to experience the violence of human feeling, / in part for its song's sake" (M 31).

At points (and especially in recent volumes such as *Vita Nova* and *The Seven Ages*), Glück has dissolved her characteristically remote perspective as oracular medium in favor of a descent into a renewed connection to the body, to sensual experience, and to the precious because fleeting details of ordinary domestic life and of nature as experienced in the company of other mortal beings. "We continued to plan; to fix things as they broke. / To repair, to improve. We traveled, we put in gardens. / And we continued brazenly to plant trees and perennials" ("Arboretum," SA 44). Her fascination with the stories of Persephone, Jesus, and Odysseus is derived from her reading of them as narratives of descent from sacred, mysterious, or nonhuman spaces back into the realm of the human, the quotidian, and the earthly. The more human-sounding, less mystical version of Glück, however, remains indebted to a modernist aesthetics of impersonality, for the self is something made "in part for its song's sake" (M 31).

Glück, like Bishop, is a protean figure whose work both courts and resists an autobiographical reading. "Change is Louise Glück's highest value," according to James Longenbach.[14] Glück's writing most often evades ethnic

13. Wendy Lesser, "Poetic Sense and Sensibility," in *Contemporary Literary Criticism,* ed. Sharon K. Hall (Detroit: Gale Research, 1986), 44:217.

14. James Longenbach, "Louise Glück's Nine Lives," in Diehl, *On Louise Glück,* 136. A closeted lesbian, Bishop engaged in a famous debate with Adrienne Rich about whether to appear in anthologies of poetry devoted exclusively to the work of women.

identification, religious classification, or gendered affiliation. In fact, her poetry often negates critical assessments that affirm identity politics as criteria for literary evaluation. She resists canonization as a hyphenated poet (that is, as a "Jewish American" poet, or a "feminist" poet, or a "nature" poet), preferring instead to retain an aura of iconoclasm, or in-betweenness. "I hardly know what 'feminism' means," Glück has written. "As the term has tended to be used (at least in my hearing) it has seemed to me constricting and tyrannical."[15] Contra Glück, various critics (including myself) insist that, although the term "feminism," for example, may be reductive, it is nonetheless illuminating for critics to place her in relation to a class of authors who share ethnicity, subject matter, subject position, writing style, or relationships to literary history.

Glück's reputation among a heterogeneous group of critics, literary historians, and other poets reflects the metamorphic poetics and ecumenical relationship to the sacred and secular literatures that should be understood as part of an expanded notion of what constitutes an experimental writing strategy that troubles the border between what we think of as biographically inflected literature and what we think of as commentary or interpretation. Canons exist as an important benchmark of literary accomplishment for Glück but also as a compendium of references that enable her (not unlike Woody Allen's character Zelig) to shift the stage upon which her personal, even autobiographical, expressions can take place as a series of masked performances. Allusiveness enables her to be elusive; to at once reveal and hide the speaker's vulnerabilities through the distance afforded by referring to myths and sources. Surprisingly, Glück's idiosyncratic self-fashionings could be compared to the way the Jewish American language poet and theorist Charles Bernstein sends up the idea of identity poetry—by listing, in a seventy-four-line litany, the many categories of selfhood he is supposed to represent, or that he has been taken to represent by various critics, through his stylistics:

> I am a serial poet, a paratactic poet, a
> disjunctive poet, a discombobulating poet,
> a montage poet, a collage poet, a hypertextual
> poet, a nonlinear poet, an abstract poet,
> a nonrepresentational poet, a process poet,
> a polydiscourse poet, a conceptual poet.[16]

15. Personal correspondence with the author.

16. Charles Bernstein, "Solidarity Is the Name We Give to What We Cannot Hold," in *My Way: Speeches and Poems* (Chicago: Chicago University Press, 1999), 33.

Similarly, Glück appears to some readers as a feminist, to others a Jew, a postmodernist, a confessionalist, a modernist, a religious author, a mystic, a classicist, a romanticist, a hard-edged emotionalist, a realist, a love poet, an elegant stylist, a blunt poet, a bitter poet, an ecofeminist nature poet, a pagan poet, a cultivated poet, an elegist, a lyric poet, a narrative poet, and an antifeminist poet who "raises crucial, disturbing issues about women's complicity in their own oppression."[17] These various identifications are symptomatic of her enactment of a dialogue between identity as biological essence (a modernist notion of writing as the discovery of authenticity) and identity as a usable social construction (a postmodern notion of self-fashioning, in which identity is subject to the constant flux of verbal recastings of self in different disguise).

My argument is that Glück's reception as an author who explores multiple subject positions—and who shifts in and out of character as a "Jewish" or "female" author—revises what Geoffrey Hartman defined as the "struggle for the text," through creative commentary on canonical proof texts that range from the Old and New testaments to Homer and Virgil, and to Romanticism and Modernism. Glück's strategy is to remain close to but distinct from such categories as "Jewish poet" or "female poet." Her strategy speaks to questions about identity that have been raised by postfeminist and queer theorists such as Judith Butler and anti-essentialist Jewish feminist theorists such as Miriam Peskowitz in *Judaism since Gender,* questions concerning the "make it up" or performative side of selfhood, especially when considering gender and religious definitions of the person as a series of masks, roles, and potentialities.

Butler, for example, argues that identities are provisional and improvisatory, "a kind of impersonation and approximation . . . a kind of imitation for which there is no original." In "Contingent Foundations," however, Butler also observes that challenging the prevailing concepts of identity does not mean we can no longer claim specific positions through which to act in the world via the fiction of selfhood:

> To deconstruct the subject is not to negate or throw away the concept; on the contrary, deconstruction implies only that we suspend all commitments to that to which the term "the subject" refers, and that we consider the linguistic functions it serves in the consolidation of authority. To deconstruct is not to negate or dismiss, but to call into question and,

17. Lynn Keller, "'Free / of Blossom and Subterfuge': Louise Glück and the Language of Renunciation," in *World, Self, Poem: Essays on Contemporary Poetry from the "Jubilation of Poets,"* ed. Leonard M. Trawick (Kent, Ohio: Kent State University Press, 1980), 123.

> perhaps most importantly, to open up a term, like the subject, to a reusage or redeployment that previously has not been authorized.[18]

When seen in the context of Glück's lyric meditations on the significance of literary sources and myths to her speaker's evolving sense of self, terms such as "Jewish," "female," "reader," even "contemporary poet" no longer appear aspects of a universal human subject that exists out there in the "real" world. Instead, subject positions function as figurative spaces, enabling the author to operate within the frame of literary conventions that convey established values from the past, through texts, even as these conventions are recast to remain relevant to the author's experience in the present tense. Glück's poetry and, for that matter, her relationship to such patriarchal constructs as the Western literary canon and to the Jewish God, Yahweh, are traditional in that she employs the voices of characters from ancient narratives and sacred texts to amplify her experience beyond personal circumstance. Understanding literary tradition as a mode of inquiry into the composition of personal identity, however, Glück can interrogate the source material and make it conform to aspects of her own experience without having to "confess" to the reader the details of her autobiographical existence, the disclosure of which defines the speaker's vulnerability in most recent lyric poetry.

Glück is also an author who has from the beginning been inspired by nature. Her lyric voice may suggest an emotional detachment from life, but her work often addresses such crucial bodily experiences as giving birth, having sex, observing her father die, then burying his body in a Jewish cemetery on Long Island. A poet who expresses concerns for nature and the meaning of the human body, Glück nonetheless challenges the biological given of the author's life by privileging culture, or the inscription of nature and voice as strategies to transcend embodied experience. In *The House on Marshland,* for example, she depicts the aftermath to her mental break from the body as being indelibly bound to phenomena, that is to say, as being of things and events as these are delivered by the senses. The nature poems in her second book reflect her debt to Wordsworthian Romanticism, evident in her emphasis on comprehension through analysis. Knowledge may arise from experience, but it is not grounded in experience. Her nature poems in *The House on Marshland* are not empirical documents; they are not meant to capture, as the

18. Judith Butler, "Imitation and Gender Insubordination," in *Inside/Out: Lesbian Theories, Gay Theories,* ed. Diana Fuss (New York: Routledge, 1991), 21; Judith Butler, "Contingent Foundations," in *Feminists Theorize the Political,* ed. Judith Butler and Joan W. Scott (New York: Routledge, 1992), 15.

lyric often wishes to do, a fleeting moment of time in the frozen permanence of words. Like her poems on the Hebrew Bible, the Christian Gospels, and Homer, these nature poems are commentaries on a figurative environment made intelligible through reflections that impose coherence, organization, and structure. Disagreeing with the confessionalists, she states specifically that she does not mean her poems to be read as reflections of a phenomenal life experienced outside the text. Glück eschews associations of her self with nature and the female body, in order to become what the feminist scholar of Romanticism Margaret Homans describes as a bearer of the word.[19] Glück's poetry illustrates Stephen Greenblatt's description of "self-fashioning," as "the power to impose a shape upon oneself," as "an aspect of the more general power to control identity."[20]

Glück attempts to "control identity" through lyric self-fashioning, but her poetry appeals to different audiences and for different reasons (as a survey of her appearance in literary anthologies would indicate). Her poems appear in Norton poetry anthologies, as exemplary works of twentieth-century writing; in collections of Jewish poetry, such as the recent *Telling and Remembering,* edited by Steven Rubin; in collections (such as *Gods and Mortals*) of contemporary poets who work on classical themes; and in feminist anthologies. Her poetry also appeared in *Americans' Favorite Poems,* in which Mary Ellen Bryan, an administrative assistant from Kansas City, Missouri, describes how "The Queen of Carthage" (VN), Glück's poem about Dido's suffering over the loss of Aeneas in Virgil's epic poem, "spoke to" her and helped her to "move on" after a passionate relationship with a scientist who "over time let me go."[21] Glück might be pleased to know that her commentary poem on Virgil has resonated with a mourning lover in Kansas City, but overall, she has not been pleased with these attempts at categorization, especially with those anthologies that are organized by an author's subject position. In conversation with me, she regretted having her poetry associated with an adjectival sign of a special categorization ("Jewish") that she considers misleading. She believes her poems can and should exist outside any systematization via religion, gender, or ethnicity.

Like Bishop in published interviews, Glück in conversation and in print chafes against descriptions of her poetry as "feminist." Given her comments

19. Margaret Homans, *Bearing the Word: Language and Female Experience in Nineteenth-Century Women's Writing* (Chicago: University of Chicago Press, 1986).

20. Stephen Greenblatt, *Renaissance Self-Fashioning from Moore to Shakespeare* (Chicago: University of Chicago Press, 1980), 1.

21. Robert Pinsky, ed., *Americans' Favorite Poems: The Favorite Poem Project Anthology* (New York: Norton, 2000), 101.

in "Education of the Poet" on the extravagant degree to which her parents encouraged her to "recognize and honor and aspire to glorious achievement," Glück has stated that she and her sister Tereze were "never given to believe that such achievement was impossible, either to our sex or our historical period" (PT 7). Her disclaimer of a feminist agenda, however, must be placed alongside the fact that she appears in anthologies such as *No More Masks,* which takes its title from a line written by Muriel Rukeyser, a book edited by Florence Howe, cofounder of the Feminist Press. More important, Glück's poems often represent a female speaker, as in "Mock Orange" (TA), who struggles to fashion an identity through words in the face of a tradition in which her voice and vision have been effaced or ignored, usually through the will of paternalistic male characters ranging from father, to Yahweh, to ex-lovers and ex-husbands who wished to inscribe the meaning of her life on her behalf, as if they had the authority to do so through their imagination of a silent and silenced other. As Lynn Keller remarks on a poem such as "Mock Orange," where a man's kiss "might as well [be] a hand over [the woman's] mouth": "gendered roles and heterosexuality itself silence and suffocate, perhaps even impose starvation on a woman."[22] My discussion of Glück's relationship to such ambiguous terms as "Jewish" poet, "feminist" poet, and "nature" poet indicates that whatever sense of authenticity she achieves in poetry is not some discovered essence but, rather, a discursive production of the self through the interrelated acts of writing and of reading narratives designed by other hands.[23]

22. Keller, "'Free / of Blossom,'" 123.

23. I am indebted to John Duvall, my Purdue colleague, for this formulation, which he has applied to the work of Toni Morrison.

Chapter Two

Dedicated to Hunger

A Poetics of Desire

Throughout her career, Glück has represented speakers who are hungry. Unlike Kafka's Hunger Artist, who made an exhibition of his starvation because he could find nothing he wanted to eat, Glück's personae go hungry because the temptation to share in the good things of this world is so great that to taste would only disappoint. She has spoken of herself as an artist whose work "from the beginning" has been driven by a "spiritual hunger." She has described the impulse to make art itself as a yearning that "begins and survives as a craving, a hunger for what eludes, a beacon, a lighthouse. . . . I am simply in the hands of something, some periodic hunger," she says of her own periods of heightened creativity, which approximate what she calls "wild possession."[1] Characters ranging from a mother to a God to a Greek hero to a reader yearn to fulfill their desire for such physical needs as food and sex, but also to satisfy their yearning for attention, for abstract concepts such as honor, or metaphysical needs such as acknowledgment from a higher being. In Glück's poems, desire may be defined as a libidinal current that flows toward a love object, but which cannot meet its destination, if it is to continue to propel the speaker toward further personal expressions. When "Eros" introduces "true love" to the speaker in "The Reproach" (TA), she perceives his appearance as an illustration of Eros's betrayal. According to the "Lover of Flowers" (AR), "the face of love, to her, / is the face turning away" (22).

For desire to spur creativity, therefore, the apostrophic address to the beloved must remain unanswered. The speaker's call to the listener represents the persistence of a failure of response. Instead of writing as a facilitation of

1. Louise Glück in Diehl, *On Louise Glück,* 184–85, 186–87.

an encounter between self and other, Glück's speakers come to associate their own creative drives with a language that must replace an actual meeting between family members, lovers, a reader and her audience, or a speaker and her God. Fulfillment, the feeling of being full, becomes the enemy of desire, the enemy of the ambitious author, who must remain hungry if she is to continue to write.

Whether Glück has cast her hungering selves through the Homeric personae of classical mythology or is writing in a more overtly autobiographical idiom about a brief love affair, Psyche and Eros seem perpetually at odds. At the end of "Marathon" (TA), a nine-part poem, Glück evokes that realm of desire

> where only the dream matters
> and the bond with any one soul
> is meaningless; you throw it away. (FFB 185)

More recently, in "The Destination" from *The Seven Ages* (2001), Glück describes how a love affair that lasted "only a few days" can "live almost completely in imagination" when the speaker concentrates, not on her regret that the actual contact with the beloved was so brief, but instead on the fact that it "was never permitted to develop / into tolerance or sluggish affection":

> The days were very long, like the days now.
> And the intervals, the separations, exalted,
> suffused with a kind of passionate joy that seemed, somehow,
> to extend those days, to be inseparable from them.
> So that a few hours could take up a lifetime. (SA 28)

Like the love affair in "The Destination," the lyricist's distance from the beloved, in time and space, informs the linguistic significance of an erotic experience that is otherwise characterized as inconsequential because fleeting. Paradoxically, the speaker's renunciation of contact with the lover becomes a measure of an event's value for her as a source of imaginative reverence.

In this chapter, I focus on how Glück transforms the deficit states of hunger and desire into terms that correspond to literary productivity. The chapter divides into three fairly separate but interrelated topics: renunciation of sex, renunciation of battle for the sake of honor and humanity, and renunciation of food for the sake of gaining attention. Although these topics deal with separate forms of desire and renunciation, which range from the literal hungers of the body to the figurative yearnings of the spirit, each topic becomes emblematic of how Glück identifies hunger as a poetics, the posture necessary for literary accomplishment. I will start with literal physical hunger as a figure in the sequence of poems collectively entitled "Dedication to Hunger" (DF), for the child's desire for love and parental recognition; then we move to the more abstract hunger for fame (in *The Triumph of Achilles*) and conclude with her authorial poetics of hunger and love-longing.

In poems such as "Appearances" and "Lost Love" (both in AR), two sisters—one alive, one dead—compete for the scarce resource of a mother's affection. The logic of triangulated desire becomes emblematic of the strategy of midrashic interpretation (see Chapter Three). Like the living child, who believes she must renounce her desire for the mother by denying her need to be in a position to receive love, Glück turns poetry into commentary, or commentary into poetry, as a way for an author interested in taking her place in the literary canon to assert control over a previously valued textual tradition, but without appearing to wish to possess its authority in her own text. Her poetics of desire, then, may be linked to the commentary tradition, because commentary is a form that converts the frustration of working in the secondary mode of explanation into the primary mode of original creativity.

In an essay in praise of the Objectivist poet George Oppen, Glück states her partiality toward a poetry that approaches silence and that verges on disappearance:

> As a reader, consequently as a writer, I am partial to most forms of voluntary silence. I love what is implicit or present in outline, that which summons (as opposed to imposes) thought. I love white space, love the telling omission, love lacunae, and find oddly depressing that which seems to have left out nothing. (PT 29)

Like Oppen, Glück prefers spare outlines for her poems, emphasizes voice over image, expresses a "love of white space," and remains fascinated with the nuance of what is left unsaid. Her poetic manner thus conveys a desire to have a lyric voice that is somehow not constrained by a physical manifestation on the page.

In part 4 of "Dedication to Hunger" (DF), entitled "The Deviation," Glück connects the psychology of female adolescent anorexic behavior to her persona as a mature poet, who, as she stated in the Oppen essay, is "partial to most forms of voluntary silence" (PT 29).

It begins quietly
in certain female children:
the fear of death, taking as its form
dedication to hunger,
because a woman's body
is a grave; it will accept
anything. I remember
lying in bed at night
touching the soft, digressive breasts,
touching, at fifteen,
the interfering flesh
that I would sacrifice
until the limbs were free
of blossom and subterfuge: I felt
what I feel now, aligning these words—
it is the same need to perfect,
of which death is the mere byproduct. (FFB 133)

In "The Deviation," the speaker recalls the anxiety she felt about her body when she examined her breasts while lying in bed; this examination of a part of the female body associated with maternity and eroticism leads her to a declaration about her own poetics. As Suzanne Matson explains: "the speaker metaphorically relates the hatred of her developing body with language's betrayals. Like an editor of a text, she will pare away 'digressions'; breasts are seen to be leading away from the argument of the self."[2] Aesthetics—the quest for beauty, the "need to perfect"—is viewed as anathema to the speaker's experience of a healthy relationship to her body as a source of procreation and erotic pleasure.

At fifteen, she became "dedicated to hunger" as a way to control her identity as an autonomous being by postponing the ability to bear children; the frightened teenager reasoned that she could then resist maturation by starving herself. As Lynn Keller explains: "Anorexia is both a retreat from adult sexuality and a childlike state safe from sexual drives, and an assertion of control—two desirable things for those who share Glück's sense of woman's powerlessness."[3] What Keller does not emphasize is Glück's perception that the physical state of not having ("the retreat" from an association of significant personal identity with the female body) is in the speaker's mind directly

2. Suzanne Matson, "Without Relation: Family and Freedom in the Poetry of Louise Glück," *Mid-American Review* 14.2 (1994): 107.
3. Keller, "'Free / of Blossom,'" 123.

related to her entrance into another arena of power and control—the space of literary accomplishment.

Further, Glück could stem "the fear of death" because the maternal body, which the teenaged girl has associated with sex and birth, will "accept / anything," and therefore "a woman's body / *is* a grave" (FFB 133). To stave off death by, paradoxically, courting it through starvation (or, in her terms, to avoid becoming "a grave"), she must exist outside "the interfering flesh" through a "sacrifice / until the limbs were free / of blossom and subterfuge." The speaker wants to exist, but in an idealized fashion or textual form that asserts her spiritual ideal or moral integrity as a self "purified" of the raw bodily needs for food and sex. Comparable to lyrics from *The Wild Iris,* where flowers speak of human themes, here human limbs are compared to the limbs of a flowering tree. But these limbs are terribly vulnerable because they lack the blossoms that attract insects, which would allow for pollination, and lack protection from predators because they have no camouflage (for subterfuge). Ultimately, the speaker hopes to emerge altogether free of the engendered body, of which the maternal figure is for her the main symbol.

In the last four lines, she connects her poetics to the childhood fear of entrapment in a body marked as female:

> I felt
> what I feel now, aligning these words—
> it is the same need to perfect,
> of which death is the mere byproduct. (FFB 133)

The speaker is an idealistic metaphysician who views the female body and natural existence itself as enemies to the achievement of sublimity through language. She believes having a body, and especially having a female body that can produce human life, will block her entrance into the sublime realm of poetic accomplishment, the place where ephemeral speech becomes a form of writing that lasts beyond the biological given of the author's life. The mature poet fears—as the anorexic teenager feared—that the nature of material life (the poem as a physical entity, the body as a mutable container of spirit, the maternal body that becomes both a self and an other in the act of bearing children) will limit access to an ideal form of existence.

In its literal sense, hunger is the acute physical sensation of desire for the nourishment that will sustain the body, but in "Lost Love" (AR) and other poems such as "Moonbeam" (SA) and "Metamorphosis" (TA), Glück has converted "appetite" into a symbolic term to describe a desire for love or recognition that discounts the body, the realm of the biological given. The speaker's comment about being "willing to destroy herself" in "Dedication to Hunger" (DF) resonates with Glück's displacement, onto the infant sister in "Lost Love" (AR), of her own fascination with negating the self through starvation. In a poem expressing the speaker's conflicted feelings about her own survival, she accuses her sister of intentionally destroying herself, so that the dead sister could draw the mother's affections away from the speaker:

> My sister spent a whole life in the earth.
> She was born, she died.
> In between,
> not one alert look, not one sentence.
>
> She did what babies do,
> she cried. But she didn't want to be fed. (AR 27)

The outrageous and outraged statements in "Lost Love" about the sister who did not survive into adulthood but whose absence lingers heavily around the author, in the speaker's contest for the mother's affection, should be read as an example of how literal, physical hunger transforms into the child's desire for love and parental recognition.

The sister and her premature death haunts the surviving family; she turns the mother into an expert at grief. The Glück persona is left in the unenviable position of survivor, who, raised as a guilty substitute for someone remembered as sacrificial victim, cannot compete with the lost image in her quest for the mother's affection. The speaker understands, or perhaps willfully misunderstands, the baby's death as a consciously willed act of self-starvation: "But she didn't want to be fed."[4] In "Lost Love" (AR), the buried sister possesses a talismanic power over the mother, whose heart had become small and not human, "like a tiny pendant of iron," and is drawn, as if by a magnet, toward the cemetery plot.

René Girard, in *Violence and the Sacred,* has discussed what he calls "triangulated desire," the idea that desire is always already mediated before we cast our eyes upon an object. According to Girard, we can only want an object if we know it has been claimed as valuable by someone else. Hegel spoke of the

4. "Appearances" occurs in the midst of another traumatic episode in the speaker's life, the first anniversary of her father's death. The poem's comment about the sister's death is in part a reflection of the grief the speaker is experiencing. She writes in the midst of observing how her mother has become numbed, watching TV, playing cards with her sister, also a widow, and only going through the motions of life. As her father's death seems to be draining the mother of life, Glück feels compelled to explore the prior incident that caused the mother to shut down her emotional life.

foundation of master-slave relations as stemming from the "struggle for recognition," by which he meant what Francis Fukuyama (following Alexandre Kojève in his ***Introduction to the Reading of Hegel***) refers to as "***a desire for a desire,*** that is, a desire that that person who evaluated us too low should change his opinion and recognize us according to our own estimate of our worth."[5] In Glück's case Girardian "triangulated desire," the Hegelian "desire for a desire," occurs through fantasies she constructs about the enjoyment her mother experienced for one of the speaker's sisters. Glück writes about her sister in the essay "Death and Absence," noting that she "died before I was born," and therefore her "death was not my experience, but her absence was" (PT 127).

Throughout *Ararat,* Glück imagines herself a guilty survivor, someone guilty merely because she is alive while someone near her is not. Thinking magically and through the logic of sacrificial violence, she believes her birth was contingent upon a substitution of her life for her sister's. Desire for the beloved's attention (in this case from a mother who seems capable of loving only one child at a time) becomes cast as a zero-sum game, from this point of view. Someone must sacrifice her will to make room for another's will. Ironically, it is the dead sister, not the living one, who wins the battle for the mother's attention, making it difficult for the reader to know whether it is the living sister (Glück's alter ego) or the dead sister who is the scapegoat, the sacrificial victim.

Glück writes in an essay that "it seemed wrong to forget the dead child," but she nonetheless expresses disdain for the sister who receives the mother's care, which the speaker believes was intended for her (PT 127). "Anyone can love a dead child, love an absence," she declares in "Appearances" (AR 32). Her dismissive tone suggests outrage at the mother's decision to love the memory of a dead child rather than attend to the needs of the living, but the speaker also understands, at least on a theoretical level, that absence is the prerequisite for desire. To return to "Lost Love," for example, she writes:

> Then it seemed to me my sister's body
> was a magnet. I could feel it draw
> my mother's heart into the earth,
> so it would grow. (AR 27)

5. Francis Fukuyama, *The End of History and the Last Man* (New York: Free Press, 1993), 165 (Hegel quoted p.135). See also Alexandre Kojève, ***Introduction to the Reading of Hegel,*** trans. James H. Nichols Jr. (Ithaca: Cornell University Press, 1969).

The "it" in the final line here seems to refer to the sister, suggesting that her death and burial in the ground, like the bulbs that become glorious flowers in *The Wild Iris,* must precede her reappearance as an object of affection that can be nurtured through maternal love. The poem is ironic because, in order to create a fantasy space where the speaker can hope for warmth and love from the mother, she must sublimate her claims for attention by forging a stoic disposition. She must pretend to have a cold heart, not a bleeding one. Glück will return to address, and also challenge, the logic of the same dynamic of desire for the beloved's attention being sublimated through stoicism, in "Midnight" (M), where the wife chastises herself for trying to "communicate" with her husband by "not answering / when he calls" (M 26). In "Moonbeam" (SA), Glück's autobiographical persona at once expresses and ironizes her concentration on yearnings that can be satisfied only on the metaphysical level of ideas, when she writes that "hunger is not for experience / but for understanding, as though it could be had in the abstract" (SA 5). Her emphasis on biological and metaphysical types of hunger implies a self that is empty (like the moon, which draws its apparent light from the sun), a nothingness that remains in need of a sense of identity or awaits content that would lend meaning to her natural existence. In "Metamorphosis" (TA), Glück links her anorexic behavior as a child to her fascination with a transcendence of the body, associating her malady with her dying father's renunciation of the world in his "excitement" about death:

> My father has forgotten me
> in the excitement of dying.
> Like a child who will not eat,
> he takes no notice of anything. (FFB 157)

In this poem Glück expresses her tendency to deal with metaphysical types of hunger that cannot be satisfied by a given, existing thing. She deals with a metaphysical "hunger" that suggests what she calls in an essay on T. S. Eliot a "religious mind":

> [T]he religious mind, with its hunger for meaning and disposition to awe, its craving for the path, the continuum, the unbroken line, for what is final, immutable, cannot sustain itself on matter and natural process. It feels misled by matter; as for the anecdotes of natural process, these it transforms to myth. (PT 21)

In "Appearances" and "Lost Love" (AR), and "Midnight" (M), then, Glück understands desire to be a state that pits the wish to gain recognition of one's humanity from the beloved (an abstraction that does not exist in nature) against the natural drives for food, love from a parent or spouse, and self-preservation. The conflict between the instinct to satisfy one's biological existence and the desire to prove one's mastery over animal nature through self-denial (or by seeking recognition in the fight that Hegel said was for "pure prestige," a nonbiological desire, an abstraction) infuses her attitude toward love—secular and sacred, maternal, familial, and erotic.

Glück's philosophy of desire sheds light on her poetics, especially on her blunt, reticent tone of voice in individual lyrics from a rock-hard book such as *Ararat.* It also sheds light on her interest in the book-length sequence that resists a close (or semantically closed) reading of the lyric, as a well-wrought urn, an autonomous product that exists in splendid isolation from other texts. Her disregard for confessionalism or what she calls the "specimen man"—in favor of a style that records with "the camera's cool, compensatory voyeurism and the clinician's dispassion"—becomes a strategy for authorial appearance, at once transparent and opaque, that is comparable to how she imagines her desire for recognition from readers (PT 49).

Her use of "hunger" as a metaphor for desire also places her work in a tradition of Jewish American women authors who have sublimated their desire for nourishment to signify their affection for their loved ones, and especially for their children. Erika Duncan observes:

> In Jewish literature by women, mothers are the "bread givers" who try to make feeding into a replenishing ecstatic act. But the mothers are themselves starved in every way, sucked dry and withered from being asked almost from birth to give a nurturance they never receive. . . . They are starved not only for the actual food they are forced to turn over to others, but for the stuff of self and soul, for love and song.[6]

The socioeconomic and cultural position of Glück's upper-middle-class suburban speaker, residing in the last three decades of the twentieth century in Vermont, Cambridge, or on Cape Cod, is hardly comparable to that of the main character in Anzia Yezierska's ***Bread Givers,*** the story of a desperately poor immigrant woman growing up in a Lower East Side ghetto in the early twentieth century. At the same time, as Susannah Heschel writes: "the image of hunger unites the mothers in Jewish fiction, both the hunger these women strive to satisfy in others through their constant self-sacrificing, and the hunger they themselves experience as their sensitivities are neglected and

6. Erika Duncan, "The Hungry Jewish Mother," in Heschel, *Jewish Feminist,* 28.

their emotions starved." The imagery of the Jewish mother who "feeds others because it is the only access she knows to a little bit of love" is highly evocative, as we come to terms with how the logic of desire works itself out in Glück's poetics as a form of hunger.[7]

Her clinically dispassionate appearance in poems conforms to her understanding of desire as a state of having by not having, ***a restraint so passionate that [it] implies possession,*** to borrow her observation about two swans silently circling each other in the pond from "Palais des Arts" (DF). Glück compels many readers to become fascinated with the mythic personae she has created, and destroyed, by connecting her biography to classical and biblical sources via her commentary. She does so, however, with extreme diffidence, as a hovering figure, a "voice / without a body," as she says in "Circe's Grief" (M 46).

In "Dedication to Hunger" (DF), Glück dealt with self-starvation and the withering away of the female body in ways that, in subsequent volumes, would resonate with her mature efforts to understand desire as a form of restraint, or as a desire for absolute knowledge, power, or truth that is contingent upon a breaking with the desiring side of life altogether. In "The Triumph of Achilles," Glück connects her poetics of desire (which pits symbolic recognition of one's humanity against the satiation of physical appetites) directly to her repulsion toward bodily hungers and also to her guilt-filled desire for self-preservation.

"The Triumph of Achilles" concerns a figurative type of hunger. In this poem Glück addresses her own view of the desire for recognition as the product of a struggle for something supernatural, or something antinatural, something beyond or other than the wish for personal happiness in mere being, the "good life," or physical security, which the poet attempts to celebrate, as Stephen Burt points out, in "Parable of the Gift" and "Otis" (M).[8] Her paradoxical theory of desire as best expressed through a renunciation of the desiring part of the self may become clearer when we put it into practice by contrasting her interpretation of Homeric battle in "The Triumph of Achilles" (1985) with its modernist precursor, "The Shield of Achilles" by W. H. Auden (1952).

In books 16 and 17 of *The Iliad,* Achilles lends his armor to his companion Patróklos. Thus, when Patróklos is slain by Hector, Achilles loses the sign of his own symbolic value. While Achilles mourns his friend and mentor, the

7. Anzia Yezierska, *Bread Givers: A Struggle between a Father of the Old World and a Daughter of the New* (1925; New York: Persea Books, 1975); Heschel, *Jewish Feminist,* 7.

8. Stephen Burt, "'The Dark Garage with the Garbage': Louise Glück's Structures," in Diehl, *On Louise Glück,* 86–87.

goddess Thetis, Achilles' mother, travels to Mount Olympus to beg Hephaestus, the god of fire, to forge a new suit of armor for her son, including the splendid shield that Homer describes in book 18 (lines 478–608). On the armor Hephaestus depicts a harmonious cosmic vision that includes the heavens, the earth, and the sea, surrounding images of two cities, one at peace and one at war.[9]

In his version of the shield, Auden reflects upon the catastrophic middle decades of the twentieth century and so sets his poem up as an ironic revision and bitter commentary upon Homer's ekphrastic writing. Far from a mandarin exercise in art appreciation, however, Auden's "Shield of Achilles" joins his "Musée des Beaux Arts" (1938) as an ethical critique of life from an artist's perspective. Whereas, in Homer, mortal combat was the way an individual warrior could demonstrate his inner strength and superior character through the readiness to sacrifice himself for an idea, an abstraction such as imperial glory or personal honor, in Auden, the risk of life in a bloody battle has become "an experience forced on masses of men, and ultimately women and children as well," that leads "not to the satisfaction of recognition, but to anonymous and objectless death."[10]

Initially an anonymous female in Auden's poem (Thetis is named as the character who "cried out in dismay" only in the final stanza), the goddess looks at the work of an anonymous armorer (Hephaestus is only named as he "hobble[s] away" in the last stanza). A figure for the ethical reader who has turned to *The Iliad* for instruction during a period of catastrophic modern warfare on a scale unimaginable during Homer's time, Auden's Thetis expects to find depictions on the shield of the City of Peace: vines, olive trees, "Marble well-governed cities," religious altars, "athletes at their games," "Men and women in a dance." Instead she finds only images of the City of War that fail to connote the dignity of warfare. Achilles' shield lacks the heroic images of individual warriors pitted against one another in hand-to-hand battle to win recognition and everlasting fame.

Writing during the height of the Cold War, less than a decade after the exposure of the Holocaust atrocities and the atomic bombings of Nagasaki and Hiroshima by the United States under President Truman, Auden suggests that human behavior and the technologies of warfare have changed since Homer's time. Persons may no longer prosecute war on a scale

9. W. H. Auden, "The Shield of Achilles," in Jon Stallworthy and David Daiches, eds., *The Norton Anthology of English Literature: The Twentieth Century* (New York: Norton, 2000), 2511–12. (References to this poem will be given parenthetically in the text.)

10. Fukuyama, *End of History,* 335.

available to representation, even in so massive and majestic a form as the classical epic. In Auden, warfare is no longer balanced with peaceful images of domesticity but, rather, consists of faceless acts of savagery:

> A plain without a feature, bare and brown,
> No blade of grass, no sign of neighbourhood,
> Nothing to eat and nowhere to sit down,
> Yet, congregated on its blankness, stood
> An unintelligible multitude,
> A million eyes, a million boots in line,
> Without expression, waiting for a sign. (9–15)

Auden refers to conflicts between iconic warriors in Homer in order to contrast these acts by distinguishable agents, engaged in a struggle for recognition, with the loss of agency in the World War II context of totalitarian regimes and total warfare. The culture of scapegoating that contributed to the Holocaust, Cold War persecution, and the Russian gulags, he argues, links the crucifixion of Jesus Christ during a period of apocalyptic fervor and state terror in Jerusalem two thousand years ago to the Holocaust and Stalinist purges that characterized mid-twentieth-century Soviet, European, and American history. His poem remains powerful at the beginning of the twenty-first century as an elegy that mourns the loss of individual responsibility for the crimes against humanity perpetrated by members of genocidal regimes.

In Auden's poem, state violence is mediated through the disembodied voice of a dictator, via the radio, the instrument that exerted ideological control in the first half of the twentieth century. Critiquing what Nietzsche referred to as a "herd mentality," Auden observes that "out of the air a voice without a face" dictates that citizens may freely commit terrible acts without guilt or blame. Because no individual can be singled out as perpetrator and, therefore, held responsible for the crime, actions are blameless because not localizable.

> Barbed wire enclosed an arbitrary spot
> Where bored officials lounged (one cracked a joke)
> And sentries sweated, for the day was hot:
> A crowd of ordinary decent folk
> Watched from without and neither moved nor spoke
> As three pale figures were led forth and bound
> To three posts driven upright in the ground. (31–37)

However desperate he may be about "the banality of evil," as Arendt put it, Auden holds out a spark of hope when Thetis articulates the voice of protest. Her empathetic imagination allows her to mourn for Achilles, and cry for the crippled state of humanity, as Hephaestus has represented it on the shield. Thetis is Auden's figure for the political poet and social critic. Through her vision, he expresses the persistence of human values in the face of a modern world that has evacuated such moral concerns. Thetis is the exception to the totalitarian rule dominating Auden's poem, which registers the massive hardening of hearts.

Thetis imagines the world from the position of the human other, but she is a sea goddess, she is not human. The "ragged urchin" in the penultimate stanza becomes the emblematic modern character, a shelled sea creature like the crab described by Eliot in "Prufrock": "I should have been a pair of ragged claws / Scuttling across the floors of silent seas."[11] Auden's "urchin" ends the poem throwing stones at birds, for no other reason than to inflict pain on a vulnerable creature that will not hit back. Unlike Thetis, he considers rape, and boys knifing each other, to be "axiomatic" of life, not atrocious peculiarities worthy of outraged testimony. He is more cave man than civilized. Auden parodies Frost's paradigmatic statement from "Stopping by Woods on a Snowy Evening" about individual responsibility through keeping promises: "[He'd] never heard / Of any world where promises were kept / Or one could weep because another wept" (57–59).

Glück displays an empathetic imagination that is comparable to Thetis's, and Auden would probably have admired "The Triumph of Achilles" had he lived another decade or so to read her lyric commentary on the Homeric tale. Glück, however, seems less at ease with Auden's late modernist viewpoint—the sweeping social, political, and martial critique from a demigod's perspective, the aerial view of history seen in poems such as "The Shield of Achilles," "The Musée des Beaux Arts," or "September, 1939." Writing to achieve personal clarification concerning her desire for affection from other human beings and in the minor tonal key of postmodernism, which treads lightly when speaking on behalf of the other's experience, Glück in "The Triumph of Achilles" nonetheless picks up where Auden's poem left off. Her poem resembles Auden's because it attempts to recover the speaker's ability (all but erased in Auden) to register desire for another person, to express that which is most precious because most vulnerable, and to "weep because another wept." In her interpretation of warfare as a legitimate forum through

11. T. S. Eliot, "The Love Song of J. Alfred Prufrock," in Ramazani et al., *Norton Anthology* 1:464.

which the warrior may risk his personal safety for something beyond or other than his own physical security, moreover, Glück expresses her position on desire by engaging in her own interpretative warfare with Auden over the meaning of Homer's epic poem. In so doing, she reclaims the aristocratic version of battle as a meaningful example of the struggle for recognition among poets, a position on conflict that Auden condemned as irrelevant in an age of nuclearism and mass war.

Like Auden's Thetis, who empathizes with her son's fate, Glück imagines Achilles' strife because Patróklos has perished, especially because his companion has suffered a defamation of his body that signals the reduction of his symbolic value. Tellingly, Glück replaces the "shield" found in the title of Auden's poem with the "triumph" in her title, because she is celebrating a return to human feeling for another person as a prompt toward agency that involves risking one's own life for a symbolic cause. While her expression of empathy is welcomed in the wake of postmodern skepticism about one's ability to enter into the subject position of another, Glück's interpretation of Achilles' desire for Patróklos as based in loss, war, and death transforms the triumphant empathy into a bittersweet expression of yearning for the beloved's safety at the cost of one's own physical presence.

In Homer, Achilles becomes enraged—to the point of sadistic madness and the creation of an environmental disaster—by Hector's desecration of Patróklos's body, because it has damaged his friend's value in a culture that takes the measure of personal dignity through the degree of fame or honor bestowed at burial. Infuriated by the image of Hector's circling the walls of Troy, dragging the body of Achilles' companion behind him in the dust as if it were carrion, Achilles chooses to recover the armor he had lent to Patróklos, but also to go on a wild killing spree, clogging the river with dead Trojan bodies. By so doing, he accepts warfare as a manifestation of the struggle for recognition and links his own value to the recovery of his friend's mangled corpse.

Achilles engages in what Hegel called the "struggle for recognition," which animates heroic behavior when the warrior pursues the abstract value of recognition of his humanity and freedom from control by another person above his desire to preserve his life. For Hegel (as his foremost modern commentator, Kojève, has observed), history began with the test of the first man's humanity, which occurred when he agreed to a fight that would leave the victor in the role of master and the vanquished, who feared death and so was willing to capitulate to his opponent out of a desire for self-preservation, in the role of slave. Glück makes clear that, by entering battle against Hector, Achilles knows he seals his fate as subject to the early death Thetis had prophesied:

What were the Greek ships on fire
compared to this loss?

In his tent, Achilles
grieved with his whole being
and the gods saw

he was a man already dead, a victim
of the part that loved,
the part that was mortal. (FFB 168)

Glück avoids critiquing the mechanized warfare and slaughter of nameless foot soldiers surrounding the death of the individual warrior that so fascinated and appalled Auden, who no longer believed with Homer and Hegel that war could be the meaningful expression of the desire for recognition. Glück interrogates, and finally dismisses, a macrocosmic condemnation of war focused on "the Greek ships on fire," on a panoramic view of the cost of war. "The Triumph of Achilles" instead focuses on the power of grief to motivate heroic action. It also looks into the politics of friendship in a way that reaffirms the master-slave dynamic, showing Achilles to be moved into battle against Hector in pursuit of an abstraction: the good name of his friend, as linked to signs that connote honor—the return of the armor and a proper burial of the corpse.

Glück's "Triumph of Achilles" sets the relationship between Achilles and Patróklos at the intersection between friendship—defined by the principle of democratic sameness (they wear identical armor)—and the hierarchical principle of difference that characterizes both the feudal model of master-slave relations and the aristocratic attitude toward warfare that produces the significance of few individual warriors at the cost of the destruction of the anonymous many whose stories are left untold. Superficially but not insignificantly, Patróklos resembles Achilles because "they wore / the same armor." Glück notes, however: "Always in these friendships / one serves the other, one is less than the other: the hierarchy / is always apparent" (FFB 168). She presents a complex friendship. It is based, on the one hand, in a competition for mastery over the companion and, on the other hand, in an empathetic identification with the partner, in friendship, for both share the same fate as mortal human beings. She addresses how the trauma of losing the beloved friend contributes to the narrative tone of the testimony; the speaker is transformed into a witness, whose authenticity, paradoxically, is related to his unreliability: "the legends / cannot be trusted— / their source is the survivor, / the one who has been abandoned." Most important, however, "The

Triumph of Achilles" describes what it means to be a human being, who nonetheless desires an existence apart from the limitations of the body, when Glück contrasts Patróklos's physical defacement with his transformation into a linguistic figure underwritten by his death. "[N]o one survives" the story, but Achilles remains an important character to Glück—in fact he is "triumphant"—because he has extended his desire for recognition beyond self-preservation. His empathy toward Patróklos was unavailable to anyone in Auden's poem except Thetis, a goddess.

In contrast to the gods in *The Iliad,* the speaker's wish to retain what he cannot possess and yet survive defines the human condition as tragic, but not vain. Glück interprets the part of Achilles "that loved" Patróklos—and so was willing to die in order to recover the body and armor that signified honor—as "the part that was mortal." Peter Stitt has observed: "One would expect the triumph of Achilles to be found in his battle with Hector, but such is not the case. Instead, Glück locates it in his loss of Patroclus, an event that makes Achilles human."[12] Driven to recover the mutilated body, Achilles concludes his exile in the tent on the shoreline of Troy after the "Embassy" scene, when he agrees to battle with Hector. In the same act, he transfers his identity from a physical presence to the lines of value conferred upon him by Homer. According to Glück, Achilles is not triumphant because he is the most powerful warrior on the battlefields of Troy, having achieved mastery over all competitors seeking recognition of their humanity through the willingness to fight to the death; nor is he triumphant because his name will be preserved in Homer's poem. Instead, he is triumphant because, in pitting his life against the symbolic value of his friend, he affirms his dignity. Desire for the recognition of the beloved and desire for self-preservation are put at odds. According to the bitter logic of heroic activity as expressed in "The Triumph of Achilles," the illogical (self-defeating rather than self-preserving) yearning to possess what one cannot ever obtain in life distinguishes the human hero, who is willing to risk his life for a symbolic value that stems from the gods, a value apprehended by the immortal fame of poetry.

In *Looking Awry,* Slavoj Žižek interprets Achilles' revenge against Hector as a ceaseless chase around the ramparts of Troy. The never-ending chase scene reminds him of John Keats's depiction in his ekphrastic ode, when Keats imagined the lovers' race on the Greek urn as frozen into a visual composition at once static and inconclusive. Besides being a verbal response to a funerary object, Keats's poem registers a detachment from life, because the scene appears through a visual idiom that lacks the time interval necessary

12. Stitt, "Contemporary American Poems," 215.

for verbal narrative to occur. Focusing on book 22 of *The Iliad,* where Achilles tries to catch up with Hector as they circle the outskirts of Troy, Žižek analyzes the surreal quality of "the pursuer [who] never succeeds in catching up with the fugitive whom he is after." The scene illustrates Xeno's paradox: that "we never can cover a given distance X, because . . . a goal, once reached, always retreats anew."[13]

Like Žižek, Glück imagines desire to be a drive that produces subjectivity rather than an emotional state produced by her speaker's response to the world existing outside her gaze. Žižek speaks of the "vicious circle of a desire, whose apparent satisfaction only widens the gap of its dissatisfaction." Similarly Glück, throughout her career, imagines desire as the state of being physically close to but emotionally removed from—or else physically removed from but emotionally attached to—the beloved. Both situations produce grief and tension, because each combines nearness with a remoteness that is characteristic of what Žižek refers to as "the subject's 'impossible' relation to *a,* to the object-cause of desire."[14]

For Glück, as for Žižek, absence and loss become strangely productive states of creative endeavor, when they assist the author in the patterning of her life into a narrative. The object of desire cannot be attained in Glück's poetry, but as Žižek explains, "the searching and indecision proper to desire" are meant to defer getting too close to the object of desire, which would paradoxically make the object of desire disappear and so become worthless. Postponing satisfaction, Žižek writes, is the "state that reproduced the lack constitutive of desire."[15]

Glück's treatment of characters who renounce their desire for affection as a strategy to achieve their goals of making themselves known to the beloved also connects to her poetics of commentary. As the Bible scholar Michael Fishbane has observed, the midrashist sublimates the desire for recognition of his or her originality by performing the apparently subservient role of commentator.[16] At the same time, the self-effacing acts of analysis and explanation become a veiled statement of freedom, creativity, aggression, and originality, which emerge in relationship to reading the Torah. The midrashist intends to reassess the Bible's meaning by filling in its

13. Slavoj Žižek, *Looking Awry: An Introduction to Jacques Lacan through Popular Culture* (Cambridge, Mass.: MIT Press, 1991), 4–5.

14. Ibid., 209, 6.

15. Ibid., 8.

16. Michael Fishbane, "Inner Biblical Exegesis: Types and Strategies of Interpretation in Ancient Israel," in Geoffrey H. Hartman and Sanford Budick, eds., *Midrash and Literature* (New Haven: Yale University Press, 1986), 19–40.

gaps and hollow places, thereby reconstructing scripture as a polysemous text, while appearing to submit to its influence through appraisal of its timeless values.

Glück turns to midrash to gain insight into the nature of desire as a struggle for mastery in "A Fable" and the "Yellow Dahlia" (AR). The volume's title, *Ararat,* refers to the mountain upon which Noah's ark rested after the flood subsided in Genesis (6:9–9:29), but each poem recalls another well-known tale from the Hebrew Bible, which concerns Solomon, not Noah. They both specifically refer to the story found in I Kings (5:9–14) of the judicious ruler who used his native wit to determine the birth mother of a baby whose biological origin remained in doubt and so must be decided upon by law. The contestants before Solomon were prostitutes who had lived together when each was carrying a son. They gave birth within three days of each other, but one of the children subsequently died, possibly suffocated by the other mother out of jealousy. Challenging the logic of possession as a sign of desire for the beloved, Solomon threatens to cut the living child's body in half with a sword so that each contestant could share the corpse of the slain infant. "Each of you says, 'The living one is mine; the dead one, yours,'" he says. Grasping the logic of desire as a willingness to forgo possession of the beloved, the birth mother establishes her dignity by surrendering her son. In the process she illustrates her maternal legitimacy to Solomon: "Please, my lord, give her the living child! Do not kill him!"[17]

In early poems such as "Dedication to Hunger" (DF), Glück deals with hunger and the renunciation of desire for food and sex by specifically addressing her battle with anorexia nervosa, a form of "hurting" the self by attempting to diminish the body to the point of disappearance. "Yellow Dahlia" (AR) owes something to Glück's earlier more literalized version of hunger, when her speaker's ambivalent feelings for her sister gain expression in a literalized version of the desire in "A Fable" (AR) to control the beloved by denying the speaker's relationship to the body. *Ararat* documents how, as an adult, Glück has felt in competition with a powerful void, the nearly palpable absent presence of the late sister, as well as in competition for affection with a third sister, who did survive into adulthood. In "Yellow Dahlia," she comments on the famous biblical tale of King Solomon and the two mothers to describe how she has hurt herself (through self-starvation? through emotional withdrawal? through the psychological pain associated

17. Ellen Frankel, *The Illustrated Hebrew Bible: Seventy-Five Selected Stories* (New York: Stewart, Tabori and Chang, 1999), 183–84.

with the survivor's extreme feelings of guilt?) in order to sublimate her aggression toward the living sister:

> I had to hurt
> myself instead:
> I believe in justice.
>
> We were like day and night,
> one act of creation.
> I couldn't separate
> the two halves,
> one child from the other. (AR 51–52)

According to this brutal confession, the speaker's obsession with death and the urge to destroy herself through fasting as an expiation of guilt are symptoms of her unwillingness to let go of her identification with a sister whom she has perceived simultaneously as a competitor for the mother's love and as a double, whose existence in the speaker's psyche is indelibly linked to her own sense of a self intimately acquainted with death and loss. The relationship between the living daughter and the dead one parallels that of the link between Achilles and Patróklos in "The Triumph of Achilles," for in that case, the hero must risk his life to recover the armor associated with the dead friend, whose existence mirrors the survivor's.[18]

Glück retells the tale in "A Fable" (AR), in which desire involves sublimation, loss, triangulation, and emotional restraint. She has turned to the Solomonic tale to understand the struggles for her mother's affection, which flows toward the sister who died before the author was born. This is a primary theme throughout *Ararat.*

18. "Animals" (AR) comments from another, more earthy perspective on the theme of desire as a sentiment attached to loss, as presented in "A Fable," and in "Appearances," which first announces the contest between daughters for the limited resource of maternal love. The penultimate image of "Animals" interprets family life as if it were part of an economy of scarcity. This is comparable to the world imagined in "A Fable" and "Appearances," but in "Animals" affection is symbolized as food:

> We were like animals
> trying to share a dry pasture.
> Between us, one tree, barely
> strong enough to sustain
> a single life. (AR 48)

Affection is figured as food, but there is not enough to go around to make a meal for the two sisters, who appear in this parable as young animals struggling to survive in a drought-stricken environment.

Unlike the allusiveness characteristic of modernists, Glück's myth-making in *Ararat* does not attempt either to conceal or to deny the relevance of the proof text in the anguish of her personal life. Instead, she amplifies the meaning of her biography by transforming an element of her story into a myth that merges familial conflicts with the structure found in scriptural narrative. In her retelling, however, there are not two mothers, but one, and not one child, but two:

Suppose
you saw your mother
torn between two daughters:
what could you do
to save her but be
willing to destroy
yourself—she would know
who was the rightful child,
the one who couldn't bear
to divide the mother. (AR 36–37)

In the Bible, the birth mother's renunciation of her son revealed her identity to Solomon. In "A Fable," Glück reconfigures herself as the daughter who must abandon the beloved object, in this case the mother. The Solomon story as it appears in "A Fable" involves a living child and a dead one, but more important, Glück reverses the narrative dynamics so she can apply its message about desire and detachment to her contest with the sister. The reader (the "you" referred to in the poem) can interpret her withdrawal from the conflict as a sign of her desire for maternal affection, but also as a sign of her desire for the reader's attention. We have moved from literal to figurative hunger, but can we not connect the statement about the one "willing to destroy" herself in "A Fable" (AR) to the comments about the anorexic teenager in "The Deviation" (DF)?

In Glück's experience as an author, a family member, a religious supplicant, and a grim analyst of love in a secular realm, expressing affection for the beloved—or announcing the desire for recognition from the reader through a textual re-creation of self as a work of performance art—involves a having by not having, a coming into view as a textual figure by taking the self out of the flow of natural life. To assert autonomy, so closely linked in her mind to authorship, Glück must distance the self from nature and from the beloved, by taking on different personae, thereby establishing impenetrable boundaries between lyric speaker, nature, and a biographical impression of the authorial self. As Don Bogen observes, Glück goes "beyond standard romantic visions to show how desire ultimately isolates as much as it unifies."[19] In short, her poetry expresses desire for the persons and things she wants to possess in this world by saying no to them instead of yes. Glück is the poet of the thwarted speaker because, she reasons, to remove the obstacles that frustrate a meeting between self and other in the world outside the text would be to erect a block between the author and control of the text, that is, her control of the site upon which her identity as a literary figure depends.

Glück's commentary on authorship thus demands a reading that acknowledges distance between writer and reader. She implies a schism between, on the one hand, her image and voice as these aspects of identity appear in the text, and on the other hand, the reader who would perceive these signs of her presence as if they were a script corresponding to an actual version of herself. She asserts that writing produces a gap between author and narrator, between what she calls "the authority of event" or the "natural arrangement" of life and how she may substitute her experience for the textual appearance (PT 25). "The empowering distance of the poet from his materials repeats itself in another equally useful distance: that of the poem from its reader," she writes in an essay on T. S. Eliot, "The Idea of Courage" (PT 26). Glück's position on authorship—based as it is in experiential deficit, or on what she calls "the impossibility of connecting the self one is in the present with the self that wrote" (FFB 26)—links writing with her desire for recognition from readers together with her characteristic tonal detachment, the inscription of a voice on the verge of disappearing altogether as a sign of the utterly unapproachable.

One aspect of what she calls "the artist's most stubborn dilemma" is, therefore, a contemporary version of what the New Criticism once labeled the "authorial fallacy." Returning to the High Modernist mythos of impersonality, while at the same time dispelling the confessionalist plan to recover the self in text by reducing the distinction between language and natural reality, Glück refers to "the distance between the remote artist self, miraculously fluent, accidentally, fleetingly perceptive, and the clumsy, lost self in the world" (PT 27). She wants to please readers, she says, but her hunger "for praise" has not led her to feel satisfied with what she has accomplished (PT 10).

How can hunger ever satisfy us? To the contrary, her self-contempt at experiencing the need to fulfill the body's drive for food and for sex veers toward a guilt-filled embarrassment at having a body at all, especially when she interprets her need for approval from readers as a sign of vanity, or as the

19. Don Bogen, "Review of 'The Triumph of Achilles,'" *The Nation* 2 (1986): 53–54.

sinful desire to be recognized by others as better than they are. For her pride is earned by accomplishing a difficult task. In essays and poems she goes so far as to attach her loathing herself for needing recognition to her revulsion at the existence of her body, and, as a displaced version of her rejection of physical appetites, the need for food and sex.

At various points in her career, but especially in her first three books, Glück has interpreted the literary meaning of anorexia nervosa, a disease she has confronted since a teenager. Even turning an illness that involves the disappearance of flesh into a metaphor for the relationship between writing and desire, she regards her eating disorder as a symptomatic expression of the author's ambivalent drive toward receiving attention from readers through the ultimate act of self-denial, thus suggesting a deep affinity between poetry and death. Anorexia becomes a traumatic symptom, "written" onto the body (as if the author's physical being were a manifestation of the textual self), that signifies she is willing to sacrifice anything with body and physicality for her art. "Out of terror at its incompleteness and ravenous need, anorexia constructs a physical sign calculated to manifest disdain for need, for hunger, designed to appear entirely free of all forms of dependency, to appear complete, self-contained" (PT 11).

In the essays in *Proofs & Theories,* she understands desire for recognition not only as best achieved through a physical detachment from the object of affection, but also as an instinct that remains valuable to her as an author. Why? Because it propels the impulse to write as a sign of her freedom from the physical limitations of natural life, as well as a registration of symbolic agency, and the wish, however displaced and fanciful, to communicate with others in a peculiar form that is at once intimate and remote. In "Education of the Poet," Glück interprets desire as a painful necessity:

> Most writers spend much of their time in various kinds of torment: wanting to write, being unable to write; wanting to write differently, being unable to write differently. In a whole lifetime, years are spent waiting to be claimed by an idea. . . . It is a life dignified, I think, by yearning, not made serene by sensations of achievement. (PT 3)

Later in the essay, she acknowledges that the poem—an object that manifests the desire for recognition as a material fact, in this sense, like a human body—may defer the need to communicate momentarily, but this satisfaction will, paradoxically, be forgotten at the moment it is experienced. For her, desire is anticipatory of execution; the goal, if we can call it that, is to be in a position to write, not to finish, not to have written:

> It seems to me that the desire to make art produces an ongoing experience of longing, a restlessness sometimes, but not inevitably, played out romantically, or sexually. Always there seems something ahead, the next poem or story, visible, at least, apprehensible, but unreachable. . . . [T]he poem embodying that sound seems to exist somewhere already finished. It's like a lighthouse, except that, as one swims toward it, it backs away. (PT 16)

In "Education of the Poet" Glück can articulate—in, by her standards, lavish detail—the frustrating silence that the poet must endure, often in her case for years, prior to the achievement of the next comparatively brief period of creative flourish, when she can make "the poem embodying that sound."

For Glück such a phase was the ten-week period in the summer of 1992 when she composed all of *The Wild Iris.* Glück associates the image of fluid writing after long stretches of silence with the body that flickers into appearance for brief stretches and then out of appearance for much longer ones, but also with the difference between the body and the "sound" of the human voice. Form is seen as a necessary manifestation of lyric, but also as a kind of trap, a vehicle for transplanting the author's voice and placing it out of her reach, as if it were now an alien physical being that would have to relinquish the security of isolation and endure the give-and-take that occurs after the reader acquires and begins to consume the published work. Her dislike of the "body" of her text resonates with her desire to exist somehow outside of the gendered roles of wife and lover, for these positions imply to Glück a loss of control that she considers suffocating, violating.[20]

By contrast to her vivid discussion about the endurance of long periods of silence when she is unable to write (the "fundamental experience of the writer" that she defines as "helplessness" [PT 3]), she has fewer words to offer about the mysterious process of literary creation, the instant when she is actually doing the work of the poet to bring form to voice by putting pen to paper. This is so because the poem as embodiment of the desire for recognition inevitably transforms the tense and helpless state of wanting to reach an audience, a state she compares to a libidinal impulse, into the unsatisfying and guilt-filled state of having made an attempt to connect with readers by manifesting her wish in the grossly physical form of the poem: "as long as one is working the thing itself is wrong or unfinished: a failure" (PT 16). Once she has completed the craft stage of editing the poem, or the period that she calls "working," the depressing sensation of "failure," deferred

20. Keller, "'Free / of Blossom,'" 123.

during the act of composing, sets in, only to be replaced by an amnesiac state of forgetfulness that negates her knowledge of having produced anything of literary value. "And then the poem is finished, and at that moment, instantly detached. . . . No record exists of the poet's agency. And the poet, from that point, isn't a poet anymore, simply someone who wishes to be one" (PT 16). Amnesiac forgetfulness corresponds to the states of absence and detachment that Glück has identified as signs of having entered her experience into language. Considering how she distinguishes between language and authorial presence, it is not surprising that Glück interprets desire for recognition as a source of heartbreak throughout her poetry. At the same time, desire for recognition remains essential to her definition of authorship as a sign of her willingness to struggle to express her mastery over nature (including the embodied self) through the transformational work of making a figure of the self in a work of art.

Chapter Three

Visions and Revisions

Commentary and the Question of Being a Contemporary Jewish Poet

Werner Sollors in ***Beyond Ethnicity*** (1986) foregrounds ethnicity as a cultural and aesthetic designation, a consensual approach to identity formation rather than an essential (descent) category of selfhood bestowed upon the person at birth.[1] Considering Jewish identity as a consensual relationship to the recollection of personal history through literature allows a consideration of Glück's creative readings of poets from Homer to Dante to Wallace Stevens as a type of commentary expressing her version of Judaism as a way of thinking about canonical texts. The literary inheritance is not considered sacred and so becomes available to variations through the author's willingness to talk back to it.

My intention here is both to unpack how and to interrogate why Glück refers to a variety of proof texts as a series of shifting stages upon which to perform her life story, in the form of sequences of lyric meditations and dramatic monologues that nonetheless suggest interrelated cultural references and pluralized perspectives. Glück's "Jewishness" is bound up with how she interprets canons both secular and sacred as multiple networks of identity construction. Other recent, and to my mind powerful, accounts of the relationships between canon and contemporary authorship concentrate on the Jewish tradition of creative commentary, or midrash. In "Commentary in Contemporary Jewish American Poetry," for example, Jonathan Barron argues that poets have followed the rabbinical tradition of oral commentary and interpretation (the Talmud) by making the Torah a part of their

1. Werner Sollors, *Beyond Ethnicity: Consent and Descent in American Literature* (New York: Oxford University Press, 1986).

generation's experience. Contemporary Jewish American poets perceive their writing as an expression of human speech that activates the "Total Book" of the sacred text, the Torah:

> According to the rabbinical tradition, *transcendence,* as the very definition of God, prohibits any one person from absolute knowledge. For to claim such knowledge would put one in the mind of God as the mind of God. Nonetheless, it is in the nature of the mind to want to know. Therefore, against the human urge toward such knowledge, rabbinical Judaism developed an oral tradition of commentary and interpretation—the Talmud—that avoids the danger of totalizing, absolute, idolatrous knowledge. It sets itself always in the spoken voice of a singular individual commenting, and interpreting. Commentary, unlike a pronouncement, a law, does not replicate, make, or substitute itself for, or even challenge the transcendent Law. Rather, commentary seeks to reveal and uncover the meaning of that law, now, in the context of human time.[2]

The term "midrash" derives from the Hebrew root "to search out." It was once limited to defining an early rabbinical (400–1200 C.E.) commentary tradition. Classical midrash was not concerned so much with dynamism and contemporaneity as it was with the continuing revelation of the Lord's Word. However, as Barry W. Holtz has argued, there is "no single book called the Midrash." Holtz advises readers to think of midrash as a verb rather than a noun. He describes midrash as a reading process, an interpretive activity, a creative cast of mind, not a single book or movement. He argues that midrash has occurred in Judaism at points of crisis and cultural change, so it became a way for diasporic Jews to deal with tensions and discontinuities—such as how to redefine the roles of sacrifice and sanctification after the Temple was destroyed in 70 C.E. Given Erich Auerbach's famous description in "Odysseus' Scar" of the Bible's laconic nature, especially when compared to Homeric epic, we should not be surprised that a tradition of commentary and interpretation has arisen. Midrash, then as now, "comes to fill in the gaps, to tell us the details that the Bible teasingly leaves out."[3]

At least since 1986, when Geoffrey Hartman and Sanford Budick published *Midrash and Literature,* a growing number of Bible critics such as James

2. Jonathan Barron, "Commentary in Contemporary Jewish American Poetry," in Barron and Selinger, *Jewish American Poetry,* 234.

3. Barry Holtz, *Back to the Sources: Reading the Classic Jewish Texts* (New York: Summit Books, 1984), 177, 180; Erich Auerbach, *Mimesis: The Representation of Reality in Western Literature,* trans. from German by Willard R. Trask (Princeton, N.J.: Princeton University Press, 2003).

Kugel and Robert Alter and literary theorists such as Jacques Derrida and Gerald Bruns have tried to make sense of the wide band of modern and contemporary Jewish writers, and especially Jewish women writers, who have written about their lives by filling in the aporias in the biblical narratives.[4] The midrash movement has captured much critical attention because it offers a way for previously disenfranchised readers such as secular humanists and Jewish women to create dynamic works of art, by encountering Bible stories that may have seemed in past eras to belong to an exclusive heritage. From the point of view of contemporary literary theory, midrash is also a significant approach to texts from the sacred and secular canon. When one reads poetry as midrash, the rigid hierarchies and classificatory systems that informed an older critical model—systems such as primary and secondary works, originality versus commentary, divinely sanctioned authority versus human endeavor, canonical and noncanonical categories, concepts of sacred and profane—are challenged in ways that open up of the tenets of canon formation. More important for this study, how to repair the rift women have felt between themselves and Jewish source texts remains in question, especially since midrash traditionally functioned to reveal rather than contest the Lord's Word. As Holtz points out, the rabbis most likely felt free and flexible when interpreting Bible narratives and legal codes because they also felt they were inspired to uncover what they believed *was already there,* written by the perfect author in an "eternally relevant book."[5] Glück's strong denial of the influence of Judaism on her life and work, even as Old Testament stories and the commentary tradition have clearly influenced her as an artist, speaks to the large gap between rift and repair.

Publishing her first book in 1968, Glück expresses herself in the midst of a paradigm-shifting examination of the secular canons of British and American literatures by feminist theorists such as Judith Fetterly, Sandra Gilbert, Susan Gubar, Elaine Showalter, and Jane Tompkins, as well as by poets such as Adrienne Rich, Elinor Wilner, Alicia Ostriker, and Maxine Kumin. Many of the prominent female senior scholars teaching in the academy today—and those who led the way for a generation of younger scholars in revising the canon of English and American literatures in the 1970s and 1980s—are Jewish. Although born into Jewish families, these female poets and scholars tended to sublimate their ambivalence toward Judaism, a patriarchal religion in which women have occupied a second-class position, by transferring their reactions to a religious system to how they approached the

4. Hartman and Budick, *Midrash and Literature.*
5. Holtz, *Back to the Sources,* 185.

canon they confronted upon entering graduate programs of English and comparative literature in the 1960s and 1970s.

In a retrospective essay that is especially forthcoming on this point, Susan Gubar discusses her bittersweet feelings about Judaism as a text-centered religion that foregrounds justice and human rights but is written from a perspective that often excludes women as significant figures in its primary narrative and commentary traditions. Writing some two decades after coauthoring *The Madwoman in the Attic,* Gubar reflects on the then unacknowledged connections between her reactions to a 1980 Passover Seder and the impulses that led her to feminist literary criticism:

> Although at the time I did not know it, my personal anger at this particular seder resembled the responses of a generation of women writing during the seventies, eighties, and now in the nineties, feminists reacting to gender asymmetries in the legal, liturgical, and spiritual traditions of Judaism.[6]

Like Gubar, who has published a book on the impact of the Holocaust on English and American poets, Glück may be defined as a secular author who is working to revise the canon in the academy in the second half of the twentieth century. Glück has tended not to emphasize Judaism as a religious practice (although her book *Ararat* centers upon the burial of her father in a Jewish cemetery) or Jewishness as an ethnicity (although her poem "Legend" [TA] concerns her paternal grandfather's emigration from Hungary to the Lower East Side of Manhattan). Glück is an assimilated Jew who seems as comfortable writing about Achilles, or a red trillium growing between rocks in a suburban garden in Vermont, as she does about Moses or David or Solomon. Her revisionary impulses in addressing Homer and parts of nature nonetheless relate her to critics such as Gubar who have redefined the meaning of key literary works outside the Jewish canon as a displaced version of their relationship to Judaism in contemporary America.[7] By revising canonical materials of all sorts, Glück joins hands with what Gubar calls the

6. Susan Gubar, "Eating the Bread of Affliction: Judaism and Gender," in *Critical Condition: Feminism at the Turn of the Century* (New York: Columbia University Press, 2000), 72–73.

7. According to David Bleich, "the more consequential gestures to restore a living Jewish identity and culture are taking place through the study of history, the Biblical texts, and the attempts, primarily through Jewish feminism, to recast some of the values that have compromised the strong themes of social justice in Jewish history." David Bleich, "Learning, Learning, Learning: Jewish Poetry in America," in Barron and Selinger, *Jewish American Poetry,* 187.

tradition of Jewish women who "explored their bitterness about their secondariness in their own heritage"—while affirming ways of reading and thinking that resemble Jewish traditions of reading which suspend rigid boundaries between primary and secondary texts, between a fundamental set of sacred works and the commentary portions found in the oral Torah.[8]

Robert Alter, in *Canon and Creativity,* has challenged the definition of canonicity as "the simple and assured phenomenon of enshrining doctrine in text that it is often assumed to be."[9] Applying principles of "literary canonicity" to the Bible, Alter finds that a canon can be and, historically, *has been* "much more flexible, and less ideologically binding, than prevalent conceptions allow" (5). He quarrels with the confidence with which scholars such as Harold Bloom in the *Book of J* have adopted the nineteenth-century German "Documentary Hypothesis," or historicist approach, to determine biblical authorship, but Alter does argue that the Bible should be received as a text, a kind of bibliographic library composed of many, often contradictory and clashing voices, assembled together by editors "sometime around the turn of the Christian era" (22):

> The primary [Hebrew Biblical] narrative is . . . composite, a redactor's orchestration of tensions among divergent or even clashing views of the represented figures and events. It is thus both a report of what happened and a puzzling, an interpreter's struggle over the reported action. One readily understands how such a narrative would generate three thousand years of exegesis, with no end in sight. (16)

Like Harold Bloom, Alter champions T. S. Eliot's well-known conception of the "individual talent," who turns away from canons as doctrine to interpret them as common idioms, facilitating idiosyncratic responses to scripture ranging from playful transformation to ideological challenge. By redefining the Hebrew Bible as a polysemous compendium of narratives, poems, proverbs, prophecies, and other genres of writing, compiled by many editors over time, Alter upends the dyad of acts of producing and consuming literature.

Defining a Jewish canon as "a transhistorical textual community" (5), Alter confronts definitions of the scripture as an approved list of authoritative works that should be preserved intact by priestlike keepers of the gate. He reads such "problem-books" as Job and Ecclesiastes as "philosophical

8. Gubar, "Bread of Affliction," 73.

9. Robert Alter, *Canon and Creativity: Modern Writing and the Authority of Scripture* (New Haven: Yale University Press, 2000), 4. In the following discussion of this book, page references will be given in the text.

challenges to views generally accepted in the dominant body of beliefs of ancient Israel" (28–29). Within the proof text itself, he finds a practice of bold critique that anticipates the efforts by modern writers—from Franz Kafka (in *Amerika*), Thomas Mann (in *Joseph and His Brothers*), and the poet Haim Nahman Bialik to contemporary Jewish women poets such as Alicia Ostriker, Jacqueline Osherow, Chana Bloch, and Glück. This is a rather disparate group. What they have in common is their desire to investigate social life and to explore their own drive to assert a freedom from the past through a creative reframing of the proof texts in order to extend "the range of meanings of the textual community in which they participate when they use the biblical canon . . . to express vitalistic pantheism, or an individual fate of hapless victimhood, or a vision of cosmic pitilessness, or a notion of eternal recurrence" (5–6).

Following Alter's commentary on the relationships between secular literary expression and the Bible, I see Glück's poetry as an expression of a Jewish way of thinking about canons—or an expression that, in Alter's terms, illustrates the tendentious and dynamic "culture of exegesis" that characterizes "the Hebrew imagination, as early as its founding biblical phase" (15). Glück revises scriptural and classical texts in order to explore her spiritual autobiography from shifting points of view. Especially in book-length sequences such as *Ararat, Meadowlands,* and *The Wild Iris,* she follows in the midrashic tradition of generating further discussion about individual utterances (individual texts) by supplying a context in which other texts, and other voices, offer interpretations on common subject matter. Shira Wolosky has written that, in midrash, "multiple interpretations emerge alongside each other, without the compulsion to harmonize them or render them consistent. . . . Always and through all, interpretation is conceived fundamentally as text responding to text, interpretation to interpretation, a procedure that begins within the corpus of Scripture itself." Glück's increasing interest in supplying multiple interpretations of her main lyric speaker's experience—through the voices of the characters of Telemachus, Circe, and Penelope in *Meadowlands,* or through the voices of the various flora that respond to the main speaker's quest for signs of a divine presence in *The Wild Iris*—enacts what David Stern calls "the typical midrashic predilection for multiple interpretations rather than for a single truth behind the text."[10]

10. Shira Wolosky, "On Contemporary Literary Theory and Jewish American Poetics," in *The Cambridge Companion to Jewish American Literature,* ed. Michael P. Kramer and Hana Wirth-Nesher (Cambridge, England: Cambridge University Press, 2003), 250–68; David Stern, *Midrash and Theory* (Evanston, Ill.: Northwestern University Press, 1996), 3.

Glück's poetry is indebted to quests for access to divine knowledge and to secular power that are found in the Bible (both "Old" and "New") as well as in Homer, Virgil, and Dante; in fairy tales; and in historical legends such as Joan of Arc, whose prophetic stance and willingness to sacrifice herself for an abstract principle or impersonal cause such as the national liberation of France appeals to Glück. Like the story of Gretel, the Joan of Arc narrative displays a desire for recognition at the cost of the will toward self-preservation. Primarily influenced by "high cult" sources, Glück draws also from popular culture—and especially from musical traditions ranging from soul to klezmer to opera. In *Meadowlands,* a book devoted primarily to matching the speaker's contemporary experience with the story of Odysseus and Penelope, for example, Glück refers to the influence of an Otis Redding record upon her when she was a young woman. She also refers to members of the New York Football Giants such as Lawrence Taylor and Phil Simms as latter-day versions of Greek warriors.[11] However much she is a poet of vision and revision of classical texts, Glück is also very much an author of this world, at this time, in this place.

By connecting poetry to criticism and interpretation and in basing poems on Bible stories, Glück joins more overtly Jewish feminist poets such as Wilner and Osherow. She thus expresses what Matthew Baigell describes as the "Jewish habit [of conflating] present with past tragedies, [collapsing] present time into past time and [connecting] terrible contemporary events . . . with biblical events."[12] But in Glück's Bible poems, the primary interest in canons is not to promote feminist revisionism of sacred sources. Instead, her Bible poems offer nervous reflections on status, power, morality, desire, and the meaning of covenant as an exclusionary version of being chosen—issues that more often than not connect Glück's speaker to dominant male characters from the Torah such as David and Moses. Glück's challenge to canon engages with but differs from the negotiation between Judaism and gender found in work by authors such as Adrienne Rich in the essay "Split at the Root," Cynthia Ozick in "Notes toward Finding the Right Question," Judith Plaskow in *Standing Again at Sinai,* and contributors to such journals as *Lilith: The Jewish Woman's Magazine,* and collections such as Susannah Heschel's *On Being a Jewish Feminist: A Reader.* Glück's wrestling with the canon in order to forge her own literary autobiography through revising the biographies of biblical heroes has more in common with the theories of

11. In "Meadowlands 3," she protests: "How could the Giants name / that place the Meadowlands? It has / about as much in common with a pasture / as would the inside of an oven" (M 34).

12. Matthew Baigell, *Jewish Artists in New York: The Holocaust Years* (New Brunswick, N.J.: Rutgers University Press, 2002), 109.

literary influence promoted by Harold Bloom in *The Anxiety of Influence* than it does with the work of such feminist historians as Gilbert and Gubar.[13]

So, is Glück a Jewish poet? Well, the first answer is no. In a conversation, Glück denied this identity, saying that the Jewish tradition did not "speak" to her in the ways that, for example, Hellenism or nature did. In a letter, she describes her Jewish background as limited:

> We had a rudimentary Jewish upbringing. We lived in a Jewish suburb, but Jewish practice was, as I remember, casual. We all celebrated Christmas, sans tree. I think I was not especially attuned to social matters. The food at our table was French and quite polished. We didn't light candles on Friday. We did convene, with my mother's family, for the high holidays. The European and Russian roots, on both sides, were not immediate. My mother's parents were born here, as far as I know. My father's parents came from Hungary before his birth. No vestiges of other language remained in either. Only my mother's brother knew any Hebrew.
>
> I rebelled early against a religious education, partly because it was an education in addition to music lessons, dance lessons, and so on; it was the low priority, and I did not get very far; it was, in my parents' view, the expendable item.[14]

Moreover, she identifies herself, in her poetry, with other than Jewish figures, alongside Jewish ones. But inside her effusive no to the vestiges of a Jewish influence on her writings, we may also be hearing the subtle echo of yes. Does her denial manifest an anxiety of influence? Does her identification with Hellenistic and Christian figures as well as specifically Jewish ones reflect a Bloomian strategy of complementation, or "Tessera"? For Bloom, "Tessera" (the mosaic term for linking together parts of a broken vessel) reflects the later poet's anxiety about a precursor, through the process of complementing her writing or of supplying what she lacks.[15] This strategy of

13. Adrienne Rich, "Split at the Root: An Essay on Jewish Identity," in *Adrienne Rich's Poetry and Prose,* ed. Barbara Charlesworth Gelpi and Albert Gelpi (New York: Norton, 1993), 224–38; Cynthia Ozick, "Notes toward Finding the Right Question (A Vindication of the Rights of Jewish Women)," *Forum 35* (Spring-Summer 1979): 37–60.

14. Personal correspondence with the author.

15. Bloom defines "Tessera" as the second of his six "revisionary ratios": "Tessera, which is completion and antithesis; I take the word not from mosaic-making, where it is still used, but from the ancient mystery cults, where it meant a token of recognition, the fragment say of a small pot which with the other fragments would re-constitute the vessel. A poet antithetically 'completes' his precursor, by so reading the parent-poem as to retain its terms but to mean

responding to anxiety through supplementation is most akin to a specifically Jewish approach to canonical texts and figures, at least if we go along with Alter's interpretation of midrash as a tradition of creative commentary. In terms of her relationship to Judaism, we could say that Glück's denial of its influence on her work manifests in her tendency to complement the Jewish stories and characters she uses with something adversarial, with classical materials and with nature in particular.

Glück often invokes Jewish sources, but she limits their meanings so as to make room for the value, or emotional impact, of adversarial materials such as are found in Greek myth. Take "Mount Ararat" (AR). The poem discusses the family plot at the Jewish graveyard (named Mount Ararat), where her father and one of her sisters are buried. It is described as a place "dedicated to the Jewish god / who doesn't hesitate to take / a son from a mother" (AR 30). Dismissing the image of a compassionate and merciful God, described by Jonah as "slow to anger, abounding in kindness, renouncing punishment" (Jonah 4:2), she represents Yahweh as a ruthless deity, who "doesn't hesitate," who seems more interested in ritual sacrifice than in concern for the human intensities of desire, emotion, and pain upon the death of a loved one. Instead of privileging the Hebraic and setting its (anti-idolatrous, antisacrificial) truth apart from Hellenistic myth (as René Girard does), the poet seems to see the biblical narrative as mythic and sacrificial.

By contrast to Yahweh, Glück represents the God-man Achilles in "The Triumph of Achilles" (TA) as a classical figure who embraces life, suffering, and the inevitability of death with a kind of Nietzschean intensity. Unlike the Yahweh represented in *Ararat,* Homeric narrative implies an acceptance of the compatibility of pain, loss, and a life well lived. Whereas, in *The Wild Iris,* the Jewish God is cast as jealous of his divine sovereignty, a remote impersonal force not unlike the image of the first "unmoved mover" (described by Maimonides in *Guide for the Perplexed,* ca. 1200), in *Meadowlands* Glück associates the passionate intensities of human love, human struggle, and artistic achievement with Homer.

In "Saints" (AR), Glück compares the lives of her grandmother and her aunt:

> My grandmother's was tranquil, even at the end.
> She was like a person walking in calm water;

---

them in another sense, as though the precursor had failed to go far enough." Harold Bloom, *The Anxiety of Influence: A Theory of Poetry* (1973), 2nd ed. (New York: Oxford University Press, 1997), 14.

for some reason
the sea couldn't bring itself to hurt her.
When my aunt took the same path,
the waves broke over her, they attacked her,
which is how the Fates respond
to a true spiritual nature. (AR 50)

Glück associates the grandmother's life, which does not involve genuine risk, with the story of Moses and the Israelites' escape from Egypt via the Red Sea through the image of her walking on a sea that "couldn't bring itself to hurt her." By contrast, the aunt's story, which Glück links to a Greek image of female divinity (the Fates), concerns the hardships, violence, and passionate intensity of "a true spiritual nature," the "nature" of Glück's perception of herself.

Glück interprets Hebrew Bible stories first by juxtaposing them with classical myths and then by connecting the ancient sources to her own experience. She maintains a balance between the lyric, with its emphasis on a first-person retelling of subjective experience, and what Maerra Y. Shreiber refers to as a "cross-cultural exchange." By commenting on Jewish as well as non-Jewish texts, Glück imagines a more "heterogeneous, inclusive version of Jewishness," as well as a way to honor "individuated emotive experience" alongside "collective diversity."[16] In "A Parable" (TA), for example, she describes the pattern of King David's biography as following the "trace" of "a mountain." The mountain "arc" illustrates the shape of David's narrative from obscurity, to the incline of power, to a social decline brought about by the excesses of his sexual appetite and political ambition. Following the model Bloom provides of complementarity through an inclusion of adversarial material, we note that in "The Mountain" (the poem preceding "A Parable" in the collection), Glück interprets the Greek mythic character and legendary first murderer, Sisyphus, as "the artist" who

lies
because he is obsessed with attainment,
that he perceives the summit
as that place where he will live forever,
a place about to be
transformed by his burden. (FFB 194)

16. Maerra Y. Shreiber, "Jewish American Poetry," in Kramer and Wirth-Nesher, *Jewish American Literature,* 164, 165–66.

Besides linking David's story with that of Sisyphus through the image of the mountain arc, Glück also invites us to make analogies between biblical and classical figures of desire and her own struggle for recognition as an author. In "Education of the Poet," she describes the process of organizing a series of lyrics into a book as the "making of a pile of poems an arc, a shaped utterance" (PT 17).[17] By connecting David's career to the myth of Sisyphus and then by linking their histories to her own analysis of the creative process, she has turned the biblical story into a classical myth involving the themes of desire, control, violence, and ambition that reflect on her own autobiographical concerns with her status as an author.

Perhaps one reason why Glück tends not to emphasize her Jewishness when thinking of herself as an author is that she has associated the story of the Israelites' forty years of wandering in the desert prior to God's revelation at Sinai with her own silent periods, her own dread of wordlessness and meaninglessness. In a 1999 interview with Brian Phillips published in the *Harvard Advocate,* she stated:

> My compositional process almost always begins in a kind of despondency, or hopelessness, or desolation, usually born of a conviction that I will never write again. That I will at long intervals turn out little mechanical B plus poems, but that I'll never again feel that I am at the throat of the dog, that I'm at something essential. This pattern really hasn't varied, though my first book was more diligently written. But even then there were long hiatuses of silence and periods of despondency, like in the desert, that have come to seem to me the norm of my aesthetic life . . . which isn't to say those passages are not brutal. So that each of my books really begins with a prayer, you know: Appear to me again. Let me be suffused with the wish to, and ability to, make meaning out of language.[18]

An author who wishes to stress her independence and her difference from any group identification must pray to the absolute Other in order to "make meaning out of language." An author who in "Saints" (AR) associated the life of a "true spiritual nature" with an aunt who tempted the Fates has invoked the "brutal" Exodus narrative to describe the long stretches of silence that accompany her brief periods of creative flourish.

17. In "Retreating Wind" from *The Wild Iris,* the image of the arc recurs in the poet's description of a bird as it makes its arclike flight from a white birch to an apple tree. A standard symbol for the soul (as in associations of Jesus with the descending dove), the bird represents the fate of the mortal speaker (birth, growth, maturity, decline) as opposed to the perennial flowers, such as the iris, upon which the speaker meditates (WI, 15).

18. Brian Phillips, "An Interview with Louise Glück," *Harvard Advocate* (1999): 247–48.

Glück interprets canons from an unusually intimate perspective. In an autobiographical essay from *Proofs & Theories,* she describes them as her family inheritance and, therefore, as a reflection of the psychological conflicts accompanying family life. This is why I dare to connect her poetry not only to the Jewish tradition of commentary, but to what I must admit up front may seem a rather strange theoretical bedfellow, Harold Bloom.

A Bloomian reading strategy may seem anathema to a contemporary female author's attempts to discover what her own voice might sound like by recovering gaps and fissures within a range of prior texts. But who else but Bloom speaks to how "belated" authors relate to poetic generations in terms of familial conflict? Few critics—even among those such as Alter who do emphasize the creative nature of commentary as a significant literary endeavor—go so far as Bloom in considering how an author's relationship to traditions produces "a literary biography" through the esoteric and subjective perspective on the books read:

> A biography becomes *literary* biography only when literary meaning is produced, and literary meaning can only result from the interpretation of literature. Poetry begins, always, when someone who is going to become a poet *reads a poem.* But I immediately add—when he *begins* to read a poem, for to see how fully he reads that poem we will have to see the poem that he himself will write *as his reading.*[19]

By commenting on biblical, classical, as well as romantic, and modern poetry as if she were dealing with the work of family members who exist in tension with one another, Glück unsettles the idea of canon as a closed system of sacred works—by inserting a related but previously unsung voice into the conversation about traditional texts that have helped to shape her identity. As Miriam Peskowitz and Laura Levitt remind us in *Judaism since Gender,* the act of performing new readings of old sources should be considered "something less additive than transformative."[20] Glück does not so much add a new voice onto the end of the textual line as she transforms the meaning of texts by interpreting them from a new visual angle, thereby reclaiming and recovering the author's voice and vision.[21]

19. Harold Bloom, *Kabbalah and Criticism* (New York: Seabury, 1975), 106–7.

20. Miriam Peskowitz and Laura Levitt, eds., *Judaism since Gender* (New York: Routledge, 1997), xi.

21. Unlike female "language" poets such as Lyn Hejinian or poststructuralist French feminist theorists such as Luce Irigaray, Glück does not seem interested in deconstructing the conventional underpinnings of language as a communication that accurately responds in logical fashion to a world beyond the text. Her work is available to exegesis and in fact can be quite

In her introduction to *The Best American Poetry, 1993,* Glück sounds as though she had been reading Bloom on what he calls "literary biography" when she addresses the belated author's terrible realization that "[t]he world is complete without us" (PT 91):

> Intolerable fact. To which the poet responds by rebelling, wanting to prove otherwise. Out of wounded vanity or stubborn pride or desolate need, the poet lives in chronic dispute with fact, and an astonishment occurs: another fact is created, like a new element, in partial contradiction of the intolerable. (PT 91)

From first to last, her poetry confronts the "intolerable fact" of prior creation and, from this uncomfortable perspective, announces a "new element," which she claims is "in partial contradiction" to, or "in chronic dispute" with, the literary models that at once produce a forum for the appearance of her voice (in the way parents have children) and disturb her autonomy (in the way parents disturb the freedom of their children to express themselves).

Glück's reading of Old Testament narratives negotiates the vexed relationship between Judaism and gender. By reading female biblical characters against the conventional grain, Glück writes a kind of feminist midrash. In this she joins authors such as Ellen Frankel in *The Five Books of Miriam* (1996) and, before her, Judith Plaskow, whose *Standing again at Sinai: Judaism from a Feminist Perspective* (1990) reclaims the voices of female biblical characters through the open-ended process of writing midrash, a process Plaskow defines as "an expression of our own convictions, a creative imagining based on our own experience, albeit developed in dialogue with traditional texts."[22] Glück's poetry reflects this process. In "Lamentations" (DF), a long poem from 1980 loosely based on the Garden myth in Genesis, for example, Glück expresses her convictions about the Hebrew Bible's primordial story of language acquisition. Relying on her experience as a woman and mother, she suggests a feminist revision by associating bearing the word and bearing the child. In "Abishag" (HM) from 1975, Glück's dialogue with a traditional text similarly mirrors the Jewish feminist movement in its attempt to let women speak through new readings of old sources.

---

easily referenced toward male writers from the past. My point is that Glück does not wish to disavow a relationship to the canonical writings from the past, or to undermine the canon's authority to measure significance and cultural value by throwing out the old rules and inventing completely new ones. To the contrary, she defines herself and measures her stature in and through past texts.

22. Plaskow, *Standing again at Sinai,* 56.

In "Lamentations" and "Abishag," Glück is writing a distinctly feminist midrash, but in revisiting Bible stories she has by no means limited her attention to a critique of patriarchy. To the contrary, in longer poems from *The Triumph of Achilles* from 1985, Glück identifies with male characters. Instead of focusing on unacknowledged female characters from the Bible, she examines King David's use and abuse of power, in "A Parable." She discusses the life of Moses in the eight-part poem entitled "Day Without Night." In "Legend," she discusses her paternal grandfather and compares his diasporic journey with that of Joseph's bondage in Egypt. In all three cases, Glück has identified her creative struggles with those of male characters in order to reflect on her own ambivalent relationship to status, power, morality, gender, and most of all, language. She imagines as well as challenges her desire for and access to the prize of symbolic achievement.

Glück's poems deal with Old Testament narratives as various as the Garden myth, King David's mistreatment of Bathsheba and Abishag, Joseph's journey to Egypt, and Moses' rise from the status of estranged orphan to major prophet. However diverse the subject matter and personae through which she speaks, in each case she finds resonance with her own struggle to access language, often at the cost of alienating the newly empowered speaker from her natural environment and from the embodied self. Her poems based on the Jewish Bible thus emphasize what Kojève, in his brilliant *Introduction to the Reading of Hegel,* refers to as "a fight for pure prestige carried on for the sake of 'recognition' by the adversary."[23] At the same time, Glück calls into question the ethics of her own ambitions for literary mastery. In this spirit of self-scrutiny, she retells tales that involve biblical figures such as King David, whose desire for worldly power and control negates the obligation toward securing the safety of other, more vulnerable persons.

Crossing the borders of gender, victimhood, and victimization, Glück extends the range of her identifications with Jewish biblical figures to explore the ethical issue of responsibility of the self toward the other, in a context where creativity and social power merge. Published when Glück was in her early thirties and in the midst of the first wave of feminist revisions of the Bible, which included the groundbreaking work of figures such as Mary Daly and Adrienne Rich, "Abishag" (HM) reflects Glück's fascination, perhaps identification, with an unsung female character. Through the story of Abishag, Glück amplifies her own commentaries in more autobiographical poems—such as "Dedication to Hunger" (DF)—on how physical disappearance may be interpreted by a subjugated person as an expression of symbolic

23. Kojève, *Introduction,* 12.

power. Published ten years later, when Glück had achieved prominence as an author, "A Parable" (TA) performs the self through the mask of David, by imagining the psychology of the male king and his speech acts as a forum in which to address her own ambivalence concerning literary power as a form of mastery over the world around her.

"Lamentations" (DF)

Feminist critics from the 1970s such as Mary Daly interpreted Genesis as the site of female victimization because it is where "women have had the power of *naming* stolen from us."[24] Instead of reducing the Garden myth to the site in which women are cast as the silent victims of a patriarchal narrative, Glück projects her ambivalence about accessing the power to name through the Eden myth. "Lamentations" is a terse, mysterious, four-part poem that concludes Glück's third book, *Descending Figure,* and in it, Glück explores her experience as a woman and mother—by imagining the Fall myth as a linguistically productive but physically destructive and emotionally painful experience for both Adam and Eve. Estrangement from God, expulsion from nature, the split experienced by Eve between Psyche and Eros, and the division of male from female, all lead toward Glück's discussion of human entrance into sexuality in "Lamentations" part 1, and especially to the advent of maternity in part 3. In part 4, Glück specifically connects writing and maternity, as two forms of human agency, when Adam's and Eve's wounded bodies are converted into texts only after Eve has given birth.

The quartet of poems takes its overall title, "Lamentations," from the five-part elegiac prayer in the "Writings" (Ketuvim) section of the Torah, which records the destruction of the First Temple in Jerusalem and the seventy-year Babylonian exile. The biblical "Lamentations" applies the extended anthropomorphic metaphor of a widow who asks God to forgive her for committing unspecified sins. It questions why God has bestowed such suffering upon the Jews. Resonant with this allegory about the Babylonian exile, through an invocation of the Garden narrative Glück's poem comments on the primordial story of guilt and alienation from a sacred place.

She addresses issues central to her own poetics, and especially to her perception of the physical, social, and emotional costs involved in acquiring

24. Mary Daly, *Beyond God the Father: Toward a Philosophy of Women's Liberation* (Boston: Beacon Press, 1973), 8.

identity through language. These themes will reappear in *The Wild Iris* (1992), where the supplicant's assertion of subjectivity through language imperils her sense of being at home in nature or at one with God. Through the Fall narrative, both in "Lamentations" and in *The Wild Iris,* Glück examines the costs of autonomy, as well as of a transforming understanding of the self from something given to something made.

Glück divides her narrative into four parts—"The Logos," "Nocturne," "The Covenant," and "The Clearing." Anticipating *The Wild Iris,* she creates a dynamic portrayal of the shifting relationship between persons and God. Yahweh is Himself a protean figure, cast variously as furious, negligent, creatively powerful, emotionally needy, resentful, and voyeuristic. Whatever His mood, until the final section the divine maker is represented as immanent. In part 1, "The Logos," God projects "flowers on the landscape" and fills the world "with his radiance." In part 2, "Nocturne," the God who earlier "was watching" Adam and Eve with "his gold eye" becomes so jealous of human sexuality and the human authority of biological reproduction that "He divided them: / the man, the woman, and the woman's body" (FFB 148). At points God is an anthropomorphic being of intense feeling, especially when He is described as "furious," "negligent," a disgruntled "monster" who feels the need to be "understood" by ungrateful and unruly human creations. He is also cast as a helpless outsider, who can only observe human affairs from a distance. Having absconded from the garden to the sky at the end of the poem, God becomes recast as a disembodied abstraction, a product of the human imagination.

The feminist theologian Adrienne Munich points out that, according to

> Scripture's second (but earlier) account of creation, Adam was the first philologist, interpretive as well as onomastic: "the Lord God formed every beast of the field and every fowl of the air, and brought them unto the man to see what he would call them; and whatsoever the man called every living creature, that was the name thereof" (Genesis 2:19). By naming creation, he possessed for himself language's power. To validate further his authority and to avoid possible controversy, he performed these acts before Eve was created.[25]

Many critics, including feminist ones, find in this fable a paradigm for male dominance over language. In part 3, "The Covenant," by contrast, Glück

25. Adrienne Munich, "Notorious Signs, Feminist Criticism, and Literary Tradition," in *Making a Difference: Feminist Literary Criticism,* ed. Gayle Greene and Coppelia Kahn (London: Methuen, 1985), 238.

revises Genesis 2:19 by allowing both Adam and Eve to respond to the fact that their expulsion from the Garden must precede their authority as language-bearers.

Glück's primordial couple responds to their estrangement from God and alienation from nature. They forge a compact, not with God (as in Exodus) but with each other. Glück's creation myth thus emphasizes human authority in the forms of building, childbearing, and language acquisition. In the book of Genesis, it is man, not woman, who gives birth, and not to an infant but to a contemporary: "This one shall be called woman / For from man was this one taken" (2:23). Munich points out that Adam "allows woman her function as life-bearer only after the Fall, when this female power bears the taint of sin, pain and death."[26] In "The Covenant," by contrast, Glück emphasizes the relationship between female creativity, in the embodied form of childbearing, and human authority, in the disembodied form of language. She does so by depicting the couple shaping their environment when "out of fear, they built a dwelling place," but then also through the image of Eve bearing a child with Adam at her side:

> As it reached its hands
> they understood they were the mother and father,
> there was no authority above them. (FFB 149)

The couple simultaneously recognize their freedom from God and their estrangement from nature, in the aftermath to Eve's birth-giving.

In part 4, "The Clearing," Glück celebrates their acquisition of language as well as the expression of Eve's authority through bearing a child. Her narrative also involves estrangement from the unself-conscious—if panic-stricken—sense of dwelling in the world on an animal level, an awareness that characterized the couple's relationship to nature and to God in the first three parts of "Lamentations." Besides their separation from animals, nature, and each other, Glück describes how the couple's own bodies change form, becoming metamorphosed from animal skin ("the fur disappeared from their bodies") into "white flesh."

> Nor could they keep their eyes
> from the white flesh
> on which wounds would show clearly
> like words on a page. (FFB 150)

26. Ibid., 241.

Glück reinterprets Adam's entrance into language through his power to name the animals in Genesis 2, by applying the linguistic displacement from nature to Eve as well. Both the man and the woman must convert alienation into a means of clarifying their own experience through language. Metaphor thus enables the speaker to turn human skin into a parchment, which serves as the scene of a self-impression. Glück has described a traumatic break from a prior state of atonement with nature and unself-consciousness about one's physical existence. She also imagines people with the power not only to name the world around them but also to imagine themselves as texts.

The couple perceive their bodies as linguistic constructs, the scars on "white flesh" resembling "words on a page." Their new self-images precede their rendering of God as an abstract concept, and this is an attitude toward divinity that replaces the "Logos" of God's creation of the world in part 1. No longer the immanent "Monster," God is recast as a vanishing ephemeral figure, something rising from the "meaningful browns and greens" (stanza 3, part 4). This figure of divinity, portrayed as having absconded from the Garden, becomes a projection of the author's desire to acquire a visionary perspective, an aesthetic disposition, at the cost of renouncing embodied life and sensual experience: "How beautiful it must have been, / the earth, that first time / seen from the air" (FFB 150).[27] Both God and human beings are subjects of language, but God's vantage point seems little more than a nostalgic projection of the human speaker's desire to possess a transcendent perspective on her own loss of innocence.

Glück reinterprets the Fall story to examine from a mythic perspective the relationships between maternity, creativity, alienation from nature, and the struggle for personal autonomy that she had been dealing with through the confessionalist mode in *Firstborn,* her first book of poems. Margaret Ann Gordon argues that Glück's interpretation of childbearing in poems such as "The Egg" and "The Wound" (F) represents giving birth as a liminal experience. For Glück, maternity implies both the woman's deep connection to nature, through the undeniable fact of physical embodiment, and Glück's separation from nature through the association of the scarred body with the written page. Gordon emphasizes how a part of the mother's once unified body (the child) "has now become irrevocably lost and foreign to its mother."[28]

27. The speaker's comments about God's perspective on the earth reflects Vendler's description of Glück's characteristic voice: "There is something 'disembodied, triumphant, dead'—Whitman's words—about Glück's usual voice. . . . She sees her experience from very far off, almost through the wrong end of a telescope, transparently removed in space or time. It is this removal which gives such mythological power." Helen Vendler, "Louise Glück," in *A Part of Nature, Part of Us: Modern American Poets* (Cambridge, Mass.: Harvard University Press, 1980), 305.

28. Gordon, "Reconceiving the Sacred," 28.

Focusing in "The Egg" on the doctor who assists in the birth that threatens her autonomy, the speaker connects the maternal self with a torn piece of paper, suggesting linkages between creation and destruction, authority and loss:

> I saw the lamps
> Converging in his glasses.
> Dramamine. You let him
> Rob me. But
> How long? how long?
> Past cutlery I saw
> My body stretching like a tear
> Along the paper. (FFB 7)

The speaker confronts the fact that, for the mother, biological reproduction involves separation and self-estrangement, the process that Gordon refers to as the "unmaking and recreation of identity."[29]

In "Lamentations" part 4, "The Clearing," Glück's version of Eve's response to the Garden myth, involving authority and exile, recalls the mother's ambivalence toward maternity in "The Egg." Whether working in the confessionalist style or through the Genesis creation myth, Glück interprets bearing the word and bearing the child as acts that substitute human creativity for divine creativity. Language authorizes human achievement but also suggests self-estrangement. The postpartum body is transformed into a text that becomes significant because wounded or torn. Because Glück rewrites Genesis 2 as a story of both male and female authority and emphasizes the relationship between childbearing and linguistic power, "Lamentations" (DF) can be read as an example of feminist revisioning of the Jewish Bible. As Claire Satlof put it, feminist revisioning involves "recasting tradition and pronouncing a previously unspoken word."[30]

"Abishag" (HM)

In "History, Fiction, and the Tradition," Satlof argues that "writing itself, for feminists, is a form of rebellion, usurpation, or revisioning." Unlike

29. Ibid., 33.
30. Claire Satlof, "History, Fiction, and the Tradition: Creating a Jewish Feminist Poetic," in Heschel, *Jewish Feminist,* 203.

deconstructionist reading strategies that wish to obliterate the established meaning of literary works, and therefore to disregard their relevance to the imagining of present or future worlds (also understood as texts with unstable borders), Satlof maintains that a feminist poetics must incorporate a constructive principle as well as a challenging one. Feminist revisioning must discover new ways to imagine contemporary experience, without damaging the power of myth to shape and transform the experience of contemporary life. For Satlof, a feminist poetic must incorporate the deconstructivist principle of shaking up normative ways of seeing the world, but it must also "mark the beginning of a new realization and a new myth-making, for language is intimately bound up with religious ritual. More than the vehicle for performing rituals, language establishes the reality of myth."[31]

Satlof's idea of a feminist poetics has definite affinities with the specifically Jewish exegetical tradition. For example, in "Midrash, Bible, and Women's Voices," the contemporary novelist Norma Rosen has interpreted the emphasis on "aggadot," or biblical retellings through commentary, as a form of feminist interpretation. For Rosen, a feminist midrash is a type of commentary that remains true to the etymological roots of "midrash," a word that Rosen reminds us comes from the Hebrew *lidrosh,* meaning "to search, to ask, to explain, to draw out, to enlarge upon." Rosen compares the narrative techniques of the ancient rabbis—and especially the rabbis' understanding that there is "more than one way for the narrative to go, and it may go in all those ways simultaneously"—to the postmodern narrative techniques she employs in her own fictions:

> Much of what the rabbis did with midrash resembles the fiction-writing impulse. Midrashists ask themselves about motivation for what the characters do. What the text omits, they try to supply, sometimes imagining themselves into the feelings of a character. Accounting for discrepancies in the story, they make events plausible.[32]

In "Abishag," Glück performs a midrash as Rosen would define the concept. She pays attention to an absence in the proof text—how a woman known primarily as a royal concubine and nursemaid to the aging King David was not adequately imagined as a human being with a significant voice, vision, subjectivity, and desires of her own. As commentator Glück takes liberties

31. Ibid., 192.

32. Norma Rosen, "Midrash, Bible, & Women's Voices," *Judaism* 180.45.4 (Fall 1996): 442–45 (423, 428, 428).

with the biblical narrative by turning it in a new direction or into more than one direction simultaneously. In recalling a silent—because silenced—female character with a level of psychological depth and specificity not offered her in the Bible, Glück contributes to a revival of what Rosen calls "the lost voice of women," which stems from "the millennial prohibition against the voices of women in traditional Jewish culture and religious writing."[33]

Abishag is a minor character in the story of King David and his male children's contest for the throne. Glück, however, makes a strong case that Abishag deserves recognition for reasons other than that she nursed King David in his old age, or that she played a role in conflicts among members of a royal family who wished to establish their political lineage by possessing her body. If she is remembered at all in standard commentaries, Abishag remains a body with no accompanying subjectivity. Hers is the narrative of the once beautiful woman around whom were staged conflicts between powerful men. In Robert Frost's "Provide, Provide" (1936), for example, Abishag reappears as a wrinkled cleaning lady, to symbolize the disregard that follows early stardom in the modern American culture of celebrity:

> The witch that came (the withered hag)
> To wash the steps with pail and rag,
> Was once the beauty Abishag,
>
> The picture pride of Hollywood.[34]

In Kings, Abishag figures in the story of David's contested relationship with his sons Solomon, Absalom, and Adonijah. She is a character in the Bible story "The Revolt of Adonijah," in which two sons attempt a rebellion against David in order to assume the throne intended for Solomon, whose mother was Bathsheba. Glück's "Abishag" (HM) is an example of contemporary feminist midrash because of the perspectival shift that takes place between her version of the tale and traditional readings of a presumably minor character (from 1 Kings 1 and 2:13–25).

Best-known as the seventy-year-old King David's nursemaid and last concubine, Abishag is described in the Bible as being a "very beautiful girl" who "took care of the king and waited on him, but he had no intercourse with her" (1 Kings 1:4). The political significance of Abishag's beauty figures in Adonijah's second attempt to become king. Nathan (a prophet) and

33. Ibid., 425.
34. Robert Frost, "Provide, Provide," in Ramazani et al., *Norton Anthology* 1:222.

Bathsheba (Solomon's mother) warn the aging King David that Adonijah has attempted to crown himself, which leads David to abdicate his throne to Solomon. After David's death, Adonijah tries a second time to gain legitimacy as king. Adonijah asks Bathsheba to serve as intermediary so that Solomon might grant him the right to marry Abishag (1 Kings 2:18). Solomon denies the request, believing that the marriage is politically motivated, since only the king's successor is allowed to sleep with the king's concubine. Eventually, Solomon chooses the immediate execution of one of his only two remaining brothers, for fear that Adonijah has signaled a revival of his attempt to capture the throne by marrying Abishag.

Rabbi Joseph Telushkin's commentary on the significance of Abishag in terms of the fraternal conflict involving royal ambitions focuses on her role as a sacred prostitute. Telushkin focuses on her great beauty. Because she is desirable to powerful men, she gains significance only in relation to them, and she exists in the text as a source of conflict and intrigue among David's sons. In contrast to the detailed characterization of the brothers (Amnon is lustful, Absalom charming and prideful), the description of Abishag registers no psychological traits or emotional response. She is an empty female figure in a story that Eve Kosofsky Sedgwick would describe as really being "between men," a story involving fraternal struggle for political power but cast in terms of a love triangle.[35]

In Glück's version, by contrast, Abishag the silent beautiful thing becomes the speaking subject in a first-person narrative poem that also represents events before she became David's concubine. For Telushkin, Abishag's significance in Kings resides in the allegorical interpretation we still sometimes make today between the political significance of territory and a female body subject to ownership by and identification with the nation state. Access to Abishag's body through sexual privilege is understood to be a politically significant conquest, the exclusive right of the king. Upon David's death, a primary sign of Solomon's status as his successor is that he becomes the only man authorized to have access to her body, turning sex with her into a site of political control and an expression of monarchic power.[36]

The political meaning of Abishag's body as a symbol of the king's power and of fratricidal conflict recedes into the background of the story Glück tells, which registers the voice and vision of Abishag in part 1. Although

35. Eve Kosofsky Sedgwick, ***Between Men: English Literature and Male Homosocial Desire*** (New York: Columbia University Press, 1985).

36. In this analysis, I am indebted to Joseph Telushkin, ***Biblical Literacy: The Most Important People, Events, and Ideas of the Hebrew Bible*** (New York: William Morrow, 1997).

reflecting on her experience from a belated position, Abishag does not focus on the moment of fraternal conflict described in Kings. Instead, Glück takes the story farther back in time to a pivotal event of parental betrayal in a young girl's experience. The focus is on the moment when Abishag, then still living with her family in the town of Shunam in the hill country outside Jerusalem, was recruited by David's kinsmen for duty in the harem in an attempt to cheer the aging king by reviving his sexual appetites.

> At God's word David's kinsmen cast
> through Canaan:
> It was understood
> the king was dying
> as they said
> outright
> so that my father turned to me saying
> *How much have I ever asked of you*
> to which I answered
> *Nothing*
> as I remembered. (FFB 87)

"Abishag" (HM) remembers a poignant episode in a girl's life involving absence, betrayal, and male desire. Glück focuses on a time when Abishag was still young and full of potential, a period when she was not yet defined exclusively as David's nursemaid because the once passionate king could no longer "get heat" even in the company of the beautiful concubine (1 Kings 1:2). In this early time, too, Abishag lacks the power to express her desire to stay with her father in Canaan. At the same time the pain, indignation, and resignation of having no choice in her own destiny is wrapped up in her silence, her reply, "nothing."

"Abishag" testifies to Glück's understanding of the traumatic consequences that an early loss of family and home may have on a woman's subsequent relationships with men. As if it were yesterday, and not many decades earlier, she recalls the devastating conversation with her father, suggesting that the initial rupture of her home has been registered as a mental wound:

> When I see myself
> it is still as I was then,
> beside the well, staring
> into the hollowed gourd half filled
> with water, where the dark braid

grazing the left shoulder was recorded
though the face
was featureless
of which they did not say
She has the look of one who seeks
some greater and destroying passion:

They took me as I was.
Not one among the kinsmen touched me,
not one among the slaves.
No one will touch me now. (FFB 87–88)

Specifically remembering how her face and hair looked reflected in water, Abishag recalls how her "dark braid" was "recorded." Although these features are imagined with specificity, "the face / was featureless." Abishag's vision of her image as "featureless" appears to be the by-product of a social erasure that had already taken place when she was transferred from the biological father in Canaan to David the symbolic father in Jerusalem, by way of "God's word."

Abishag's transformation into an object of male desire—lacking the features of sensation and expression associated with a desiring subject (eyes, ears, mouth)—has influenced her memory of her features. In contrast to Abishag's inability to remember the features of her face, Glück imaginatively re-creates Abishag's voice and vision in the poem. In the retrospective language of the lyric, the figure of "nothing" becomes a source of potentially subversive strength, an expression of dignity in inconspicuousness that cannot be contained by Abishag's father, David, Solomon, or Adonijah. Abishag states that her featureless face reflected, not her lack of distinctiveness, but the blindness of David's kinsmen, who effaced her as a feeling individual with her own agency and imaginative prowess. Glück recovers the confidence of a visionary speaker, by characterizing the aspects of Abishag's appearance that the men "did not say" she possessed: *She has the look of one who seeks / some greater and destroying passion.*

In the second half of the poem, Abishag recounts a "recurring dream" in which,

my father
stands at the doorway in his black cassock
telling me to choose
among my suitors, each of whom
will speak my name once

until I lift my hand in signal.
On my father's arm I listen
for not three sounds: *Abishag,*
but two: *my love–* (FFB 88)

Unlike the helpless situation her father put her in during part 1, her dream presents the father, in the robe of a priest, offering her a degree of autonomy in her future, "telling me to choose / among my suitors." Patriarchal control remains evident, as the father offers her only a limited range of choices, "among my suitors," even as the power to choose is reserved for her. In the contest for her affection, which reads as if it were an ancient version of television's *Dating Game,* each suitor "will speak my name once." Instead of wanting to hear the terms of ownership symbolized by the "three sounds" of her first name, she wants to be addressed in the language of affection. In part 2, Glück grants Abishag the type of agency her father had withheld. She does this by recasting a faceless slave, given away like an inanimate object, into a feeling subject, who expresses desire through imagination and remembering, who dreams of being called the love of one particular suitor.

The last stanza further disturbs the speaker's own recollection of childhood in Canaan, by recasting her dream of marrying for love:

I tell you if it is my own will
binding me I cannot be saved.
And yet in the dream, in the half-light
of the stone house, they looked
so much alike. Sometimes I think
the voices were themselves
identical, and that I raised my hand
[to choose among them]
chiefly in weariness. I hear my father saying
Choose, choose. But they were not alike
and to select death, O yes I can
believe that of my body. (FFB 88)

This final stanza is mysterious, and certainly open to multiple interpretations. What seems clear is that Abishag's dream of choosing among suitors remains insufficient to assert her subjectivity. Abishag's dilemma remains that her dream of choosing a mate is overdetermined by the need to decide among the prescribed suitors (and perhaps by the requirement of marriage). The process conforms to what the political theorist Louis

Althusser, writing about ideological state control, has called "interpellation," or what Peter Barry calls "the 'trick' whereby we are made to feel that we are choosing when we have no choice."[37] Even in her dreams, Abishag believes her choice really amounts to no significant choice at all, because she has internalized her father's wishes. Freedom to choose a beloved based on mutual recognition of the other's humanity crumbles in the context of an endless line of sameness, dictated by the father's circumscription of the available choices.

In the last three lines, Abishag reinterprets the dream. But once again Glück stresses the problem of interpellation, as a fiction of difference that merely veils the paternal control to call the name of the game. Abishag asserts that "they were not alike," but whatever differences do exist among the suitors remain inconsequential from her point of view. Any decision she might make under the jurisdiction of her father's domain is, in the dream that signifies creative spirit, unacceptable, a pretend freedom. Suicide, or the selection of disappearance from the social context in which she feels she has already been erased, becomes Abishag's alternative to selecting a suitor in this ersatz context: "and to select death, O yes I can / believe that of my body." The poem ends in the melodramatic tones of suicidal desperation, but, by contemplating suicide as a form of resistance to a lack of freedom, Abishag asserts control over the destination of her soul, or linguistic self, because it is only "my body" that will have died.

Abishag believes that the speaker's voice can exist with or without the body. She imagines dismissing herself from participation in a social world where her subjectivity has already been effaced. Although a forbidden act in Jewish law because it is said to be destroying an entire world, suicide becomes Abishag's protest against a society that has offered no meaningful place for her to express her wishes and to explore her dreams. "Abishag" echoes "Dedication to Hunger" (DF) where, at fifteen, the speaker recalls, she believed that to control her identity as an autonomous being she must exist outside "the interfering flesh" through a "sacrifice / until the limbs were free / of blossom and subterfuge" (FFB 133). "Abishag," too, interprets the state of "nothing" or disappearance as the only way to communicate a protest over the power of the father's demands on her body, through his ability to name her and to determine her future. Suicide becomes the only action that suggests a choice that is not just another form of enslavement.

37. Althusser quoted in Peter Barry, *Beginning Theory: An Introduction to Literary and Cultural Theory* (Manchester, England: Manchester University Press, 1995), 165.

"A Parable" (TA)

Glück's lyrics expand in significance when read intertextually. This is certainly the case when reading "Abishag" as an Aggadah, or midrash, on Kings. The poem's significance increases also when we trace how thematic elements from "Abishag" resurface in subsequent volumes. If Glück expresses her interest in biblical commentary by interpreting scripture as a series of common texts that do not have a single, authoritative meaning, she also treats her own oeuvre as a lexicon that the author may revisit in order to construct new versions of the self. Her earlier poems themselves become proof texts available for commentary within lyrics found in later volumes. I want to connect Glück's revisionary poetics in "Abishag" in both these intertextual directions—by linking "Abishag" with another poem, "A Parable" (TA), which returns to the issue of sexual politics, but as it is found in another episode from the story of King David.

"A Parable" focuses on King David's treatment of women as faceless objects available merely for his sexual consumption. Instead of focusing on Abishag, a female victim of male power, "A Parable" focuses on the interpellative power of the male aggressor, David. The very first man we can call "King of the Jews" and "the sweet singer of Israel" (2 Sam. 23:1), David is nonetheless figured in "A Parable" as a narcissistic despot who extends the range of his desire for social domination and political control into the realm of sexual conquest in ways that lead to corruption and, eventually, a dynastic fall. It becomes clear, when "A Parable" is connected thematically to "The Mountain," the poem that precedes it in *The Triumph of Achilles,* that Glück's interest in the tale of David, in this commentary poem, is not so much to critique patriarchy (which may have been the case in "Abishag") but to explore a parable about her own aspirations for glory through naming.

"A Parable" begins with an almost breezy, yet lyrical, rendition of the legend of how "the childish shepherd," the youngest son of Jesse, becomes transformed, first, into an unlikely hero by killing the "towering" Philistine Goliath through guerilla tactics to revenge the murder of Jews and then, second, into a godlike ruler consumed with power and lust after taking over the kingdom by force from Saul:

> It was an epoch of heroes.
> So this young boy, this nobody,
> making his way from one plain to another,
> picks up a small stone among the cold, unspecified
> rocks of the hillside. It is a pleasant day.

> At his feet, normal vegetation, the few white flowers
> like stars, the leaves woolly, sage-green:
> at the bottom of the hill are corpses.
>
> Who is the enemy? Who has distributed
> the compact bodies of the Jews
> in this unprecedented silence? Disguised in dirt,
> the scattered army sees the beast, Goliath,
> towering above the childish shepherd.
> They shut their eyes. And all the level earth
> becomes the shattered surface of a sea, so disruptive
> is that fall. In the ensuing dust, David
> lifts his hand: then it is his, the hushed,
> completed kingdom—
>
> Fellow Jews, to plot a hero's journey
> is to trace a mountain: hero to god, god to ruler.
> At the precipice, the moment we don't want to hear about—
> the stone is gone; now
> the hand is the weapon. (FFB 195)

Writing to her "fellow Jews," Glück imagines David's biography as following the "trace" of "a mountain," with the "arc" expressing the shape of a narrative from obscurity to the incline of power to a social decline brought about by David's desires for Bathsheba, a wife acquired through adultery and murder, who will eventually give birth to Solomon, another powerful king and legendary poet whose administration was brought down by sexual desires, suggesting a transmission of these traits from father to son.

David appropriates two men's wives, but it is his adultery with Bathsheba that draws Glück's attention as an example of a failure of moral judgment due to an inability to check one's own desire, an association of an expression of power with a violation of sexual boundaries. In *Eros and the Jews,* David Biale explains that, after appropriating Abigail, the wife of Nabal, as a "reward" for not attacking Nabal and as a punishment for Nabal's "crime" of refusing to pay him protection money, David commits adultery with Bathsheba.

> This is the dark version of the Abigail story: the author roundly condemns David's theft of another man's wife. David sleeps with Bathsheba while her husband, Uriah, is at the battlefront: the king is having fun in bed while the general is in the trenches. When Bathsheba becomes pregnant, David tries to cover up his own paternity by ordering her husband back, in hopes that he will sleep with his wife. Uriah refuses,

> even when David gets him drunk. Unable to hide his crime, David has Uriah killed at the front. Bathsheba then marries David, but the child born of their adulterous union dies at the hand of God.[38]

As if through a genetic coding, David's son Solomon will, at least according to legend, compose the great mystical Hebrew love poetry of the Song of Songs. He will perform courageous acts on behalf of others only to have these gifts turned toward material gain (Solomon's gold) and erotic fulfillment (Solomon's wives). In "A Parable," Glück accepts that connections exist between different, often contradictory, aspects of the desiring self. These aspects pivot between an admirable yearning for recognition in the symbolic arenas of language and politics and the (from her point of view) abhorrent wish for satiation of physical desires such as food or sex.

In the "Covenant" section of "Lamentations" (DF), the image of the newborn baby "as it reached its hands" signified to Adam and Eve that "there was no authority above them" (FFB 149). Here, Glück figures David's abuse of his power through the "hand" that has become the "weapon." Glück also stresses David's corruption by altering his title from "hero" (a human designation that signifies striving against the limitations of mortality), to "god" (a nonhuman designation of infinite power), to "ruler" (a position that in his case involves legislating with an iron hand). In "The Untrustworthy Speaker" (AR), the speaker acknowledges her own previously concealed aggressive instincts toward her sister. Similarly, in "A Parable," the speaker observes "the hand is the weapon" that has been erased or ignored in histories of Jewish victimization. The hand of the hero that slew Goliath with the stone and the slingshot (1 Samuel) is, at the end of "A Parable," redefined as the ruling hand of a dictator that directs Bathsheba to his bed and her husband, Uriah, to his death (2 Samuel).[39]

> On the palace roof, King David stares across
> the shining city of Jerusalem
> into the face of Bathsheba and perceives

38. David Biale, *Eros and the Jews: From Biblical Israel to Contemporary America* (Berkeley and Los Angeles: University of California Press, 1997), 19.

39. The self-sacrificing drive for recognition that led David to compose the psalms and to believe he could kill Goliath with the stone from a slingshot can be directed toward composing great cycles of poems such as the Psalms or the Song of Songs, or toward the vain displays of personal satisfaction that led David to abuse his reign and to make grave mistakes in martial judgment, which imperilled the state and led to a civil war among his sons.

his own amplified desire. At heart, he feels nothing.
She is like a flower in a tub of water. Above his head,
the clouds move. And it comes to him he has attained
all he is capable of dreaming. (FFB 195–96)

Glück is both attracted to and repulsed by the libidinal aspects of David's rise to power. She identifies with David as a complex figure of agon (Robert Pinsky calls him "a poet as well as a warrior-killer" and a "wily" shape-shifter "like Odysseus"), who has willingly risked his life to assert his humanity in his battle with Goliath.[40] She also criticizes David and, by so doing, challenges her own myth-making as a form of arrogance, or "amplified desire," when she acknowledges "the moment we don't want to hear about," or the aggressive narcissism that accompanies the desire for recognition of one's symbolic value. At the end of "A Parable," she considers David's political failures as the result of his imaginative limits for what constitutes valuable attainment. By "all he is capable of dreaming," Glück means something like a lack of empathy. She suggests that David's lack of interest in the sublime realm of self-sacrifice for a symbolic cause such as national recognition has led him to focus on a narcissistic projection in the figure of the human other. David believes he can attain Bathsheba without loss of subjectivity or the extinguishing of desire.

The poem that precedes "A Parable" in *The Triumph of Achilles,* "The Mountain," affirms the connection I believe Glück wants her readers to make between David and herself. In "The Mountain," Glück interprets the Greek mythic character and legendary first murderer, Sisyphus, as "the artist" who

lies
because he is obsessed with attainment,
that he perceives the summit
as that place where he will live forever,
a place about to be
transformed by his burden. (FFB 194)

Like David in "A Parable," Sisyphus expresses his desire for control through the pointing of hands, a speech act that signifies his desire for a linguistic dominion from on high. By placing a poem in which David's career is viewed as a mountain's arc beside "The Mountain," Glück connects her authorial

40. Robert Pinsky, *The Life of David* (New York: Schocken Books, 2005), 3–4.

ambition with David's excesses. In "Education of the Poet," she described the process of organizing a series of lyrics into a book as the "making of a pile of poems an arc, a shaped utterance" (PT 17).

Compared to "Abishag," "A Parable" offers a more searching analysis of Glück's own ambivalent relationship to literary power, because now she imagines the psyche of the subject of desire, as well as the object. No longer conceiving herself through Abishag, the victim of unchecked male desire, Glück, through the stories of David and Sisyphus, questions the outcomes to her interpretation of literary power and familial relations as a zero-sum game in an economy of scarcity. Both David and Glück are at times willing to sacrifice personal safety for a symbolic cause. In both cases, she fears, pride may turn the admirable, very human struggle for recognition into a trivial pursuit, which breaches ethical commitment and involves the satiation of a yearning for glory. (David certainly does not honor the ethical commitment to the other that Levinas refers to in *Totality and Infinity.* Levinas connects the biblical commandment that one shall not commit murder to the appearance of the face of the human other as a check on one's subjectivity.)[41]

"Day Without Night" (TA)

Commenting on the relevance of the Moses tale for a contemporary audience of readers, the biblical scholar Everett Fox notes: "Such stories mirror our own longing for accomplishment and acceptance, as well as our own universal desire to overcome the ultimate enemy, Death. In the hero's triumphs, we triumph; his vanquishing of death cathartically becomes our own." In poems from different times in her career, Glück has turned and returned to the Moses story to address her own "longing for accomplishment and acceptance," as well as to clarify her speculations about death, God, and the vanity of human aspirations.[42] In "The Undertaking" (HM), for example, Glück describes Moses' trip in the basket down the Nile as fortunate, liberating, and mystical as his journey is surrounded by light. Making his way along a lush natural surrounding of lilies, shrubs, and palm, Moses even feels

41. Emmanuel Levinas, *Totality and Infinity: An Essay on Exteriority,* trans. Alphonso Lingis (Pittsburgh, Pa.: Duquesne University Press, 1969).

42. Quotations are from Everett Fox, *The Five Books of Moses* (New York: Schocken Books, 2000), 252. The story appears in Exodus 2:1–10. Abandoned by parents of the House of Levi to avoid the pharaoh Ramses' decree to slay all male Jewish newborns, Moses is discovered by the pharaoh's daughter while the baby floats in an ark made out of reeds among the bulrushes

"the waves' goodwill / as arms widen over the water" (FFB 83). I suppose that this uplifting tone of voice is fitting for a lyric that describes the miraculous childhood of the Jewish prophet, who, though tongue-tied, eventually receives the law of God on Mount Sinai and becomes among the rare few blessed to see even the back of God and then to survive this witness.

One major Glück poem on Moses is the eight-part "Day Without Night" from *The Triumph of Achilles.* It follows two other poems in which Glück's struggle for literary authority is connected to mythic tales involving male characters whose stories are found within the Greek and Jewish canons: "The Mountain" refers to the myth of Sisyphus, and "A Parable" analyzes David's rise from obscurity to kingship and then to an abuse of power as ruler. In both these poems, Glück symbolizes her desire for literary accomplishment by having her main speaker scale a mountain, such as Parnassus would be within the Greek classical tradition. Both poems graft a personal narrative upon archetypal stories recounting the desire for individual attainment. Similarly, "Day Without Night" combines biblical and classical material, imagining Moses as Prometheus and therefore as a Miltonic precursor for the poet as seeker of absolute illumination at great personal cost. From the start of the poem, Glück casts Moses as on the quest for insight, but also as desiring the political authority associated with Ramses.

> It was as though Pharaoh's daughter
> had brought home a lion cub
> and for a few weeks
> passed it off as a cat
> . . . .
> on Pharaoh's lap
> he reaches for the crown of Egypt. (FFB 197–98)

In "The Mountain" version of the myth, the action takes place in Hades, where Sisyphus is "obsessed with attainment" and "perceives the summit / as that place where he will live forever" (FFB 194). Like Sisyphus, Moses in "Day Without Night" suffers the risk of death, in this case by eating fire (in order to secure his independence from Pharaoh by proving he is uninterested

on the banks of the Nile River, where the royal Egyptian daughter has gone to bathe. As with the story of David in "A Parable," the Mosaic legend appeals to Glück because it involves a rise to prophetic status from unlikely origins. A baby abandoned by Jewish parents, Moses is raised as an Egyptian prince with his birth mother as his nurse, reversing the power relations between child and parent.

in material wealth) and by ignoring the tray of rubies that the ruler has "set before the child" in favor of the "burning embers" (FFB 198).

Gordon has noted that fire imagery appears often in the first three volumes of Glück's poetry. It signifies "the body of the mystic" as well as "the blazing illumination of revelation."[43] Examples include the body of Jeanne d'Arc, which "must be / transformed to fire" (FFB 78); the murder of the witch that haunts Gretel with memories of "that black forest and the fire in earnest" (FFB 63); and the barn "blazing in darkness" in "The Magi" (FFB 66). Perhaps the poem that most directly bears on the fire imagery from "Day Without Night," however, would be "The Inlet" (F). The poem features an indented portion that recounts the story of Shadrach as he recalls a mythical return from "the edge":

> Waveside, beside earth's edge,
> Before the toward-death cartwheel of the sun,
> I dreamed I was afraid and through the din
> Of birds, the din, the hurricane of the parting sedge
> Came to the danger lull.
> The white weeds, white waves' white
> Scalps dissolve in the obliterating light.
> And only I, Shadrach, come back alive and well. (FFB 54)

Gordon reminds us that, in Daniel 3:12–30, Shadrach is "a companion of Daniel who, with Meshach and Abednego, was thrown into the fiery furnace of Nebuchadnezzar and came out unharmed."[44]

Moses, like Sisyphus, becomes a figure of interest to Glück because his story involves a boundless desire for personal attainment at the cost of great suffering. Both Moses and Sisyphus are fated to perform a task without end; but Glück's Moses has less in common with the diffident Moses in Exodus, who hid his face because he was afraid to look at God, than with the striving figure of Moses described in a midrash, as recorded by Louis Ginzberg in *Legends of the Jews*. Reminding us of the prophet Isaiah, whose lips were cleansed with a burning coal, the child grabbed Pharaoh's crown and placed it upon his own head, leading Pharaoh to arrange the test of the jewel and the coal to see if Moses was a threat and must be put to death.[45] In Exodus, God convinces Moses to speak to the Jews, not on behalf of his own power and

43. Gordon, "Reconceiving the Sacred," 41–42.
44. Ibid., 33.
45. Louis Ginzberg, *Legends of the Jews* (New York: Jewish Publication Society, 1901), 272–74.

authority but as God's mouthpiece. By contrast, Glück's Moses wishes to attain mastery in the political sphere. Further, as Peter Stitt has argued, Glück makes Moses "an entirely human baby, without hints of demigodliness," by suggesting he was the "illegitimate offspring of the princess's unwed lust."[46]

> You did not press this woman [Pharaoh's daughter].
> She said she came upon
> a child in the rushes;
> each time she told the story,
> her handmaidens recreated
> their interminable chorus of sighs.
> It had to be. (FFB 197)

Glück's Moses resembles the biblical prophet in his willingness to accept a harrowing punishment rather than crass material wealth in order to attain visionary power and political influence.

Conflating aspects of the biblical characterization of Moses and the prophet Isaiah, Glück's Moses will lack eloquence, famously slowed into a stammer, as a consequence of consuming the fire as a sign of his prophetic stature.

> And God said to him,
> "You can be the favored one,
> the one who tastes fire
> and cannot speak,
> or you can die now
> and let the others
> stay in Egypt: tell them
> it was better to die in Egypt,
> better to litter the river
> with your corpse, than face
> a new world." (FFB 199)

As a child, Moses chose the tray of burning embers, and the "image / of truth is fire," as Glück defines it in part 1 of "Day Without Night." The source of illumination is associated with a Satanic or Promethean quest, but Moses seeks an illumination that Glück describes as unreal: "Are you taken in / by lights, by illusions?" (FFB 200). The title "Day Without Night" by

46. Stitt, "Contemporary American Poems," 215.

itself refers to an illusion, signifying personal insight, not a way to God that requires the dissolution of self. Unlike the sun, which is subject to the diurnal course, the day without night occurs with a static sun that "burns in hell." I take this image to refer to the path of the individual imagination (figured most famously as Satan in Milton's ***Paradise Lost***). The romantic path toward self-discovery is, then, unrelated to the gnostic realm, which Glück seeks to identify as "your path to god," a negative way characterized by silence, invisibility, namelessness, and darkness.

"Legend" (TA)

For the most part, Glück, a secular Jew yet mystical poet, eschews definitions of her Jewishness along ethnic lines. "Legend," another poem with a Jewish theme, is a rare illustration of how she connects her identity to the family "legend" told of her paternal grandfather—and so by extension to the archetypal "legend" of the early twentieth-century Jewish American immigration narrative associated with the Ellis Island experience. As much as Glück may wish to resist an ethnic identification of the self, because of her fear that it would limit her scope, "Legend" reveals the degree to which such an escape from one's familial background is not possible.

In an interview with Ann Douglas at the time Glück was writing ***The Triumph of Achilles,*** she admits: "My tendency—as is obvious—is to very promptly build mythic structures, to see the resemblance of the present moment to the archetypal configuration. So that almost immediately the archetypal configuration is superimposed."[47] In "Legend," Glück doubles the "superimposition" of "archetypal configuration" by layering a legend of family history and one from the Bible upon her own self-portrait. Herself a metamorphic figure, she records how her grandfather left behind the beloved pastoral setting and intimacy of an Eastern European shtetl for the hope of a better life in New York City, where the American Dream turned into a nightmare, as a series of misfortunes transformed a man who was once "a scholar" and property owner into a modern version of Joseph, a stranger in a strange land:

> My father's father came
> to New York from Dhlua:
> one misfortune followed another.

47. Ann Douglas, "Descending Figure: An Interview with Louise Glück," ***Columbia Magazine*** (1980): 123.

In Hungary, a scholar, a man of property.
Then failure: an immigrant
rolling cigars in a cold basement.

He was like Joseph in Egypt.
At night, he walked the city;
spray of the harbor
turned to tears on his face. (FFB 209)

Glück alludes to the story of Joseph's bondage in Egypt (Genesis 39–47). He is imprisoned on false charges of coveting Potiphar's wife, but this eventually leads him to become a viceroy, because he is able to interpret dreams, first those of the king's cupbearer and baker and then those of the pharaoh himself, foretelling the seven years of success and seven years of famine that Egypt would experience. Glück imagines her grandfather as Joseph, who survives physical hardship and spatial dislocation because of his skill as a dream weaver and fortune-teller. Read as a reenactment of Joseph's narrative of imprisonment and insight, the grandfather's story becomes a source of inspiration for the author. Drawing him as a reincarnation of Joseph enables her to meditate upon her own situation, that of a Jewish author who focuses on abstractions and whose willingness to "speak the truth gives / the illusion of freedom" (FFB 210) in a situation she considers to be emotional bondage to a world not always subject to her will.

In "Legend," the grandfather's exile from his pastoral shtetl home in Dhlua—"forty houses, / a few cows grazing the rich meadows" (FFB 209)—becomes transformed into an opportunity for him to fashion a new version of himself through the power he has to reconstruct the past into a scene of Edenic peace that contrasts with his bleak life in New York City. She imagines Hungary from the perspective of a hungry, urban dweller who has lost touch with the signs of his previous identity as a scholar and landowner. He now merely survives, doing menial tasks in a cold factory basement. Unlike Stevens's "roller of big cigars" in "The Emperor of Ice-Cream," the grandfather is not a fat cat but a displaced immigrant laborer.[48]

Dhlua, the imaginary Dhlua, becomes a dual site. One site is actual, one a fiction recast as an oasis of freedom and personal visibility, a dream space that exists for the grandfather on such an abstract level that it cannot be destroyed or erased by the mind-numbing work of rolling cigars. In imagination, the lost country of his youth is returned to him as a fantasy

48. Wallace Stevens, "The Emperor of Ice-Cream," in Ramazani et al., *Norton Anthology* 1:248.

space worthy of Chagall, a painter of floating musicians, who Stephen Fredman regards as one of the Jewish archetypes of hybridity:[49]

> From the factory, like sad birds his dreams
> flew to Dhlua, grasping in their beaks
> as from moist earth in which a man could see
> the shape of his own footprint,
> scattered images, loose bits of the village. (FFB 209–10)

The grandfather becomes a nostalgic symbol of inspiration for Glück. He is an example of another family member from an earlier generation on her father's side for whom experiential deprivation—physical hunger and metaphysical despair—could also be revisited as a source of what Keats referred to as soul-making, or what Glück refers to as desire. The grandfather displayed a willingness to continue to "feel / the grandeur of the world" through the realm of dream and imaginative reveries, even as history's unfortunate circumstances fell upon him "like a heavy weight." His endurance of hardship enabled him to forge his soul into something hard, durable, and therefore not subject to damage through external circumstance. His soul eventually resembles "a diamond: in the world there is nothing / hard enough to change it" (FFB 209). The speaker's grandfather is unlike the biblical Joseph in that his ability to dream and to speak honestly about his dreams through interpretation does not lead him to wealth, status, or an eventual reconciliation with his relatives. Glück nonetheless perceives her grandfather as a modern version of Joseph because of the richness of the internal life. He is able to defy the unkind external circumstances he faces in New York City where his soulful qualities go unacknowledged in the context of urban and industrial life.

Conclusion

In "The Untrustworthy Speaker" (AR), a poem from a book that bears an eponymous reference to the Noah story, it is as if the speaker recognizes that, for all her commentary on her childhood in other poems, Glück has only partially imagined herself in poetry, by adopting the mantle of victim:

49. Stephen Fredman, *A Menorah for Athena: Charles Reznikoff and the Jewish Dilemmas of Objectivist Poetry* (Chicago: University of Chicago Press, 2001), 51.

> I never see myself,
> standing on the front steps, holding my sister's hand.
> That's why I can't account
> for the bruises on her arm, where the sleeve ends. (AR 34)

As Melissa Brown explains, it is as if in these lines Glück "had suddenly awakened from a hypnotic trance during which she therapeutically mumbled the story of her miserable childhood. Because she has not seen herself as both victim and victimizer, the gifts of language have not been able to heal the wound."[50] In her commentary poems on David and Moses, Glück does not go as far as she will in "The Untrustworthy Speaker" to announce in overtly autobiographical terms the way her lyric self-fashioning as victim has veiled from readers her own aggressive instincts and violent impulses. She does turn to biblical commentary in several instances in order to critique the kind of abuse of authority discussed in "The Untrustworthy Speaker" as the misuse of language and victim status to conceal aggression. She connects her commentary on the Bible to expressions of imaginative power in a secular culture, in which the literary canon may be understood as a paradigmatic site to display in writing the aggressive instinct for personal recognition that Glück at once conceals and reveals through the proof text.

A radically individualistic author, Glück nonetheless maintains an uncanny relationship to the Bible in her struggle for recognition. For this reason, her work is a form of midrash, which emphasizes the interpreter's voice as revealed in commentary. A system that has tended to exclude the female point of view, Judaism, when thought of as interpretive practice rather than as an essential identity formation, has nonetheless provided Glück with a model of revision. The commentary tradition allows us as readers to notice how Glück brings gender, Jewishness, and identity together as fluid constructs. Her poetry, like the Hebrew commentary tradition in which it participates, favors dialogue and revision over fundamental law or essentialist categories of selfhood and communal identification. She is close and familiar, yet distant and estranged from the scripture that gives a public weight to her experience of personal anguish. At the same time, by referring to the canon, Glück can detach herself from the daily life that she characterizes as painful and isolating.

50. Melissa Brown, "The Love of Form Is a Love of Endings: Poetic Hunger and the Aesthetic Body in Louise Glück" (Ph.D. diss., University of Iowa, 1997), 50.

Chapter Four

The Wound in the Word

Trauma Theory and the Question of Witness

Contemporary psychoanalytic theorists have challenged traditional conceptions of accurate testimony. They question the idea of reliability when we refer to statements made by a witness who documents extreme physical suffering, psychological disorientation, or metaphysical despair. In *Unclaimed Experience,* Cathy Caruth explains:

> For history to be a history of trauma means that it is referential precisely to the extent that it is not fully perceived as it occurs; or to put it somewhat differently, that a history can be grasped only in the very inaccessibility of its occurrence.[1]

For the victim of a catastrophe, distinctions between remembering, forgetting, and misremembering become moot. What happens to living witnesses to terror in death camps, for example, is unspeakable, if speaking implies the expression of a legible discourse and if the definition of survival refers to personal liberation from memory in the form of a recovered sense of identity as a whole.

Writing disaster into the muddled or stammering tone of one's testimony—rather than writing objectively about a disaster as documentary reportage—involves the problem of temporal undecidability. How can we even say something has happened if, as Caruth argues, "it is not fully perceived as it occurs"? How do we verify facts when the witness may never have consciously registered the event in the first place? The unreliability of testimony, therefore, can be interpreted as a psychic tremor that exemplifies how the witness may

1. Cathy Caruth, *Unclaimed Experience* (Baltimore: Johns Hopkins University Press, 1996), 187.

regard the present moment as a painful repetition of the long-ago. Metaphorically speaking, testimony may be "written" onto the body of the witness. A kind of truth about how the pain of the past has literally intruded upon the present-tense existence of the speaker may be expressed as a facial tic, as tears, or even as the silence that follows an interviewee's refusal to answer a question. As is the case with many of the survivors interviewed in Claude Lanzmann's documentary film *Shoah* about their experience of the Nazi death camps, trauma can be announced as a stutter, a discursive interruption, a sudden unwillingness to continue the story one has agreed to tell. We can interpret inarticulateness, or narrative "failure," as indicating that what went before has intruded and impinged upon the present self.

It would be a major overstatement, and highly inappropriate, to claim the significance of a historical catastrophe such as the Shoah as a lingering trace on Glück's poetry. Making any more than a glancing nod toward a link between that event and her poetry is definitely not my intention in reading her as a trauma artist. There are moments, however, where we do glimpse the author directly addressing or at least alluding to Holocaust scenes and imagery. In "Memoir" from *The Seven Ages* (2001), Glück speaks in an autobiographical register as well as on behalf of a class of comparably situated persons, that is, other prosperous, assimilated Jews who grew up on Long Island after World War II:

> I grew up on an island, prosperous,
> in the second half of the twentieth century;
> the shadow of the Holocaust
> hardly touched us. (SA 62)

In this statement of denial, the speaker avoids disclosing any personal details about her childhood. She ends up speaking in the first-person plural about how the Holocaust was personally insignificant to her entire group. "Memoir" seems to be an ironically titled poem.

"Memoir" also seems to be a reply to Muriel Rukeyser's "Poem" ("I lived in the first century of world wars").[2] With intimate detail, Rukeyser remembers her passionate struggle to gather and pass on news of conflicts occurring across the globe, via an American mass media she accuses of being saturated with the task of selling products. With a mixture of fondness and anxiety, Rukeyser recalls the risks and frustrations that accompanied her life as a

2. Muriel Rukeyser, "Poem," in *Twentieth-Century American Poetry,* ed. Dana Gioia, David Mason, and Meg Schoerke (Boston: McGraw-Hill, 2004), 506.

concerned citizen in an otherwise complacent urban American environment during the turbulent era of World War II. Writing "in the second half of the twentieth century" (that is, in the aftermath to the cataclysmic events of the "first century of world wars"), Glück claims to have been "hardly touched" even by the "shadow" of the Holocaust.

In "The Fortress" (HM), Glück hints at how the shadow of the Shoah does make itself felt in an oblique form. This is a poem based on her interpretation of a Tarot card that signifies "war." The card features images of prisoners being released from a destroyed fortress. The speaker sees in her reading of the card the image of "ovens manned by wives" (FFB 93). Images of the incineration of bodies in ovens, and of death by burning, appear rather frequently in Glück poems. In "Gretel in Darkness" (HM):

> I hear the witch's cry
> break in the moonlight through a sheet
> of sugar: God rewards.
> Her tongue shrivels into gas. (FFB 63)

We as readers of "The Fortress" and "Gretel in Darkness" may not help but be reminded of the newsreel imagery of the death camps. In both poems, however, Glück's speaker is focused on family matters—on the speaker's agon with a maternal figure in "Gretel," and on a grotesque version of marriage as involving incarceration and incineration in "The Fortress." As in "Daddy" by Sylvia Plath, which characterizes the speaker's father as a "Panzer man," Holocaust imagery serves to mark the intensity of the speaker's agon with family members.

Although direct reference to a historical catastrophe such as the Shoah are rare in Glück, her texts do represent, in their tone and style, her experience of a profound psychological wound that at times mirrors survivor testimony. Whether its root cause is physical, psychological, or metaphysical, Glück speaks of a "wound" that has altered her speaker's ability to clearly differentiate between "now" and "then." Throughout her career, whether working in confessionalist or mythopoetic mode, Glück has focused on traumatized speakers: the mother suffering from postpartum depression in "The Egg" (F), the anorexic teenager almost starving herself to death in "Dedication to Hunger" (DF), the emotionally numbed and therefore linguistically reticent daughter mourning for her father and sister in *Ararat,* the enraged and defiant wife who must face the end of a once passionate marriage in *Meadowlands.* Glück writes about these traumatized subjects with insight that comes from personal understanding. But we need to distinguish these personae from the author, whose project involves survival and recovery from trauma through lyric and narrative reflection.

As Margaret Ann Gordon has pointed out, Glück's archetypal narrative quest figures often descend into a traumatic psychic landscape characterized by spatial and temporal disorientation.[3] There is the Persephone of "Pomegranate" (HM), the Odysseus of *Meadowlands,* and the Gretel of "Gretel in Darkness" (HM). The story of the autobiographical anorexic teenager who courts death in "Dedication to Hunger" similarly fits the pattern of a descent into a literal or figurative underworld. Gordon notes that the journey taken by many of these figures of descent also involves a return from the edge of total loss. Persephone, Gretel, and the anorexic teenager all return from the edge of personal destruction, even if their new identities are marred by traumatic memory. Glück's narration of their grief implies the possibility of a reconfiguration of the self in testimony that takes the form of lyric.

Casting the lives of her speakers as damaged texts that require commentary if they are to become legible, Glück emphasizes the lucidity, the preternaturally calm state of comprehension, that occurs at the end of a traumatic episode. She is attracted to commentary as a mode of self-analysis, and she has expressed her "love of endings." In the relationship between trauma and recovery, then, Glück's application of language, myth, and narrative to what are, for her, traumatic sites—both the legacy of the great literary masters and her own physical and metaphysical struggles—bears out Gordon's point. The author must return to the site of a traumatic memory in language in order to allow the recovery of her speaker's personal identity. Glück's increasing fascination with the book-length sequence, in such works as *Meadowlands* and *The Wild Iris,* speaks to her understanding of the relationship between narrative and survival. The way she shapes the self through the disguise of one persona and then revises this identity, through another characterization related to literary or personal history, speaks to her embrace of the idea of narrative as a form of personal recovery, of survival through the acceptance of linguistic transformation.

The truth is that the typical external and internal sources of grief in Glück poems have little to do with historical atrocities. Divorce, the death of a parent and a sibling, the terror of a house fire in Vermont, ambivalence about having children—these are primary sources of suffering for Glück speakers. Other Glück speakers express a kind of metaphysical anxiety about the status of the female body, leading to an acute awareness of the nearness of illness and a courting of death. While distressing, a divorce or a house fire is

3. Gordon, "Reconceiving the Sacred."

hardly analogous to the disasters we encounter when reading Holocaust testimonials. By referring to her as a trauma artist in this chapter, then, I will address her perception of the inadequacy of language and of myth to respond to loss through representations that evoke psychological wounds. The critical theory on trauma that has been applied to the fractured accounts of survivor testimonials by theorists of Shoah such as Caruth, Dominick LaCapra, Dori Laub, and Geoffrey Hartman can be meaningfully applied to Glück's invocation of the untrustworthy speaker. For Glück, as for the Shoah theorists, the untrustworthy speaker is a paradoxically reliable witness to trauma, precisely *because* unreliable. The speaker does not so much write about terrors from the past as display the repetition of terror in the form of what Hartman refers to as "a disaster notation."[4]

We can find evidence of poetry as a "disaster notation" in "The Racer's Widow" (F), which tells a story that is, on the surface, not autobiographical. Yet, with its use of the first person and with its observations about the impact violent memories have upon the speaker's ability to address what went before as history, the poem resonates with the persona poems and the autobiographical trauma poems from *Ararat.* Stating, "It is not painful to discuss / His death," the racer's widow at first seems able to discuss her husband's crash as if it were ancient history. "I have been primed for this, / For separation, for so long—" (FFB 24). But then the speaker can no longer detach herself from the past. She is overcome by the sights and sounds of his last race:

> But still his face assaults
> Me, I can hear that car careen again, the crowd coagulate on asphalt
> In my sleep. And watching him, I feel my legs like snow
> That let him finally let him go
> As he lies draining there. And see
> How even he did not get to keep that lovely body. (FFB 24)

Robert Miklitsch has discussed how Glück combines style and sentiment in these lines to create the impression that the speaker has been taken back to the past. "The loose, run-on sentences and sometimes violent enjambments (especially 'his face assaults / Me,' which has an almost tactile quality) mimic the speaker's involuntary recollection, and cathartic recreation, of the 'scene of pathos.'"[5] Miklitsch captures how Glück's first volume previews the more autobiographical trauma writing in *Ararat.*

4. Geoffrey Hartman, *The Longest Shadow: In the Aftermath of the Holocaust* (New York: Palgrave Macmillan, 2002), 164.

The temporal undecidability of traumatic experience and the fragmented quality of the literature of trauma are paradigmatic elements of Glück's poetry. This is the case in "The Racer's Widow" (F), where Glück distances herself from her subject of traumatic memory through the account of someone else's inability to heal a great pain. It is also the case when she is writing in a variety of other modes, including her confessionalist address to familial history in "The Untrustworthy Speaker" (AR); in "Archipelago" (HM), which employs a Homeric frame; and in "Gretel in Darkness" (HM) a persona poem with roots in Grimm's fairy tale.

The Troubled Narrator in "Archipelago" (HM)

"Archipelago" brings its readers before the troubled and troubling kind of narrator defined by Caruth, the one whose "history can be grasped only in the very inaccessibility of its occurrence."[6] Glück narrates the aftermath to an ill-fated sea journey and a foiled return home. Unlike in *Meadowlands,* where *The Odyssey* exists in relation to the speaker's domestic strife in postmodern American suburbia, in "Archipelago," the specific details of the mythic frame are blotted out and left spectral. Through the tone of the poem, Glück casts her narrator as compelling, precisely because unreliable. The reader must question whether accuracy is the primary quality to note when interpreting a testimony as true to the past.

"Archipelago" follows the Homeric narrative pattern by beginning in medias res with a set of mariners trying to dock upon an island. The poem begins after "the tenth year":

> we came upon immense sunlight, a relief
> of islands locked into the water. These became our course.
> Eleven months we drifted, toward the twelfth
> wandered into docile ocean, a harbor. We prepared for peace.
> Weeks passed. And then the captain saw
> the mouth closing that defined our port—we are
> devoured. Other voices stir. Water

5. Robert Miklitsch, "Assembling a Landscape: The Poetry of Louise Glück," *Hollins Critic* 19.4 (Oct. 1982): 3.

6. Caruth, *Unclaimed Experience,* 187. In Italian, an "archipelago" refers specifically to the Aegean Sea, and so Glück's title puts us in mind of the regional setting for *The Odyssey,* a text that in *Meadowlands* becomes crucial to her interpretation of marriage, desire, and the role of the imagination in reconfiguring reality as a compensation for experiential loss.

> sneers against our ship, our shrunk number runs
> in two packs: madness and suicide. The twelfth year
> the captain calls his name, it has no meaning, and the crew
> shrieks in its extremity. (FFB 65)

The archetypal scenario of a decade-long delay prior to a homecoming may frame the lyric, but the poem's subject is how trauma influences memory and narration. Where Odysseus returns to Ithaca, at first in beggar's disguise but then to wage a battle with the suitors (108 of whom he kills to reclaim his wife and kingdom), the sailors in Glück's poem must combat a dangerous but anonymous adversary. Where Odysseus knows that his destination is Ithaca, even if his arrival is long delayed, the crew in "Archipelago" have wandered into uncharted waters as they head in an unknown direction. There is no safe harbor in this poem; there is no home base. Although the islands have no meaning for the crew prior to their sudden appearance, they gather significance as they "became our course" only after being sighted. Odysseus triumphs by destroying the suitors; Glück tells the story of a crew who are hopelessly lost, and "devoured" by their opponents.[7]

As in *The Odyssey,* Glück organizes her lyric by rapidly collapsing time frames into smaller increments. The time frame shifts from the "tenth year," to months of drifting into the harbor, and then to passing "weeks," when, "preparing for peace," the ship instead encounters resistance and, suddenly, "we are / devoured." Shifting from the anticipation of conflict through the ongoing verbal forms of "drifting" and "devouring," to an abrupt conclusion to the battle, which leaves the crew stunned in the present tense, but after the violence has occurred ("we are / devoured"), Glück has described the conflict by erasing the central event. Following Caruth, we could say that the event never occurred to the traumatized victims, or else that it has never stopped occurring.

Like Caruth, Glück wants to attend to the way trauma influences testimony in the aftermath of combat. Her focus is squarely on the period after the ship has been destroyed, the crucial time frame in terms of the issue of testimony. The time after the ship is destroyed is when survivors must grapple with what has happened to their ability to express themselves, or even to remember what precisely they have been through, or where they have

7. Homer's definition of courtesy is the host's sharing of food with the guest, which is the fundamental distinction between civilization (Phaecians) and barbarism (Cyclops). "Archipelago," on the other hand, depicts victims devoured by barbaric hosts, rather than guests granted the privilege of eating before their hosts have eaten.

been. The poem turns in the last five lines to address the problems of recollection, representation, and the survivor's weakened sense of identity:

> our shrunk number runs
> in two packs: madness and suicide. The twelfth year
> the captain calls his name, it has no meaning, and the crew
> shrieks in its extremity. (FFB 65)

One among the "devoured," the speaker offers a survivor's tale related to *The Odyssey* in its broadest outlines. But Glück suggests that living through an assault, and achieving liberation from memories of defeat in battle, may not coincide. Either the captain or his crew has suffered aphasia because one or the other cannot remember his name when it is called out. The crew's language has devolved into "shrieks," a term that suggests animal cries in response to extreme discomfort as much as it does human speech. The speaker testifies to defeat, through the blotting out of the account. A survivor, the narrator should nonetheless be counted among the "devoured," because his speech registers the fact that he has been, like those who perished at sea, irreparably damaged.

George E. Dimock Jr., in "The Name of Odysseus," argues that the Greek hero has endured the trouble, pain, and "weariness of rowing" to "achieve the goal of recognition and identity."[8] By contrast, the crew's return in "Archipelago" leads to "madness and suicide." An existential strangeness has replaced the scenes of recognition by Odysseus's loved ones: the nurse who notices the scar on his thigh when bathing him; the swineherd who treats Odysseus, then in the guise of a beggar, with the kindness normally bestowed upon an honored guest; the dog who keels over when he spots his old master; and Penelope, the patient and cunning spouse. In "Archipelago," the speaker relates a story of disorientation, through the idiom of a mythic resource, even as the theme of the poem is the diminished reliability of the lyric voice or the mythic frame in the aftermath to trauma.

The speaker in "Archipelago" represents trauma through the unreliable narrator in a way that is uncannily reminiscent of Geoffrey Hartman's analysis of Freudian theory:

> Freud . . . demonstrated that trauma was the result of living through extreme experience without experiencing it—without being able to

8. George E. Dimock Jr., "The Name of Odysseus," in *Homer: A Collection of Critical Essays,* ed. George Steiner and Robert Fagles (Englewood Cliffs, N.J.: Prentice Hall, 1962), 116, 114.

> integrate it emotionally or mentally. The disturbances associated with trauma are, according to Freud, an attempt of the system to prepare retroactively for a shock that had already taken place, to catch up with and master it.

Glück effaces details that might allow us as readers to link "Archipelago" to a specific historical event or autobiographical incident, or even to assert a more definitive connection between the incident described and the Homeric epic. This erasure of detailed reference is part of her expression of what Hartman calls "the wound in the word," referring to the way prior disturbance spills over into the present tense, resisting the containment of rhetoric or narrative pattern. "Archipelago" enacts what Hartman calls "a style that marks an absence" and that, by so doing, may become "a form of testimony."[9] As Glück puts it in "Decade":

> A void
> appears in the life
> A shock so deep, so terrible,
> its force
> levels the perceived world. (SA 38)

An unsettling kind of survivor's tale, "Archipelago" (HM) illustrates the theme of the wounded speaker who is, paradoxically, reliable as a witness to trauma because unreliable as a storyteller. As in "Archipelago," Glück represents speakers who do not "see anything objectively" (AR 34) in "Gretel in Darkness" (HM), a persona poem based on the fairy tale, as well in the overtly autobiographical "The Untrustworthy Speaker" (AR). Examples of remembering and forgetting, these three poems represent a living witness to trauma.

"Gretel in Darkness" (HM): A Traumatic Fairy Tale

The child psychologist Bruno Bettelheim has demonstrated that, far from being trifles or merely frightening episodes of horror without symbolic significance, fairy tales are vehicles through which childhood attitudes, fears, and beliefs are enacted and potentially worked through. In *The Uses of Enchantment* (1976), Bettelheim interpreted fairy tales from a Freudian perspective by focusing on childhood development and familial relations:

9. Hartman, *The Longest Shadow,* 158, 161.

"They speak about [the child's] severe inner pressures in a way that the child unconsciously understands, and—without belittling the most serious inner struggles which growing up entails—offer examples of both temporary and permanent solutions to pressing difficulties."[10] According to Bettelheim, fairy tales address "existential dilemmas" faced by children on a conscious and preconscious level. They are especially concerned with "the need to be loved and the fear that one is thought worthless; the love of life, and the fear of death" (10).

In a chapter devoted to "Hansel and Gretel," Bettelheim reads psychological meaning into the trip to the forest undertaken by the brother and sister, who leave a poor woodcutter's family residing on the edge of the woods to go to the gingerbread house, which the siblings begin to eat, before they are nearly devoured by the witch who lives there. In the forest, Gretel outwits the witch by tricking her into the fireplace where she, not they, burns to death. After this harrowing encounter, the children return home to their parents, who, Bettelheim argues, they had feared would devour or abandon them. Having overcome "oral or oedipal problems" during their adventures with the witch in the forest, the children can now return home to "successfully mature into adolescence" (165).

According to Bettelheim, the siblings have run away from home because they "believe that their parents are talking about a plot to desert them"; they are "convinced that their parents plan to starve them to death" (159). Characterizing the father as "a shadowy and ineffectual figure throughout the story," Bettelheim argues that the more clearly drawn "Mother is all-important, in both her benign and her threatening aspects" (160). The trip to the woods, where the children devour the gingerbread roof and window, is a symbolic regression to "destructive orality" (162). Eating the house represents a fantasy return to the "good mother," who provides endless nourishment and sensual pleasure through nursing. By contrast the witch, who wants to eat the children as revenge for their destruction of her dwelling, is for Bettelheim a complementary image of the evil mother, whose reaction to their gluttony teaches them an important lesson about "the dangers of unrestrained oral greed and dependence" (162).

The children turn the table on the witch by luring her into the fireplace, then by disguising a bone as a child's finger. Bettelheim reads this substitution of bone for finger as a sign that the children have freed themselves from the

10. Bruno Bettelheim, *The Uses of Enchantment: The Meaning and Importance of Fairy Tales* (New York: Vintage, 1976), 6 (further quotations from this work will be cited parenthetically in the text). I do not argue for Bettelheim's direct influence on Glück's version of this fairy tale, but she is aware of his work. She quotes a statement of his concerning a child's knowledge of the difference between good and evil as an epigraph to *The Triumph of Achilles*.

oral gratification stage. Having erased the image of the evil mother, they may now return to their parents with a "greater wisdom," symbolically registered in the jewels the children bring home. In the end Bettelheim understands the fairy tale as therapeutic, as a story of trauma and recovery through which children can work out their "immature dependence on [their] parents." By entering into the symbolic work of the tale through reading, children can reach the "next higher stage of development: cherishing also the support of age mates" (166).

In "Gretel in Darkness," Glück joins Bettelheim in comprehending the psychological significance of the fairy tale, but she is far less sanguine than Bettelheim about its therapeutic value. Approaching a story of matricide through the distancing device of a mask, which nonetheless places the speaker (and, therefore, the reader) inside the narrative, Glück represents Gretel as a terrified child and as a traumatized adult. Glück interprets the adult life of the speaker, and especially her relationships with men, as indelibly marred by a childhood memory that involves the symbolic murder of the mother:

> This is the world we wanted.
> All who would have seen us dead
> are dead. I hear the witch's cry
> break in the moonlight through a sheet
> of sugar: God rewards.
> Her tongue shrivels into gas. . . .
>
> Now, far from women's arms
> and memory of women, in our father's hut
> we sleep, are never hungry.
> Why do I not forget?
> My father bars the door, bars harm
> from this house, and it is years.
>
> No one remembers. Even you, my brother,
> summer afternoons you look at me as though
> you meant to leave,
> as though it never happened.
> But I killed for you. I see armed firs,
> the spires of that gleaming kiln—
>
> Nights I turn to you to hold me
> but you are not there.
> Am I alone? Spies
> hiss in the stillness, Hansel,
> we are there still and it is real, real,
> that black forest and the fire in earnest. (FFB 63)

Glück has stated that, even as a child, she "loved the sentence as a unit: the beginning of a preoccupation with syntax" (PT 8). In "Gretel in Darkness," she enacts her childhood fascination with syntax, in the process creating a traumatic surface through syntax and enjambment. Glück lends significance to form by juxtaposing the integrity of the declarative sentence as a complete unit of meaning with the semantic possibilities of the line as a compositional unit that may disrupt the integrity of the sentence. The poem begins in the present tense, and with a complete thought, which fills the first line of the poem and is end-stopped. This literal kind of composure suggests the speaker, having vanquished her enemies, has achieved a degree of emotional closure: "This is the world we wanted." And yet, the intrusion of the past, entering the speaker's consciousness through writing, becomes evident on a formal level as early as line 2. Unlike the end-stopped first line, line 2 is disrupted through enjambment. "All who would have seen us dead / are dead." The enjambment is semantically meaningful. It implies a dissonance between the completed grammatical expression and the limited space (the line) that the author has allotted to represent the thought.

Glück picks up the story from Gretel's present-tense point of view, after the children have tricked the witch into the oven by substituting a bone for a finger:

> I hear the witch's cry
> break in the moonlight through a sheet
> of sugar: God rewards.
> Her tongue shrivels into gas. (FFB 63)

To be granted the wish to get "the world we wanted," the speaker must vanquish the enemy (the stepmother) to achieve a safe return home. Miklitsch notes that, even though "Gretel is safe at home and what she has had to do to survive is past, she is still haunted by memories of burning witches, bewitched women."[11]

The speaker's tone of voice and the form of the poem shift from the confident expression of the initial complete thought in line 1, which registered the temporary satisfaction of desire, to lines that trail off into an ellipsis at the end of the first stanza. On a formal level, Glück is enacting how painful memories have spilled over into the text as illegibility. Her confident opening address to the reader has deteriorated from a unity between grammar and prosodic form. An elliptical silence suggests the inadequacy or impossibility of language to convey meaning and coherence at the end of stanza 4.

11. Miklitsch, "Assembling a Landscape," 11.

The matricide may be a distant memory, but as with "Archipelago" (HM) and "The Racer's Widow" (F), Gretel the storyteller is haunted by the uncanny recurrence of terror in the act of telling. Paranoid, she feels estranged from her brother, the co-conspirator in the murder and escape. Wondering "Why do I not forget?" she also suggests aphasia by declaring that "No one remembers":

> Even you, my brother,
> summer afternoons you look at me as though
> you meant to leave,
> as though it never happened.
> But I killed for you. (FFB 63)

In the final stanza, Gretel turns in bed at night for comfort from a lover who she fears will leave her, but "you are not there." These lines suggest that her panic about a *future* disappearance of the beloved has, in a psychoanalytic sense, *already* taken place in the form of a childhood worry over sibling abandonment. Together, the brother and sister have endured a terrifying ordeal, but the events in the black forest have marred their perception of the present to the degree that disappearance replaces appearance. As with the shipwrecked and psychologically damaged narrator from "Archipelago," Gretel has returned from the edge of death and loss and lives to tell the tale, but the memory of gassing a mother-figure, albeit as an act of self-defense, has damaged her rapport with a man who occupies the position once held by the brother.

In the final two lines, Glück states the impact of the past on the present. Gretel addresses Hansel: "we are there still and it is real, real, / that black forest and the fire in earnest." Glück's revision of the fairy tale contrasts sharply with Bettelheim's analysis, which surmised that "children, by being ingenious, rid themselves of these persecuting figures of their imagination. By succeeding in doing so, they gain immensely from the experience, as did Hansel and Gretel."[12] In "Gretel in Darkness," authorial survival, defined as getting the "world we wanted," involves returning to childhood stories and memories that invoke a symbolic matricide. Glück implies that her speaker's recollection of that event, an example of the will to authorial power, has come at great personal cost: "we are there still and it is real, real, / that black forest and the fire in earnest."

12. Bettelheim, *Uses of Enchantment,* 166.

The Art of Losing in *Ararat*

In "The Triumph of Achilles," Glück continues to explore the impact of trauma on her writing and her self through the distancing devices of myth and persona, even as she writes that "the legends / cannot be trusted / their source is the survivor, / the one who has been abandoned" (FFB 168). In *Ararat,* however, she removes the mask of a persona associated with myth or fable to disclose the undisguised symptoms of traumatic shock in her own language: "Long ago, I was wounded," she says in the opening line to the first poem, *"Parodos"* (AR 15). The title refers to the choral opening of a Greek play and so suggests a move toward theatricality, detachment, and allusiveness. But the communal aspect of the classical frame she has chosen cannot contain the unspecified disturbance afflicting the individual speaker. Melissa Brown notes that the poem "alerts us to the separating individuality of the discontinuous being whose struggle begins at birth, the break into existence creating a wound that never heals."[13]

"Parodos" characterizes the narrator as having lived through a disturbance that unsettles the border between life and death, between social discourse and the cryptic tones of a speaker who perceives herself as an oracular vehicle, a medium who has paid dearly for her clairvoyance:

> I was born to a vocation:
> to bear witness
> to the great mysteries.
> Now that I've seen both
> birth and death, I know
> to the dark nature these
> are proofs, not
> mysteries— (AR 15)

The speaker describes herself as being "out of touch / with the world," as "a piece of wood. A stone." Through these images, Glück characterizes her speaker's emotional condition as psychic numbness and spatial disorientation. She may compare herself to inert parts of nature, but she is disconnected from her literal environment. She exists more as a voice that runs through her mind than as a complete person with a mind and a body.

Ironically, the more she confesses to psychological disability, the more we believe, as with Dickinson in "After great pain, a formal feeling comes," her

13. Brown, "Love of Form," 39.

pain has acquainted her with "the great mysteries," including the discourse of the gravely ill and the deceased. Defining herself as "a device that listened," Glück's speaker is reconfigured as a damaged medium. She is like the "half-destroyed instruments / that once held to a course" in "Diving into the Wreck" by Adrienne Rich. In Dickinson, Rich, and Glück, we understand the admission of damage ironically. It is a registration, not of humility or self-contempt, but of how the symptoms of trauma upend the notion of veracity and produce authenticity through an unreliable narration.[14]

Ararat characterizes three generations of women in Glück's family, who have all recently suffered the death of a father, a young sibling, a husband, a daughter, and an uncle. "The Untrustworthy Speaker" represents the epicenter of the speaker's grief over these familial losses through an admission that her text incorporates what Hartman refers to as "the wound in the word":

> If you want the truth, you have to close yourself
> to the older daughter, block her out:
> when a living thing is hurt like that,
> in its deepest workings,
> all function is altered.
>
> That's why I'm not to be trusted.
> Because a wound to the heart
> is also a wound to the mind. (AR 35)

Defining her character as untrustworthy, Glück encourages us to separate deceitfulness from insincerity. In trauma writing, disingenuousness lends veracity to the account of how the "wound to the heart" becomes articulated as the "wound to the mind":

> Don't listen to me; my heart's been broken.
> I don't see anything objectively.
> . . . .
> In my own mind, I'm invisible: that why I'm dangerous.
> People like me, who seem selfless,
> we're the cripples, the liars;
> we're the ones who should be factored out
> in the interest of truth. (AR 34)

14. Emily Dickinson, "After great pain, a formal feeling comes," in Ramazani et al., *Norton Anthology* 1:36; Adrienne Rich, "Diving into the Wreck," in *Norton Anthology of Modern and Contemporary Poetry,* vol. 2, *Contemporary Poetry,* 3rd ed. (New York: Norton, 2003), 469.

The speaker defines herself as an archetypal figure of persecution, one belonging to the category of the scapegoat who should be "factored out / in the interest of truth."

The badge of "liar" or "cripple" signals Glück's allegiance with the Gypsies, Jews, Cripples, Radicals, Homosexuals, those classes of abject persons labeled by the Nazis as dangerous to the "pure" aesthetic principles of the Aryan nation, and so erased from view. As in "Daddy" by Plath or in some of the *Dream Songs* by John Berryman, Glück—who is, to speak for the moment in terms of ethnic designations, Jewish—encourages the reader to number herself as an *imaginary* Jew. She is one among the victims of genocide, an event I believe this poem signifies in a displaced form through its reading of invisibility as the outcome of persecution. Her poem confronts personal loss through the figure of the broken heart. The poem can also be read as a response to the aftershocks of Shoah on someone who in "Memoir" (SA) denied the significance of the event in her life. Certainly the Holocaust is not foregrounded as it is in "second generation" poetry by contemporary Jewish American poets such as the "Dead Man" series by Marvin Bell and, more recently, *Dead Men's Praise* by Jacqueline Osherow.

In addition to admitting that her speaker bears "false" witness, Glück upends traditional conceptions of lyric authenticity by imagining the "Untrustworthy Speaker" as "invisible." In traditional versions of lyric, "voice" functions to recuperate the image of the unacknowledged self by rectifying the problem of invisibility. Unlike writing, the spoken word is associated with the body, specifically with the mouth and lungs, which literally produce sound through the inspiration and aspiration of air. By contrast, "The Untrustworthy Speaker" emphasizes expiration and disappearance as the outcomes she desires for her efforts.

"Lost Love" (AR) represents the speaker as a victim of a family tragedy. She is the one lacking love and attention from parents too involved in their grief over another daughter's early death:

> Something did change: when my sister died,
> my mother's heart became
> very cold, very rigid,
> like a tiny pendant of iron. (AR 27)

The poem describes how the speaker's childhood was in effect stolen by the sister, who took her mother's affection with her into the grave. "The Untrustworthy Speaker" admits that her self-portrait as an innocent victim of tragic circumstances in "Lost Love" has concealed, rather than illuminated, a crucial part of her identity:

> I never see myself,
> standing on the front steps, holding my sister's hand.
> That's why I can't account
> for the bruises on her arm, where the sleeve ends. (AR 34)

She suggests that recovery from trauma in part involves accepting responsibility for why her language has in the past failed to reconstitute the self. In this case, she admits that for recovery to take place she must come to terms with her aggressive impulses and violent behavior toward her sister when both were children.

Like "The Untrustworthy Speaker," the "Widows" (AR) are a group of emotionally stunted characters who nonetheless are coming to terms with their aggressive instincts toward each other through the moderating form of a deadly serious card game:

> My mother's playing cards with my aunt,
> Spite and Malice, the family pastime, the game
> my grandmother taught all her daughters.
>
> Midsummer: too hot to go out.
> Today, my aunt's ahead; she's getting the good cards.
> My mother's dragging, having trouble with her concentration.
> She can't get used to her own bed this summer.
> She had no trouble last summer,
> getting used to the floor. She learned to sleep there
> to be near my father.
> He was dying; he got a special bed.
>
> My aunt doesn't give an inch, doesn't make
> allowance for my mother's weariness.
> It's how they were raised: you show respect by fighting.
> To let up insults the opponent. (AR 23)

As on the chivalric battlefield in Homer, personal identity and the dignity of the opponent are established through "fighting," rather than through any empathetic identification with the weariness of the wounded, weakened adversary. Archetypal Glück women, the sorority endure great pain, renouncing their desire to taste the richness of what life might have to offer them should they risk an immersion in the burning heat of midsummer. "They have cards; they have each other. / They don't need any more companionship" (AR 23).

Like the Glück authorial persona, the women interpret personal invisibility as the source of their symbolic power over the pain, loss, and insecurity that accompany life:

> My aunt's been at it longer; maybe that's why she's playing better.
> Her cards evaporate: that's what you want, that's the object: in
> the end,
> the one who has nothing wins. (AR 24)

In "Dedication to Hunger" (DF), the teenager considered inconspicuousness in body and pared-down language as signs that she could be in charge of her identity in an unstable environment. In "Widows" (AR) the mourners have circled the wagons, withdrawing to a card table in order to protect themselves from more grief after their husbands have died. The widows think it "good to stay inside on days like this, / to stay where it is cool." Avoiding the outside, the hot summer sun, in this poem signifies the refusal to risk forging new love relationships with men. Each sister has constituted herself as an emotional void, which also represents her independence from the vulnerability entailed in reliance upon others outside the family.

Depicting characters detached from the painful growth of mutability, "Widows" may be read as a nihilistic statement, but it reflects a stoic disposition, illustrating one option for surviving a traumatic episode. With its long and confidently declarative end-stopped lines, Glück's poem is suggesting, as such extravagance would suggest in Whitman and Ginsberg, a personal transformation that does imply an acceptance of change by the aunt, for example, who has redefined herself from wife or mother or woman or sister to widow. The aunt has revised her self by reconfiguring her social position. Her new title reflects her memory of the prior status as wife, but it also corresponds to her acknowledgment of the hard facts of current realities.

Certainly the emphasis placed by the widows on the ritual of a card game demonstrates their adherence to a secular example of collective mourning. The group communicates grief by playing games that channel despair into a manageable, if displaced, form:

> My grandmother thought ahead; she prepared her daughters.
> They have cards; they have each other.
> They don't need any more companionship. (AR 23)

The sisters have substituted a pastime that requires a group—the speaker says this game is "better than solitaire"—for more aggressive versions of acting out their rage upon each other, or developing tactics to injure themselves when unaccompanied. The widows focus their attention on the small aspects of life that happen to have fallen in front of them, on the literal and figurative cards that fate has dealt them. Concentrating on the cards, and not letting up on the distracted opponent, the sisters do not allow themselves to dwell on memories of the marriages that have died with their spouses, nor do they speculate about a future to take place after the mourning process has ceased.

"Widows" depicts a massive sublimation of spleen, and therefore, an inadequate recovery of what these women were like before they suffered their major losses. Learning to accept bereavement—in part by renouncing the desire to move on—could be described as the name of "the game / my grandmother taught all her daughters." Exhibiting humorously grotesque bitterness, moodiness, and competitiveness for recognition, "Widows" examines the camaraderie found among a community of isolates, the shaping of their tough exterior personae, and the displacement of fury into the development of an allegorical game with cards entitled "Spite" or "Malice" that at once exhibits and reins in aggressive instincts.

The card table—with the rules of a game where winning, fighting, and disappearing seem to go hand in hand—becomes a metaphor in *Ararat* for the writing table and for poetry as Glück has imagined the act of writing as an expression of renounced desire. Like the "Widows," Glück has chosen to come to terms with grief over loss through a surface demeanor that implies poise, cool, and indifference. In early poems such as "La Force" (F) and "The Fortress" (HM), Glück relied on archetypal imagery from the Tarot card pack to begin what Gordon calls a "process of comprehension."[15] The reading of Tarot cards may be likened to the self-examination that goes on in psychoanalysis.

In "Education of the Poet" (PT), Glück recalls how she learned in therapy to regard the autobiographical self with the kind of detached intensity that she brought to her idiosyncratic readings of the Tarot pack:

> Analysis taught me to think. Taught me to use my tendency to object to articulated ideas on my own ideas, taught me to use doubt, to examine my own speech for its evasions and excisions. It gave me an intellectual task capable of transforming paralysis—which is the extreme form of self-doubt—into insight. (PT 12)

15. Gordon, "Reconceiving the Sacred," 48.

Like the young poet who attempts to come to terms with her experience through a reading of the Tarot cards as well as through viewing her life as a text in psychoanalysis, her mother, her aunt, and, before them, her grandmother are portrayed as fierce cardplayers who interpret the cards as texts, external objects deeply related to their inner lives. They at once display and rein in their strongest emotions by projecting their inner lives onto the figures and faces that turn up in the deck, which then become part of the hands they must interpret if they are going to survive.

Lamenting Lamentation in *Vita Nova*

Responding to what the Jewish poet and theorist Allen Grossman calls a "culture of nuclearism," and to the totalizing rhetoric of modernism, most contemporary American poets have followed Robert Lowell and W. D. Snodgrass in developing what Charles Altieri refers to as an "immanent" poetics. By so doing, Grossman argues, contemporary poets have shied away from the voice of the great modern lyricists of the sublime—Yeats and Hart Crane are foremost among those poets willing "to open their throats, to speak both directly and with a full sense of the privilege of the art that they practice."[16]

By limiting voice, Grossman believes contemporary poets have reneged on their ancient responsibility to speak on behalf of the value of the individual and the survival of the human community as a whole, even as the poet may not feel comfortable speaking for other individuals, as in modernism. "It is my intention to open my throat, and by doing so, to open your eyes as a reader," Grossman tells Mark Halliday in "The Winter Conversations."[17] Grossman is probably correct to say that most contemporary poets go in fear of speaking too loudly about the social function of their office. In spite of the fear, Maerra Shreiber warns that metadiscursive systems such as poetry and religion cannot be diminished without cost. These structures have been instrumental in creating images of persons as valuable:

16. Allen Grossman, *The Sighted Singer: Two Works on Poetry for Readers and Writers* (Baltimore: Johns Hopkins University Press, 1992), 34 (Altieri), 54. In an essay, Grossman argues that the nuclear threat continues to exist as a virtual type of annihilation even as the concern for nuclear war seems to have diminished in the aftermath of the Cold War. See Allen Grossman, "Nuclear Violence, Institutions of Holiness, and the Structures of Poetry," in *The Long Schoolroom: Lessons in the Bitter Logic of the Poetic Principle* (Ann Arbor: University of Michigan Press, 1997), 168–178.

17. Grossman, *Sighted Singer,* 112.

> Both these institutions are committed to the "eidetic" or presence-making function: for poetry, like religion and its rituals, helps us structure and regulate human relationships. That is, both poetry and religion work to confer meaning and presence to a particular life, thus providing it "personhood."[18]

In addressing how Glück writes about the recovery from trauma in *Vita Nova,* I want to emphasize Shreiber's distinction between the "particular life" of human beings and the concept of "personhood," for it is only the latter that may be conferred by the poet.

A trace of an absence, "personhood" reconstructs "particular life" as an artifact. Poetry may confer the dignity of visibility in the form of personhood, but Glück in *Vita Nova* critiques her prior lyric practice as having been another disaster notation. She expresses reservations about her enactment of identity in language of such an impersonal form that nature, erotic desire, and the nuances of material existence disappear into the ethereal realm of abstraction. Because "personhood" is a category of representation (not a form of human presence) and located in the mind (not the body), much of *Vita Nova* laments the art of lamentation. By "lamenting lamentation," I mean to say that Glück reconsiders a literary endeavor that is, ironically, precipitated by the speaker's grief over the death of the beloved.

Dante tells us in the prose section of *La Vita Nuova* that he is compelled to write poetry as a way of dealing with the absence of Beatrice, who dies before he is ever able to meet her face to face. The pain of seeing the beloved's face as a mental picture, but of not having her physically with him, causes in him "a desire to write more poetry."[19] In poems such as "Relic" and "Orfeo" (VN) that revisit one of the founding stories of male lyric ordination, the myth of Orpheus and Eurydice, Glück's speakers confront the posthumous dimension to poetry. These poems critique the art that she has practiced with such outstanding results since her first book appeared in 1968 when she was only twenty-five years old. In this her final sequence from the 1990s—Glück turned fifty-seven in 2000—she interprets her lyric practice through an unforgiving calculus involving much loss and little gain.

18. Maerra Shreiber, "'Spiritual Warfare': Allen Grossman on the Relation between Poetry and the Institutions of Holiness, with Special Reference to Reznikoff's *Testimony,*" in *Poetry's Poet: Essays on the Poetry, Pedagogy, and Poetics of Allen Grossman,* ed. Daniel Morris (Orono, Me.: National Poetry Foundation, 2004), 183.

19. Dante Alighieri, *Vita Nuova,* trans. Mark Musa (Bloomington: Indiana University Press, 1973), 28.

Interpreting poetry itself as a traumatic site she must recover from, Glück also suggests that poetry may be redirected toward recovering a fresh appreciation of life outside the text. In *Vita Nova,* she tries to imagine a new destination for writing, which points toward the adequacy, the good, the richness of mere being, of a descent into life. A poet who has tended to write narratives of descent involving mythic heroes and heroines such as Persephone and Jesus Christ, Glück attempts in *Vita Nova* to accept her own mortality, to accept the cost of the precious beauty she finds in being human through a descent into the immanent realm.

In "Relic" (VN) the archetypal figure of the female beloved whose death precedes lamentation, Eurydice revisits her traditional mythic role. She critiques the Orphic exchange of her presence for the compensation that his language is supposed to provide:

> How would you like to die
> while Orpheus was singing?
> . . . .
> I think sometimes
> our consolations are the costliest thing. (VN 36)

Having dealt with the myth as an example of female objectification, Glück also recalls the cost of the exchange of life for lines in a memorable poem from the perspective of the grieving lover or singer. Orpheus urges Eurydice to speak on his behalf to the Furies in the underworld:

> Tell them I have lost my beloved;
> I am completely alone now.
> Tell them there is no music like this
> without real grief. (VN 18)

Glück's version of the Orpheus myth differs from the feminist revisionism found in "Eurydice" by H.D., in which the heroine scolds Orpheus for his failure to bring her back to life. In *Helen in Egypt,* H.D. creates a defense for Helen by claiming that she was never even in Troy, that the Greeks and Trojans fought for an illusion. As Terence Diggory remarks, Glück, by contrast to H.D., offers a "general critique of the sign as substitution" for natural human life.[20] A commentary, on her own practice, that takes into account

20. Terence Diggory, "Louise Glück's Lyric Journey," *Salmagundi* 124–25 (Fall 1999–Winter 2000): 308.

the perspectives of both Orpheus and Eurydice, "Orfeo" appraises the idea of lyric compensation for experiential loss. She revises the connection between poetry and survival after trauma to include the tragic dimension of writing itself. Unlike traditional elegiac poetry, "Orfeo" (VN) focuses less on the singer's success or failure at commemorating the dead beloved through memorable speech than on the problems faced by the speaker. He is trying to find the resources to sing an elegy in the face of "real grief."

In "Lute Song," Orpheus has become transformed from a living, grieving human being into a figure in a legend:

> the ardent
> spirit of Orpheus, made present
> not as a human being, rather
> as a pure soul rendered
> detached, immortal,
> through deflected narcissism. (VN 17)

Orpheus cannot revive Eurydice, but he also cannot save himself as a real presence with his "lute song." What he can do is to reanimate his voice through the reader's experience of the text. However much it is detached from "a human being," the transformation of the speaker's voice to the reader or listener nonetheless redirects authorial "narcissism" into an immortal form—by taking into account the vital act of interpretation that occurs whenever another person reads a poem. As Diggory remarks, the "change" of the natural voice into the artificial medium of lyric provides a "transmutation" of the self into a fact of another's memory through reading. Glück creates a "new life" for poetry, and by extension for the poet, beyond the registration of "personhood"—by contextualizing "voice" in narrative form through the expansive frame of the book-length sequence. Taking the reader into account, Glück asserts the author's freedom to reposition herself in a psychological sense away from the epicenter of trauma.

As with Dante's *Vita Nuova,* Glück lists "real grief" as the prerequisite to "songs of a high order" in her *Vita Nova.* She also pursues a new direction, which she will build upon in *The Seven Ages* by associating poetry with an enhanced attention to the pleasures derived from accepting a descent into ordinary life. In many poems from *Vita Nova* and *The Seven Ages,* Glück imagines her speaker taking part in the social exchanges and goings-on that constitute the mild kind of happiness many people take as life's daily joy. "Nest," "Ellsworth Avenue," "Lute Song," "Formaggio," and the concluding poem, "Vita Nova," all signal that the author wishes to challenge her emphasis in

"Orfeo" on Grossman's "personhood" as a textual self that requires the "pure soul rendered / detached, immortal, / through deflected narcissism" to signify symbolic accomplishment. Whereas her poetry from the 1970s pitted the authorial imagination against nature in lyrics such as "All Hallows," "To Autumn," and "For Jane Myers" (HM), in "Nest" she imagines how poetry may contribute to the visibility of nature in a literal sense.

The Voice of Mourning and the Morning of Recovery in *Vita Nova*

Like "Archipelago" and "Gretel in Darkness" (HM), *Ararat* registers the continuing impact of trauma upon the "untrustworthy" narrator through the opaque and inconclusive texture of the lyric testimony. If "Widows" offered an unsatisfying recipe for surviving loss through stoicism, reducing one's desire for companionship to a morbid game of cards, then *Vita Nova* represents the speaker at a later stage in mourning. She does not foreclose the desire to explore what life might have to offer her in the future.

Instead of positing silence as an evacuation of memory, and as the ultimate destination for the human voice, *Vita Nova* illustrates the psychoanalytic critic Judith Herman's theory of writing as a forum to recover memory in the present tense of the lyric address:

> Memory, and especially the memory that goes into storytelling, is not simply an afterbirth of experience, a secondary formation: it *enables* experiencing, it allows what we call the real to enter consciousness and word-presentation, to be something more than trauma followed by a hygienic, and ultimately illusory, mental erasure.[21]

Following Dante in this regard, Glück speaks about her experience in the context of "new life"—emotionally, mentally, geographically, aesthetically. In *Vita Nova,* her speaker risks falling in love again after her shattering divorce and her Vermont house fire that were discussed, obliquely, through the Homeric foil in *Meadowlands.* Moving to the literary center of Cambridge, Massachusetts (as the author had in fact done), she nonetheless represents her appreciation for a life that exists outside of the figurative space a move to Cambridge from Vermont might imply. Ironically, the speaker seems to become more alive to nature in the suburban world of North Cambridge than she was in the pastoral, if equally suburban, setting of Plainfield, Vermont.

21. Judith Herman, *Trauma and Recovery* (New York: Basic Books, 1992), 158.

In various poems she regains her appetite for food, appreciates nature, expresses fondness for the shopkeepers and pedestrians she happens to pass on the street, even (in the final poem) rekindles her desire for romantic love. The narrative sequencing in *Vita Nova* creates the groundwork for an emotional renewal that appears in several individual lyrics, adding a dynamic element to the static quality of the individual lyrics. On a psychological level, the energy I am associating with the narrative sequencing enables the lyric speaker to "escape the entropy created by the continuous repetition" of prior loss and to "create forward movement toward recovery."[22] As Herman has argued, a return from madness—or the recovery from trauma—requires a willingness to release oneself from the private, self-reflexive view of a shocking event.

A series of poems from *Vita Nova* express the speaker's sensation of having woken up to life following a period of invisibility. The speaker remembers feeling as if she had become unborn, and in "The New Life," she speaks of guilt, of seizure, of banishment from the material world for an unspecified sin (I suspect it is that of survival itself):

> I slept the sleep of the just,
> later the sleep of the unborn
> who come into the world
> guilty of many crimes. (VN 12)

In "Mutable Earth," she follows the lessons of the aunt in "Widows." She endures guilt and loss through a lack of warmth, but she then challenges the adequacy of that abrupt model of survival:

> Are you healed or do you only think you're healed?
>
> I told myself
> from nothing
> nothing could be taken away.
>
> But can you love anyone yet?
>
> When I feel safe, I can love.
>
> But will you touch anyone?
>
> I told myself
> if I had nothing
> the world couldn't touch me. (VN 29)

22. Karen DeMeester, "Trauma and Recovery in Virginia Woolf's *Mrs. Dalloway,*" *Modern Fiction Studies* 44.3 (Fall 1998): 652.

These lines recall Cordelia's refusal to follow her venal and deceitful sisters in expressing exclusive love for her father in Shakespeare's *King Lear.* Specifically, "Mutable Earth" (VN) recalls the fateful conversation between Cordelia, who "cannot heave / My heart into my mouth," and Lear, who says, "Nothing will come of nothing" (scene 1, act 1). The conversation between Lear and Cordelia occurs after the youngest daughter, alone among the three sisters in caring for her father, refuses to use language in a manner that will disguise her true intentions and feelings. She says "Nothing" when asked to express her love for him (and for no one else but him, including a future husband) in exchange for part of his kingdom as dowry. Invoking the tragic consequences of Cordelia's reticence to speak and emphasizing mutability, regardless of one's desire to escape change through inconspicuousness in speech and bearing, Glück suggests that figuring self-control by paring away language in the name of absolute truth is merely a fiction of safety.

The poet argues that we must face the change of life and the eventuality of death regardless of how we use words. She revises her argument in *Ararat,* about how to mourn the beloved by accepting change as part of what she calls "the patterns of my nature," even if such intense feelings may only lead to inconstancy, uncertainty, and increased pain:

> I had nothing
> and I was still changed.
> Like a costume, my numbness
> was taken away. Then
> hunger was added. (VN 30)

Glück admits to appetites that "numbness" merely shields from view but does not extinguish, like a garment covering a naked body. "Mutable Earth" imitates—but also challenges through its questions—the aunt's brusqueness as a sign of emotional control in "Widows."

In "Ellsworth Avenue," the speaker at once yields to "hungers" for various kinds of sensual experience in Cambridge and resists the numinous perspective that at times was apparent in *The Wild Iris.* Although gravitating toward the fleeting moment, she continues her affection for abstraction, which she uses to detach herself from a life she associates with loss. Glück, after all, is still Glück:

> Across the street, a small boy
> threw his hat into the air: the new

ascending always, the fresh
unsteady colors climbing and rising,
alternating
blue and gold:

Ellsworth Avenue.
A striped
abstraction of the human head
triumphant over dead shrubs. (VN 41)

In the final three lines, the lyric tilts away from a rendering of the unself-conscious child absorbed in play, a scene one might expect to find in a William Carlos Williams poem set on a street in Paterson or Rutherford. In the end, Glück explores her Stevensian impulse toward abstraction.

In modern painting, abstraction dismantles the features of the world into its constituent parts—lines, colors, and shapes—so that the artist can offer a self-conscious reflection on perception. In "Ellsworth Avenue," the abstract ending signifies Glück's creative engagement with the scene as a meditation on the relationship between art and life. By registering the scene through abstraction, the "human head" becomes more vital (the poet says "triumphant," as if language were in competition with nature for dominance over the scene) and the shrubs are "dead." The aftermath of shock is still evident in the oracular tone, suggesting numbness and detachment, but the speaker greets the emergence of a world outside the self that is sharpening into view.

Vita Nova includes moments of self-interrogation in poems such as "Mutable Earth" ("Are you healed or do you only think you're healed?") and in "Timor Mortis," with its rigorous self-questioning and admission of a fear of death: "Are you afraid?" and "Do you remember your childhood?" (VN 29, 16).[23] The sequence, however, also includes poems that register the speaker's connection with other human beings who exist in a public space where she cannot hope to claim to be in total control of her environment.

"Formaggio" registers the speaker's delight with the appealing grouping of small grocery stores, shoppers, and shopkeepers in North Cambridge, Massachusetts:

23. "Timor Mortis" is a title that alludes to the refrain of a line from the late-fifteenth-century Scottish poet William Dunbar's "Lament for the Makers." The full phrase is "Timor mortis conturbat me" or "the fear of death confounds [or distresses] me."

> [The world] never healed itself.
> But in the deep fissures, smaller worlds appeared:
> it was a good thing that human beings made them;
> human beings know what they need,
> better than any god.
>
> On Huron Avenue they became
> a block of stores; they became
> Fishmonger, Formaggio. Whatever
> they were or sold, they were
> alike in their function: they were
> visions of safety. Like
> a resting place. The salespeople
> were like parents; they appeared
> to live there. On the whole,
> kinder than parents. (VN 13)

"Real grief" remains the prerequisite for singing "songs of a high order," but "Formaggio" is a site for a positive transformation of the "deep fissures" into "smaller worlds." Here the shopkeepers "were like parents," only kinder, and relationships between self and other, fraught with ambivalence and fears of transgression in so many Glück lyrics, take on the safety, clarity, and relatively impersonal but friendly quality of buying groceries from a benign neighborhood shopkeeper.

Given that the poem's title may be translated into English as "cheese," we cannot discount an ironic reading of such happy interpersonal exchanges in a market. Is this poem kitsch? No longer associating disappearance with desire, however, the quaint version of consumerism described in "Formaggio" does speak to the author's warming trend. She draws a world of getting, spending, and brief but cordial social relationships that are mediated through the common idiom of money and goods in a market transaction that comes into relief in the course of the poem.

Glück goes beyond food shopping in a cheese shop as a sign of appetite for life, however. She expresses renewed desire as a sign of healing old wounds by progressing. "*I thought my life was over and my heart was broken. / Then I moved to Cambridge*" (VN 51). The speaker does not tell us what happened when she "moved," but the important point seems to be that narrative time has entered her lyric testimony, enabling a shift from then to a now that does not merely repeat the past, as would be the case in traumatic testimony.

In "Nest," Glück associates poetry with the site of nature, home, and birth by comparing her writing to a bird "making its nest." In a dream vision, she imagines the small bird gathering twigs and thread in early spring as a figure for the poet, who constructs a dwelling space in a world described in terms of scarcity, not abundance. Expressing its "efforts to survive" in the Stevensian context of "late desolation" and the "steady coldness / of the outside world," the bird fashions a dwelling out of leftovers: "It took what it found after the others / were finished" (VN 38, 39).

As other contemporary poets (such as the late A. R. Ammons in *Garbage* and Charles Simic in his study of Joseph Cornell, *Dime-Store Alchemy*) and American "found" artists (such as Robert Rauschenberg, David Smith, Louise Nevelson, and Jasper Johns), Glück figures the work of identity reconstruction as a task that involves refashioning the debris of artifacts of a prior world that has gradually lost its significance. The bird is described as taking "what it found in the yard, / its base materials," its "available material," and then, out of debris, in early spring, building its nest (VN 37). Glück's actions resemble the bird's in some ways, but her self-conscious position in the world is incomparable to instinctual acts of necessity.

Glück's speaker, like the bird, is a Penelope-figure, a weaver who survives being alone through creative acts on the loom in the face of dwindling resources and temporal restraints. Glück, however, sets limits upon her own comparison of poet and natural nest-maker. Where the bird has a bit of nature (twigs) and a bit of cultural material (thread) with which to build, the speaker must somehow forge a meaningful voice and vision out of her own existence without any tangible ground (either natural or cultural) on which to base her speech. The speaker may be compared to a part of nature depicted in literature, the spider that spins a web out of its own substance in Whitman's "A Noiseless, Patient Spider." "I had nothing to build with," she writes. "And I didn't know how I came here." Where the bird builds upon an "existing mass" of "collected twigs," the speaker asks, rather humorously, "when was there suddenly *mass*?" (VN 38). The registration of authorial consciousness in the form of a comic voice seems to have appeared out of the thin air of language itself. A poet who has spent much of her career working in the secondary mode of creative commentary, Glück declares her independence from all sources of creative strength outside the self. Through the text, the poet imagines a return from a state of invisibility toward the "vita nova" where the speaker finds herself "inexplicably happy" with her "bag of groceries" (VN 39).

As the authorial voice wraps itself around a visible world of street names, fruit stands, and other people, including the friendly shopkeepers, we learn that "the nest" that the poet has constructed manifests an externalization of the speaker's inner self:

And as I peered out my mind grew sharper. . . .
My eyes fixing on each thing
From the shelter of the hidden self:

first, *I love it.*
Then, *I can use it.* (VN 39)

Whatever precisely the "hidden self" may represent to Glück, it is certainly something that remains a lyric construct, that is put in the service of producing more constructs as the "I" and "eye" move from affection to possession. The lyric "I" is, to paraphrase Stevens, something made out of words to the end of it. It is not something given to her naturally by the world outside her—or else it is language reacting to and transmuting the world.

In "Orfeo" (VN), Glück expressed concern about the traumatic disposition of lyric as a compensation for lack. At the same time, she considers poetry a medium that promotes the survival of the personal voice and, in "Nest," she associates the poetic lines with the lineaments through which the individual speaker can perceive the natural world. In part she trusts poetry with the task of enabling the person to survive, because poetry has been understood for so long as the way to transmit human presence and to create a lasting voice.

Grossman has associated poetic lines with the very formation of the distinguishing features of the human face, lineaments. "All Orphic machines are versions of the countenance under the conditions required for poetic utterance," he writes in *The Sighted Singer.* "Text as Orphic machine is countenance as speech alone. Reading therefore is the inference of countenance from text, and the conservation of the text is the keeping of the lineaments of the countenance."[24] Like Grossman, Glück articulates her view of language as conservational in "Lute Song":

I made a harp of disaster
to perpetuate the beauty of my last love.
Yet my anguish such as it is,
remains the struggle for form. (VN 17)

Glück enacts Grossman's call for contemporary writers to open their throats in order to form "persons." Unlike Grossman, she is not satisfied with the

24. Grossman, *Sighted Singer,* 368.

idea of poetry as commemoration, because of its association with trauma. In "Fugue" (AV), Glück will directly link a musical instrument associated with lyric poetry (the harp) with an instrument of war (the archer's bow):

> Then I was wounded. The bow
> was now a harp, its string cutting
> deep into my palm. In the dream
>
> it both made the wound and sealed the wound. (AV 33)

Commemorating personal experience through poetry is thus in "Fugue" represented as itself a traumatic process, one that simultaneously causes and conceals pain.

The speaker's lyric voice remains an indelible feature of Glück's poetry in *Vita Nova,* but Robert Hass and other critics such as Charles Berger have identified the combination of the lyric with the narrative dimension that is implied in the book-length sequence as her most significant formal innovation. As in Dante's *Vita Nuova,* which focuses on the grieving speaker's response to the death of Beatrice in poetry, and then again in a belated prose commentary, Glück combines poetry with a narrative commentary implied by the book-length sequence. In an effect similar to the one Dante produced in his first collection, Glück presents trauma (seizure, divorce, and a devastating house fire) with the shock of an immediate wound in the lyrics. She represents a later stage of working through grief by placing the lyrics within the narrative sequence. As in Dante's lamentation for Beatrice, the lyrics document one stage of the author's relationship to grief; and the narrative invests the poems with new meanings once they are drawn into the sequence that implies a belated perspective. The narrative frame implies a further temporal and spatial distance from the traumatic episode. In *Vita Nova,* Glück combines the immediacy of voice with a narrative dimension to address her new relationship to trauma. She recalls her memories through the book to the point where her voice becomes a textual trace of self, a visualization of voice as it is registered in text.[25]

25. Edmund Jabes wrote: "In the book, the Jew himself becomes a book. In the Jew, the book itself becomes Jewish words. Because for him, the book is more than confirmation, it is the revelation of his Judaism." Jabes quoted in Norman Finkelstein, *The Ritual of New Creation* (New York: State University of New York Press, 1992), 2.

Coda: "Ripe Peach" and *The Seven Ages*

The title of the full-length book of poems immediately following *Vita Nova, The Seven Ages,* refers to what James Atlas calls "the most concise summation of our progress toward decrepitude"—Jaques's seven-ages-of-man speech in Shakespeare's *As You Like It,* which begins with "the infant mewling and puking in the nurse's arms" and moves to "second childishness and mere oblivion / sans teeth, sans eyes, sans taste, sans everything."[26] Like Jaques, who states "And so, from hour to hour, we ripe and ripe / And then, from hour to hour, we rot and rot," the poet in *Vita Nova* further addresses the speaker's ambivalent descent into life. Will she continue to honor sensual experience, as was the case in *Vita Nova,* or associate herself with a textual performance that is detached from life's rich ongoingness? This question of whether to seek perfection of the work or of the life (to paraphrase Yeats) remains at the core of her own dispute with Grossman's idea of "personhood." This challenge was expressed in *Vita Nova's* conception of poetry as a traumatic idiom that displaces reality by dissociating art from life.

"Ripe Peach" (SA), with its echo of Jaques's speech in Shakespeare, is a good place to start this speculation. The poem begins with the speaker, who, noticing a peach in a bowl on a table, experiences a desire to eat the fruit. She then catches herself falling into the characteristic posture of resistance to diving into something that might offer her a moment of pleasure, so she critiques her train of thought in a bemused and dumbstruck tone:

> There was a time
> only certainty gave me
> any joy. Imagine—
> certainty, a dead thing. (SA 52)

The speaker mocks her wish to remove herself from the world of sensual pleasure. She chastises herself for having thought that by embracing life she also would be condemning herself to the anxiety of uncertainty. She then contrasts her reaction to her emphasis on "a dead thing" to the vivid reality of the peach, an object that embodies "the world / the experiment. / The obscene mouth / famished with love" (SA 52). The irony, and poignancy, of "Ripe Peach" is that Glück's speaker has begun to consider celebrating the

26. James Atlas, *My Life in the Middle Ages: A Survivor's Tale* (New York: HarperCollins, 2005).

contingent world of physical desire as joyful, rather than dreadful. She is on the verge of giving in to the erotic realm of oral pleasure—signified by eating the ripe peach—when the prospect of her own death begins to loom larger in her imagination.

The speaker finds the peach desirable when it is "ripe," which is to say when its flavor will be richest but also when the fruit has come the closest to spoiled. The finitude of time becomes of paramount concern. In a sense, Glück has always understood value as contingent upon scarcity. Her awareness of the preciousness of time (as time becomes most dear) is an example of her overall means of evaluation. It is as if Glück's voice, which is really that of an archetypal lyric speaker, can only call attention to the sensual quality of life as precious and worthy of her praise at the moment it is on the verge of vanishing. The speaker's embrace of life is clearly not without tensions and hesitations. How could a poem by Glück be without emotional complexities and tonal subtleties? For example, she still views her own mouth, the part of her body that would first experience the peach flavor, as "obscene," an object of revulsion.

Besides displaying an Eliotic neurosis ("Do I dare to eat a peach?"), the speaker has turned to the poetics of the late Yeats, to a poem such as "A Coat," with its casting away of stylistic embroideries and mythic personae. For Yeats, the spare style represented his desire to go "naked," to express himself as if lyric speech were a natural manifestation of self. In "Eros" (SA), Glück's speaker connects her divorce to the stripping bare of relationships based on institutional conventions when she takes off her wedding ring: "That was what I wanted: to be naked" (SA 58).

In "Ripe Peach" (SA), her renunciation of abstraction is meant to confess to readers that her desire "for the certainty of the end" may have been a way for her to conceal her vulnerability from readers, a way to cast off her fear of embracing life:

> So much fear.
> So much terror of the physical world.
> The mind frantic
> guarding the body from
> the passing, the temporary,
> the body straining against it— (SA 52)

"Ripe Peach" lacks the costuming of a biblical proof text or classical myth. The poet does not seek to dissuade the reader from associating speaker with author. The poem seems raw, edgy, very open and direct, almost not poetry at all. It is an example on a discursive level of the speaker's desire to follow the late Yeats by attempting "to be naked."

Like Stevens in "The Planet on the Table," the speaker views "a peach on the kitchen table" as a "replica of earth." The peach, therefore, has already become an abstraction, a metonym. In spite of the impulse to abstract, to imagine, her direction is toward the life of sensual pleasures, not away from life by emphasizing the permanence of art:

> It is the earth,
> the same
> disappearing sweetness
> surrounding the stone end,
> and like the earth
> available— (SA 53)

There is a catch to the availability of the model of earth that she now wants to buy into. The catch is that the "opportunity for happiness" through the earth's beauty and bounty goes against the grain of the speaker's need to feel that she is in control over her environment through the "possession" of life in her text. She expresses this conundrum when she admits that she wants the "earth / we cannot possess / only experience—" (SA 53).

"Ripe Peach" reads as if it were a sincere appraisal of Glück's unsolvable agon with life. It is an admission that she has not resolved the split between the mind and the body that has propelled so much of her writing, at the same time causing her so much anxiety about seeking pleasure through the body in the forms of food and sex:

> They are not
> reconciled. The body
> here, the mind
> separate, not
> merely a warden:
> it has separate joys. (SA 53)

It appears as if the poem is going to end in a kind of truce, with the speaker agreeing to give both parts of her self their due. We suspect that she will accept the balanced pleasures each part of life may afford her, but in the end, the concern with personal survival reappears. The speaker is left to hope that her "self" will not be limited to the biological given of a mortal frame:

Is there
light that survives the end
in which the mind's enterprise
continues to live: thought
darting about the room,
above the bowl of fruit— (SA 53)

Glück's speaker does not and indeed cannot answer her own question. What is clear to me is that "the mind's enterprise" should be connected to the author's desire for recognition. She is willing to give up her life to find it again in the various forms it has appeared in, disappeared out of, and reappeared again into. Glück's lyric speaker constitutes a self that remains something made, not given.

Chapter Five

Challenging Trauma Theory

Witnessing Divine Mystery

In the struggle to put words to inexpressible episodes of grief and loss, Glück's writing fits well into theories of traumatic witnessing that give priority to horrible experience. The psychological scars traced in "The Untrustworthy Speaker" (AR) and "Archipelago" (HM) give rise to the witness's fragmentary words, which signal the gap between what a survivor can say about the experience of a catastrophic event and what one cannot describe with anything like historical accuracy. Trauma theory, as Sandor Goodhart has observed, serves "as a way of talking about an interruption that comes from outside," and thus "that maintains a relation to the events preceding its appearance."[1] Trauma theory gives priority to inexpressibly horrible experience—be it war shock, the Shoah, or sexual abuse—in a phenomenal realm that the author was never able, in Caruth's formulation, to consciously "own" in the first place. In commenting on the variety of witnesses to Jesus' mysterious appearance as the fully human figure who is also fully divine, Glück adds a transcendental biblical corollary to the sort of traumatic witnessing found in "The Untrustworthy Speaker" (AR). In "Winter Morning" (TA), she writes: "And there were other witnesses / though they were all blind, / they were all swayed by love—" (FFB 163).

"Winter Morning" (TA) and several other poems dealing with the figure of Jesus can be interpreted as foregrounding the issue of witnessing, through the accounts of cathartic experiences that involve divine insight. Like the Old Testament witnesses to divinity (such as that of the stammering prophet to Hassem, who leaves His mark in the radiance of Moses' face, or in Jacob's

1. Sandor Goodhart, *Sacrificing Commentary: Reading the End of Literature* (Baltimore: Johns Hopkins University Press, 1996), 27.

disjointed hip and limp), the witnesses to the image of Christ in his "cocoon of light" in "Winter Morning" are figures of both blindness and insight. Their testimony, while unreliable in a conventional sense, need not be understood as repeating a painful wounding, nor even as emanating from a real world experience preceding a textual rendition.

Trauma theory emphasizes the inexpressibility of pain and so gives priority to the physical wounds and psychological disorientations that follow from catastrophic events, which are then repeated as stammering linguistic expressions. But Glück poems that deal with the metaphysical issue of religious mystery and holy witnessing seem to problematize the priority of experience to language. In poems focused on religious mystery and the Christian Gospels, on speakers who claim to have seen God walk on earth, it becomes impossible to state with confidence whether language, natural phenomenon, or some other extratextual experience resides as the source of the speaker's witness and commentary. "Winter Morning" suggests that the source of witness—and therefore of all subsequent commentary on what one has seen—remains uncertain and so must remain in the realm of speculation, of commentary.

Trauma theory illuminates Glück's writings about the hard facts of mortal life and the conflicted experiences of family life—in poems from *Ararat* that confront the speaker's guilty feelings after the death of a parent and a sibling. But Glück is as much a mystic poet, with yearnings for transcendence, as she is a postconfessionalist poet, who (troping on the work of Lowell, Berryman, Sexton, and Plath) imagines domestic life and family drama through the guise of Homer, folk tale, or biblical narration. When offering multiple interpretations of the meanings of Christ's appearance in the natural world in "Winter Morning" (TA), "The Magi," and "Nativity Poem" (HM), Glück emphasizes the ineffability of God. She implicitly brings up the issue of unreliable witnessing that has also fascinated trauma theorists such as Caruth and LaCapra. But since "All is commentary" with respect to such experiences of light and darkness as divine witnessing, Glück shows us the limits to trauma theory through her commentaries on biblical witnessing. In these three poems Glück interprets witnessing in ways that suggest testimony may not be only a symptom of a wound, or a sign of prior experience, or an outcry to what life has done to a victimized speaker. Testimony may be a cathartic means to treat and cure those same wounds, rather than to merely repeat them in texts that fail to differentiate between "then" and "now."

"Winter Morning" is an especially important example of Glück's exploring the life of Jesus in order to understand how the language of the witness may relate to a speaker's experience prior to the act of writing or testifying. Like the Christian Gospels, this poem offers multiple witnesses to Jesus' life.

It supplies several interpretations of the meaning of God's appearance in human form. Some of the witnesses speak to Jesus' corporality, some speak to his ineffable status, others to the natural phenomenon that may have preceded the mystic vision. Still others speak to the thoughts of a skeptical contemporary reader who remains ironical and intellectually detached when pondering the question of "why did Jesus die?" Other Glück poems commenting on Jesus' life offer other witnesses to—and therefore alternative readings of—the meaning of Christ's appearance. "Pietà" (DF) focuses on the terrible pain his life caused the mother, who must hold and mourn over the body of the baby Jesus who she understands is not long for this world. "Nativity Poem" (HM) pays attention to the peripheral role of Joseph, and "The Magi" (HM) shows how power relations determine that certain testimonies are privileged while others are ignored. Glück, by way of Yeats's poem "Magi," attempts to recover a previously unrecognized perspective on Jesus' birth. Glück's witnesses in "The Magi" include the voices of the unheralded folk (the "we"), which have been overshadowed by the privileged witness of the visiting kings from the East in the Gospels, as well as in the work of a modernist forebear.

At first, Glück in "Winter Morning" stresses those witnesses who perceive Jesus' humanity through attention to his corporality and his physical desires. Understood as a Jew (that is to say, as a man who walks on earth), "stopping to eat and rest, in obvious need," he traveled in "green Judea," "among us like one of us." "[C]overed with the veil of life, / among the olive trees," Jesus appears alongside "the many shapes / blurred by spring" (FFB 162). In describing the crucifixion, Glück similarly deemphasizes Christ's transcendent nature and stresses instead his common humanity through corporality and mortality:

in great flocks
birds circled the body, not partial
to this form over the others

since men were all alike,
defeated by the air. (FFB 162)

Speaking to "the disciples / in a man's voice," Jesus' voice seems comparable to that of an author in that he is "seeking / recognition on earth" (FFB 162). As much as Glück represents Jesus as what D. H. Lawrence called "The Man Who Died," she nonetheless represents her speaker's relationship to his story as ironical and, therefore, as analytical and intellectually detached from what she is describing. "Today, when I woke up," the poem begins, "I asked myself / why did Christ die? Who knows / the meaning of such questions?" (FFB 161). The speaker's self-mocking comment about her own question is interesting for what it tells us about Glück's understanding of interpretations of a divine mystery. She is less concerned with nailing down the answer to the question she has posed herself than in destabilizing the meaning of the question itself. By interrogating the answerability of the question motivating her discourse, Glück allows for the play of uncertainty and mystery to open up further speculation, multiple witnesses, and creative commentary.

The speaker's first attempt to answer her own question "why did Christ die?" emphasizes the mortal nature of a "man's voice" when describing Christ's words to the disciples. Then she offers other interpretations of the same scene, which are not so grounded in life experience, human voices, or the tangible reality of God as a desiring human being. "Other witnesses" imagine Christ as an ineffable spirit, the opposite of the mortal being and figure of human desire that she has depicted in earlier parts of the poem:

> was it the wind that spoke?
> Or stroked Mary's hair, until she raised her eyes
>
> no longer wounded
> by his coldness, by his needless destruction
> of the flesh which was her fulfillment—
>
> This was not the sun.
> This was Christ in his cocoon of light:
>
> so they swore. And there were other witnesses
> though they were all blind,
> they were all swayed by love— (FFB 163)

Glück's account of these other "blind" witnesses emphasizes the mysterious relationship between perception and commentary when dealing with unverifiable and cathartic moments. Although dealing with Christ as a figure of descent, and not Odysseus from the Homeric tradition, these lines bear a striking resemblance to Stevens's late poem "The World as Meditation." In Stevens's poem, Penelope remains unsure of whether she has in fact witnessed Odysseus's actual return from Troy to Ithaca, or whether she has projected her desire for her husband's return onto a quality of light. The poem testifies to the self-sufficiency of her creative imagination.

At the end of "Winter Morning" (TA), the unknowingness of the "blind" witnesses influences the speaker's uncertainty about her own cathartic relationship to a scene of natural splendor that verges on Christ's appearance as wind and sun in the preceding stanza.

> Winters are long here.
> The road a dark gray, the maples gray, silvered with lichen,
> and the sun low on the horizon,
> white on blue; at sunset, vivid orange-red.
>
> When I shut my eyes, it vanishes.
> When I open my eyes, it reappears.
> Outside, spring rain, a pulse, a film on the window.
>
> And suddenly it is summer, all puzzling fruit and light. (FFB 163)

The speaker has described her own "descent" into the realm of earthly existence that Christ's life implied to witnesses earlier in the poem. At the same time, the speaker's epiphany—"[a]nd suddenly it is summer"—is not unlike that of the "other witnesses" who perceived the sun as a portent of God's birth, as the "cocoon" of light from which God will emerge as spirit. Her vision is thus associated with seeing and not seeing, with impermanence and with flux—"When I shut my eyes, it vanishes"—and also with an irrational perspective on nature that contradicts ordinary perceptions of how time and space are shaped; winter becomes summer; dark gray becomes "all puzzling fruit and light."

As much as life follows from poetry when interpreted through a traumatic model that associates the ruptured language of testimony with the perpetuation of long-ago wounds, a process described in *"Parodos"* (AR), Glück tolerates the puzzling state of unreliable witnessing in "Winter Morning" (TA). Thus her multiple commentaries on a scene of witnessing that remains mysterious and of unknown origins complicate our understanding of the relationship between poetry and life, between the natural world itself that ultimately inspires the speaker and the commentary tradition of the various readings of Christ's life in the Gospels. Glück's "sudden" ability to see the winter landscape transformed into a space of fecundity and illumination—"all puzzling fruit and light"—is at once an immediate example of natural observation and a mediated epiphany. She cannot "descend" into nature, or even "see" the world around her without resorting to a meditation on sacred texts. A poem that celebrates nature's supernatural resonance, "Winter Morning" is also Glück's highly intellectualized and thoroughly textualized attempt to answer the theological question of why Christ died, by commenting on the acts of commentary and interpretation that in the end constitute our knowledge of his life.

Like "Winter Morning," Glück's poem "The Magi" (HM) foregrounds the unreliability of witnessing cathartic events, by offering multiple perspectives on Christ's nativity. Glück situates her poem, not as itself one of the unverifiable testimonies of divine witness, but as a belated forum through which she may put words to a perspective unsung in prior accounts of the Gospel motif. Elevating silence to the level of testimony, she gives voice to anonymous witnesses who, because of their lowly social status, did not feel privileged to speak of what they saw in the manger at Bethlehem:

> Toward world's end, through the bare
> beginnings of winter, they are traveling again.
> How many winters have we seen it happen,
> watched the same sign come forward as they pass
> cities sprung around this route their gold
> engraved on the desert, and yet
> held our peace, these
> being the Wise, come to see at the accustomed hour
> nothing changed: roofs, the barn
> blazing in darkness, all they wish to see. (FFB 66)

Glück's speaker parodies the eastern kings' version of witnessing a cathartic incident, as seeming all too expected, too safe, too reliable, too securely linked to archetypal structures for it to correspond to the mysterious kind of cathartic witnessing seen in "Winter Morning." Unlike the bewildered speaker in that poem, she notes how unsurprising the divine mystery seems to the Magi, and how securely the nativity story conforms to their interpretation of an event that they have been expecting would take place at an appointed time.

Unlike the unreliable, yet compelling witnessing of divine mystery and natural splendor in "Winter Morning," the Magi's journey occurs at the "accustomed hour," as the wise men "pass / cities sprung around this route their gold / engraved on the desert." The speaker clearly regards the Magi as socially privileged individuals, representing the interests of those shielded from life's vicissitudes through wealth and political power. The Magi are kings, who carry "gold engraved" or are associated with the wealth of cities that might offer them protection from the risk occurring in the winter desert. Their witness may be authoritative because of their distinguished social position, but what they see lacks the qualities of "puzzling," of uncertainty, of the mysterious relationship between language and experience that Glück associates with cathartic experiences.

Recalling the nativity scene from the Christian Gospels, "The Magi" also comments on how Glück's modernist forebears have remembered this scene in ways she finds disturbing and so worthy of a critical interpretation. If the poem is read as a revisionary response to Yeats, both to his poem "The Magi" but also to his theory of tragic significance in "Easter 1916," Glück's "The Magi" stands as a challenge to the best-known phrase from "Easter 1916": "all's changed / changed utterly / a terrible beauty is born." Her recovery of this modernist touchstone enables her to get at another significant issue, the relationship between social status and how we regard witnesses.

Like "Easter 1916," which focuses on the intersections between Christian myth and Irish modern history, mortality and literary meaning, Yeats's "The Magi" (1914) is a visionary poem that centers on the Jesus story. As in "Easter 1916," Yeats associates Jesus with the onset of revolutionary changes and with cataclysmic events of a transhistorical magnitude:

> Now as at all times I can see in the mind's eye,
> In their stiff, painted clothes, the pale unsatisfied ones
> Appear and disappear in the blue depth of the sky
> With all their ancient faces like rain-beaten stones,
> And all their helms of silver hovering side by side,
> And all their eyes still fixed, hoping to find once more,
> Being by Calvary's turbulence unsatisfied,
> The uncontrollable mystery on the bestial floor.[2]

Yeats's speaker can "see in the mind's eye" a sublime image of the Magi.

Yeats's interpretation contrasts with the traditional Christian story, in which the Magi are figured as emissaries from the East. For centuries, the tale of the three Magi (or magicians, or seers) was used as a prophecy about the Messiah. As Michael R. Molnar has written in *The Star of Bethlehem:* "During King Herod's reign there were growing expectations of the advent of the Messiah: people were watching for a sign or an omen of a great ruler who would rise up from Judea and vanquish the country's enemies, namely, the tyrannical Romans and their puppet king, Herod." In Yeats, by contrast, the Magi are not defined as prophetic witnesses to God's appearance in human form so much as they are imagined as instantiations of the author's imaginative powers. The Magi correspond to Yeats's own desire for artistic power through access to an inner vision, by way of symbolic

2. W. B. Yeats, "The Magi," in Ramazani et al., *Norton Anthology* 1:103.

language that connects incident to archetype, disrupting the stability of the status quo.[3] The kings appear and disappear by way of the speaker's inner vision in "the blue depth of the sky." They also exist as a transhistorical archetypal image that corresponds to an eternally recurrent scene: "Now as at all times." The speaker's projection of the Magi's procession in the sky, then, allows Yeats to participate in a Romanticist ethos in which the individual imagines a visionary realm in order to distinguish himself from nature and the body.

According to M. L. Rosenthal, the Magi in Yeats represent forces hostile to the repressive morality he associated with Catholicism. "Being by Calvary's turbulence unsatisfied," the Magi, like Yeats the visionary artist, hope to find "once more" the "uncontrollable mystery on the bestial floor." The image, suggesting apocalyptic power, resonates with the figure of the "rough beast" in "The Second Coming." Rosenthal reads "Calvary's turbulence unsatisfied" as expressing Yeats's desire to be released from, rather than reconnected with, the Christian mythic narrative.[4] Yeats wished he could be free to discover new meanings, related to his sense of the cyclical recurrence of violent events. In the phrase "terrible beauty," in "Easter 1916," Yeats offered his interpretation of the relationship between death and literary compensation. Despite his ambivalence, Yeats maintained the prestige of "eternally recurrent" myth as central to his understanding of contemporary history. In a note describing the impulse to compose both "The Dolls" and "The Magi," he stated: "The fable for [these poems] came into my head while I was giving some lectures in Dublin. I had noticed once again how all thought among us is frozen into 'something other than human life.'"[5]

In contrast to Yeats's investment in "other than human life," Glück's "The Magi" (HM) reflects upon an ominous, perhaps even inconsolable version of human suffering, which cannot be sublimated through the Romanticist's language of transcendence. She suggests that human suffering stems in part from the fact that a group of witnesses to a scene of divine mystery have chosen to remain silent, they "hold their peace," because they do not believe anyone of stature will listen to their testimony. The "we" who witness the nativity scene in Glück's "Magi" seem to have no stake in expectations of mythic significance or personal salvation such as the Magi associate with the birth of

3. Michael R. Molnar, *The Star of Bethlehem: The Legacy of the Magi* (New Brunswick, N.J.: Rutgers University Press, 1999), 8.

4. M. L. Rosenthal, *Running to Paradise: Yeats's Poetic Art* (New York: Oxford University Press, 1994), 118.

5. W. B. Yeats, "Among School Children," in Ramazani et al., *Norton Anthology* 1:125.

Jesus. Their peace, their terrors, their prophetic readings of apocalypse all occur but, at the same time, go unrecorded in *The Gospels*.[6]

In Yeats's poem, a speaker ("I can see in the mind's eye") wishes to assert his imaginative prowess and personal independence by venturing beyond the institutional conformity he associates with Christianity. By contrast, Glück's "The Magi" turns Christ's birth into a folk tale, emphasizing commentary by offering the pluralized and therefore common perspective of anonymous spectators who feel disconnected from the eastern kings as seers of a portentous event. Instead of following Yeats's partaking in the visionary sublime by way of an individual speaker's authorized testimony of a divine witness, Glück's speaker notices the extreme weather conditions that speak to the difficulties of human survival with the "bare / beginnings of winter" emerging in the desert.

Indeed, the folk, who represent local knowledge as well as displaying openness to life's fragility and risk, mock the Magi's visionary dispositions as being blind to the dangers the Bible has traditionally associated with divine witness. Unlike the strange men who seek a truth outside the Christian story, in Yeats's "the uncontrollable mystery on the bestial floor," Glück's speaker perceives the Magi as repeating a pattern, not revising its design to conform to current affairs by seeing the world with fresh eyes. The speaker views the fixed movements, based on celestial omen, from a wide perspective, like the circumference of a circle, which surrounds and engulfs the movements depicted in the scene.

> Towards world's end, through the bare
> beginnings of winter, they are traveling again.
> How many winters have we seen it happen,
> watched the same sign come forward as they pass. (FFB 61)

Incidental movements and archetypal patterns that Yeats associated with circular time, in "Easter 1916," match up in Glück's "The Magi." But where

6. T. S. Eliot's "Journey of the Magi" from *Ariel Poems* is spoken from the perspective of one of the Magi, who remembers the difficulty of the journey to Bethlehem. The speaker has been deeply shaken by the birth of Jesus: "this Birth was / Hard and bitter agony for us, like Death, our death." For the Magi, the Christian reversal of death as life and life as death has disrupted the king's pleasure at possessing wealth and political power in the "old dispensation." This is so to the point where he feels he is among "alien people clutching their gods," and that in the end he "should be glad of another death." Yeats finds the Christian story a narrative of repression, whereas Eliot, as a believer, writes a poem that recounts a conversionary experience to Christianity. T. S. Eliot, "Journey of the Magi," in *The Longman Anthology of British Literature,* compact edition, ed. David Damrosch (New York: Longman, 2000), 2439.

the collapse of incident and archetype created the type of meaningful violence formulated by Yeats as "terrible beauty," Glück interprets the Magi's witness to the nativity as an ironic misrecognition of the deeper representational crisis surrounding the focal event, which is supposed to signify change but in fact does not.

Glück imagines the voice of voicelessness, as "The Magi" comments not only on the Gospels' privileging of the Magi's interpretation of the nativity scene but also on a blind spot in Yeats's interpretation, which forecloses commentary by identifying the speaker's visionary desires with the Magi's authoritative witness. In the essay "To My Teacher," her tribute to the late poet Stanley Kunitz, Glück claims that "no one myth can explain all reality" (PT 137). She also states that, although "all my life there have been periods of painful silence," part of the impulse to write was that she "wanted to be heard" as a "convincing proof of existence" (PT 138). On the level of a public or political voicing, rather than of one young embattled woman who wanted to defeat writer's block and to affirm her existence on a metaphysical level, "The Magi" attempts to rewrite a religious myth by destabilizing our notions of reliable and unreliable witnessing and how we distinguish significant and insignificant commentary. With silence, rather than with words, she fills in the gaps in the canonical versions of the tale, revealing a perspective that had been erased or ignored.

In the poem, the voice of the "we" contests the significance of the Magi's astrological forecast. The magical birth does not affect the "peace" or the terror that the folk already are experiencing without divine intervention or royal visitation. The speaker comments to the reader: "How many winters have we seen it happen," but inside the poem the "we" "held our peace, these / being the Wise." In one sense of the term, holding one's "peace" can suggest a perfect tranquility, a pleasing sense of wholeness that any one of us would cherish as a sign of comfort. In another sense, however, holding "our peace" can also suggest an enforced silence in the face of persons, in this case the Magi, who represent authorized power and knowledge. In this less sanguine interpretation, "held our peace" can mean something like the following: *we did not speak out about the meaninglessness of their travels and the meaningfulness of our own troubles and apocalyptic visions because there was no one who was willing to listen to us.*

A second, more distressing interpretation of "holding one's peace" may be found in the context of what Shoshana Felman, in *Testimony,* refers to as the "new moral and political imperative of an *Age of Testimony,*" which she defines as

> an age whose writing task (and reading task) is to confront the horror if its own destructiveness, to attest to the unthinkable disaster of culture's breakdown, and to attempt to assimilate the massive trauma, and the cataclysmic shift in being that resulted, without some reworked frame of culture or within some revolutionized order of consciousness.[7]

Interpreted within the framework of Glück's poetics, which foregrounds absence as a sign of desire, and which also imagines silence as a registration of a speaker's wounded psyche and damaged spirit, the voice of the "we" in "The Magi" becomes an example of how silence can be reconceived as a form of resistance to the authorized narrative accounts of cathartic events when redescribed by "unreliable" witnesses. In holding "our peace," both a form of resistance and a sign of the power of an unrecorded perspective are at play.

"The Magi" may be read together with *The Plague,* Albert Camus's 1947 allegorical novel of traumatic testimony. Camus applies the phrase "holding one's peace" in a way that may shed light on my interpretation of the same phrase as it appears in Glück's poem. *The Plague* deals with the impossibility of directly coming to terms with the unimaginable and frame-breaking events of the German concentration camps. Camus approximates the Shoah, however, through the allegorical figure of a plague, which is of such catastrophic proportions that few townspeople besides a doctor named Rieux and a journalist named Rambert believe it to be an actual historical occurrence. At the end of the book Rieux reveals himself to have been all along the narrator of the tale, in words closely related to Glück's perspective on the Magi's visit:

> Regarding his personal troubles and his long suspense, his duty was to hold his peace. . . . Thus, decidedly, it was up to him to speak for all. . . . Dr Rieux resolved to compile this chronicle, so that he should not be one of those who hold their peace but should bear witness in favor of those plague-stricken people; so that some memorial of the injustice and outrage done them might endure.[8]

In *Testimony,* Felman has described Dr. Rieux's statement of moral obligation to "bear witness," and so not to be "one of those who hold their peace," as part of Camus's awareness that twentieth-century literature should be characterized as part of an "Age of Testimony": "The 'literature of testimony' is thus

7. Shoshana Felman and Dori Laub, *Testimony: Crises of Witnessing in Literature, Psychoanalysis, and History* (New York: Routledge, 1992), 114.

8. Albert Camus, *The Plague,* trans. Stuart Gilbert (New York: Vintage, 1991), 280–81, 286–87.

not an art of leisure but an art of urgency; it exists in time not just as a memorial but as an artistic promissory note, as an attempt to bring the 'backwardness' of consciousness to the level of precipitant events."[9] Whereas Felman denounced silence as a failure to bear witness in an age of atrocity, Glück leaves open the possibility of silence as a potentially meaningful type of witness, especially when we are dealing with exposure to divine mystery. In fact, silence becomes a form of belated linguistic power in "The Magi," a repressed part of the record of what happened, and to whom it happened, as historical witnessing is revised to include a gap in the authorized account of a sacred event.

Stating in "Easter 1916" that "all's changed," Yeats expressed his belief in the relevance of sacrificial violence to an understanding of myth and history. By contrast, Glück perceives an ambiguous scene that may represent the coming of a messiah, or may be a natural catastrophe, or may have changed nothing at all. The most important difference between Glück's version of witnessing and Yeats's version, however, is that the significance of what exactly has transpired in the manger remains a part of the open-ended, speculative realm of commentary. The events are not described as if they were fully decipherable or fully disclosed to the witnesses, whose perspectives seem limited by the horizons of their desire: "nothing changed: roofs, the barn / blazing in darkness, all they wish to see" (FBB 66). Glück also reverses the power to signify by allowing the "we" to occupy the wisdom position, the painful one of afterward. Events that more prominent actors continue to experience as meaning one thing, and one thing only, remain open to multiple interpretations ranging from trivial occurrences, to the face of a cosmic mystery, to an expression of the ongoing reality of human misery as experienced by a group of anonymous desert dwellers. Recalling lines from "A Parable" (TA), in which Glück suggested the limits to King David's empathy through his attainment of "all he is capable of dreaming" (FFB 196), the Magi see only "all they wish to see," and no more than is allowed by this limited perspective that forecloses reflection. The poem's speaker is, by contrast, willing and able to see beyond the moment of heightened existence and to the condition of silence, indifference, and dissolution.

Like the speaker who voices voicelessness by keeping "our peace" in "The Magi," Glück affirms her own characteristically calm and precise tone of voice as possessing a special linguistic authority in "Nativity Poem" (HM). In characteristic midrashic fashion, she filters her own intense and ambivalent feelings about maternity and family relationships through a retelling of Jesus'

9. Felman and Laub, *Testimony,* 114.

birth. Imagining the birth from Joseph's unsung perspective, she upsets notions of center and periphery, foreground and background, major and minor characters. "Nativity Poem" humanizes Jesus' birth by focusing on Joseph's feelings and by emphasizing the vulnerable body of the baby Jesus.

Glück is an author interested in vertical journeys, in which, as she has said, "a spirit, a soul, is permitted access to the other realm and returns to speak of it."[10] "Nativity Poem" imagines Christ's birth as a story of descent from the heavens toward the earth. The poem begins in the elevated register of the visionary realm through its short, incantatory lines:

It is the evening
of the birth of god.
Singing &
with gold instruments
the angels bear down
upon the barn, their wings
neither white
wax nor marble. (FFB 71)

The poem then describes a natural setting and emphasizes family relationships in the last half of stanza one, and throughout stanza 2:

So
they have been recorded:
burnished,
literal in the composed air,
they raise their harps above
the beasts likewise gathering,
the lambs & all the startled
silken chickens. . . . And Joseph,
off to one side, has touched
his cheek, meaning
he is weeping—

10. Describing the source of the title of *Descending Figure* Glück states: "I read an interview with Paul Simon in *Rolling Stone.* Talking about his methods of composition, he made reference to the musical term, 'descending figure.' It invokes all the mythos of journey to which I'm most drawn, wherein a spirit, a soul, is permitted access to the other realm and returns to speak of it. Not that in the title there's that 'and coming-back-figure'—yet it has that Orphic reference. Some echo of Christian mythology too, the descending from the heavens to the earth. My poems are vertical poems. They aspire and they delve. They don't expand. They don't elaborate, or amplify." Douglas, "Descending Figure," 117.

> But how small he is, withdrawn
> from the hollow of his mother's life,
> the raw flesh bound
> in linen as the stars yield
> light to delight his sense
> for whom there is no ornament. (FFB 71)

Instead of the mystical story as it has been recorded in the Gospels, or else through a visual image of the nativity scene (in the first part of stanza 1), the speaker offers an alternative witness. She comments on the small body of Jesus, on the farm animals, on the absence Mary experiences through the baby's withdrawal "from the hollow of his mother's life," on Joseph's emotional reactions, and finally, in the second stanza, on the baby as mortal child connected to a kind of text through the figure of "raw flesh bound / in linen." As in "Pietà" (DF), Glück emphasizes the vulnerable physical body of the child and the ambivalence of maternity through the emotional detachment and physical separation of the mother from her child. The newborn body is illuminated, not by the smooth, polished wings of angels, but by the natural stars in the sky that "yield / light to delight his sense / for whom there is no ornament." Glück focuses on the human feelings that surround a divine event. The birth of a god will, after all, tear this family apart. The baby has "withdrawn" from the mother, Joseph is depicted as weeping, and Jesus is described, not in terms of a disembodied spiritual grandeur, but as "raw flesh bound," which seems to be denied aesthetic consolation: "there is no ornament." As in "The Magi," which offered the perspective of unacknowledged voices, Glück's focus is on Joseph, who is "off to one side," as he "touched / his cheek, meaning / he is weeping—."

Glück's interpretations of Christianity in her poetry are paradoxical and often confusing. On the one hand, in "Winter Morning" (TA), she celebrates the birth, life, and death of Jesus Christ as if he embodied an earthbound spirituality contradicting the agonistic conflict between the Jews and their God, Yahweh, in *The Wild Iris*. Perhaps this is her version of the Jewish Jesus. On the other hand, in "Winter Morning" (TA), she does not seem to identify herself with Jesus' story even as she illustrates God's descent into phenomenal life. Rather, she represents her persona through the guise of other Christian figures. Instead of Christ, whom she regards as the archetypal fulfillment of yearning to unify the body and the spirit, she identifies herself with female characters of self-abnegation, with the nuns, saints, and female martyrs of the church.

In "Pietà," Glück comments on the painful split between representational significance and embodied life through her account of the genesis of a theological mystery. She represents Mary carrying Jesus "[u]nder the strained / fabric of her skin" (FBB 112). Mary knows that the child who "wanted to stay / in her body" will soon become a figure for the "crowd," and so a part of public significance and symbolic representation, unlike the intimate contours of biological life with the mother represented by the baby Jesus. The men who have come to worship him kneel "like / figures in a painting" (FFB 112).

In "Winter Morning" (TA), Glück reads Jesus as a corporeal figure, an ordinary Jewish man who eats, sleeps, walks on the earth among the flowers of Judea, and speaks to his disciples in a human voice. Contra Jesus, a figure of desire and corporality, the nuns, saints, and martyrs in other Glück poems illustrate her own experience of self-denial as an expression of transcendence and spirituality. Like Odysseus, Jesus appeals to Glück because he descends from the realm of the ineffable into phenomenal life, but she does not identify with his narrative in her personae as a Christian martyr, a saint, or a nun (to name three of her persistent self-characterizations when working within the Christian idiom).

The figure of the saint, who symbolizes the "memorialized suffering of the devout," has held an especially favored place among Glück's self-characterizations. It can be argued that even the battle with anorexia nervosa (described in "Dedication to Hunger" as expressing both female desire and literary productivity) may be an example of "holy anorexia," or the expression of spiritual achievement through self-denial in medieval Christendom.[11] Her fascination with sainthood, "holy anorexia," and the biographical figure of Joan of Arc—who in "Jeanne D'Arc" (HM) must be "transformed to fire, for God's purpose" (FFB 78)—suggests her equation between holiness, personal suffering, and physical absence as signs of spiritual or artistic perfection. By contrast, her commentary poems on Jesus' existence in poems such as "Winter Morning" (TA) and "Nativity Poem" (HM) emphasize the "earthly existence implied by Christ's life."[12]

In "Winter Morning," Glück interprets Jesus' life as affirming phenomenal experience in a way that her characteristic biographical persona can only imagine from a position of ironic distance and intellectual detachment. Her interpretation of Jesus as a mortal man, who expresses a desire for recognition from other human beings through his speeches to the disciples, differs markedly from her interpretation of Judaism and of its God, Yahweh,

11. Gordon, "Reconceiving the Sacred," 13, 80.
12. Ibid., 104.

whom she has cast as the heartless perpetrator of sacrificial violence against his chosen people, as one who "doesn't hesitate to take / a son from a mother" ("Mount Ararat" [AR 30]). In *The Wild Iris,* the gardener-supplicant experiences her relationship to Yahweh as one of agonistic struggle, and she identifies with Job, the prototypical figure of the Jewish scapegoat, as herself God's plaything, the victim of God's tests and destructive whims. Clearly offering Glück an alternative to Yahweh as a creative and destructive force who is, not unlike her father in *Ararat,* at once oppressive, remote, and the cause of heartbreaking longing for connection to masculine authority, Jesus integrates the material and spiritual realms in a way that moderates the difference between humans and God. In "Winter Morning" and "Nativity Poem," Jesus exists on a level of equivalence with human beings.

"Winter Morning" at points stresses Christ's human side and so affirms the earth-based spirituality that Glück has failed to achieve in works depicting her own religious yearnings. Such a failure to integrate body and spirit occurs in *The Wild Iris,* which imagines an indelible split between the author's creative aspirations and God's powers to negate all human accomplishments. Glück's attraction to Christ's story is significant as an alternative to her harsh treatment of the Jewish God, but "Winter Morning" tells us how she applies the commentary tradition to the speaker's witnessing of cathartic yet ineffable events that defy our usual notions of accurate testimony. In "Winter Morning," Glück, through a biblical corollary, reinterprets the meaning of witnessing, as different from her interpretation of trauma writing. In "Winter Morning," "Nativity Poem," and "The Magi," Glück aligns her own interest in the origins of creativity, witnessing, and commentary on biblical proof texts with narratives from the New Testament. Like Glück's poetry, which imagines belatedness as a potential source of literary power, the New Testament authors interpret lateness as possessing a priority over an "original" creation myth that is itself connected to language and commentary through God's linguistic disposition in Genesis 1. Although Glück interprets Jesus' life as affirming phenomenal experience in a way that has eluded her autobiographical persona, she is drawn toward the life of Jesus because his story offers her an antidote to the painful separation of body and spirit that is characteristic of her "second nature" poetry in *The House on Marshland* and *Ararat.* But Jesus' story also interests Glück because the Gospels emphasize the multiplication of commentary through the four authorized versions. The Jesus narrative resonates with her own understanding that personal origins are at once a commentary on authoritative texts and the fulfillment of prior texts; the New Testament refers back to the Torah but also may be read as the fulfillment that was anticipated in the prior text.

Part II

A Poet of the Book

Chapter Six

The House on Marshland

Second Nature Writing and the Entrance into the Symbolic

In *Firstborn,* Glück cast her autobiographical speaker through what Suzanne Matson has called the "Plathian stance of victimization."[1] Glück identified the perpetrator of the crimes against her person as, variously, her mortal body, her heterosexual desires, callous and domineering men, and nature itself. In "The Edge," she writes, "I tie / My heart to that headboard" (FFB 21). In "The Egg," the speaker also recasts a doctor's assistance in the birth of a child as a malevolent act of male domination bordering on rape. His "enormous hands / Swarmed, carnivorous, / For prey" (FFB 6). Addressing a boyfriend in "Labor Day" as "You pimp," her speaker expresses her enraged reply to his attempt to pawn her off on another guy at a party (FFB 13). In "Cottonmouth Country," she depicts sea and land as dangerous lovers—aspects of an allegorical figure, Death—who wish to absorb the speaker into their domain. She confronts "signs / That Death wooed us, by water, wooed us / By land" (FFB 43). At the end of "Cottonmouth Country," following her observation of a snake after it has abandoned a layer of skin on a mossy rock, "[r]eared in the polluted air," she remarks: "Birth, not death, is the hard loss. / I know. I also left a skin there" (FFB 43).

Robert Miklitsch has observed the themes of emptiness, sterility, and death evident in "The Egg" and other poems from *Firstborn.* He writes that these themes are "juxtaposed with [the] natural fertility of the physical world."[2] I need to qualify Miklitsch's comment. In *Firstborn* Glück does not so much juxtapose natural fertility with the distressing themes he lists as she expresses her contempt for the fact of living in a body that must eventually

1. Matson, "Without Relation," 96.
2. Miklitsch, "Assembling a Landscape," 2.

betray her autonomy by perishing. She regards the body as the site of entrapment, humiliation, and violation. She casts the act of giving birth as an expression of the body's control over the autonomous self.

Glück has chosen in her debut volume to employ the extreme language of hyperbole (the High Modernist idiom of Hart Crane and the early Robert Lowell) to describe the proximity of death to life, even in scenes of maternity from "The Egg." By contrast, in poems from her second volume, *The House on Marshland,* the speaker represents her condition in a tone of preternatural calm and quiet acceptance. What to make of this tonal shift? Whereas *Firstborn* expressed the speaker's outrage at physical existence in a natural environment that seemed to her to entail a loss of control, *Marshland,* which maintains nature as its setting, characterizes a speaker after she has "left a skin there," that is, after she has made a mental break with the body as the site of significant personal experience. The nature poems from *Marshland* indicate that she has come to understand personal identity as a linguistic construct, something made, not given.

In *Marshland,* Glück confronts nature in order to assert control over her personal identity through language, ritual, and myth. Her poetry continues to evoke the themes of maternity, sexuality, and the self in nature, but these aspects of the speaker's existence are transformed into symbolic landscapes and linguistic acts. In this sense, *The House on Marshland* is a breakthrough text as it anticipates Glück's persistent attempts in *The Triumph of Achilles, Meadowlands,* and *The Wild Iris* to assuage her isolation by creating a narrative of identity through myths, metaphors, and traditions of storytelling. Echoing a theme found in poems such as "Dedication to Hunger," which focuses on the author's anorexic condition as a way to pursue spiritual and intellectual ideals, Glück eschews associations of her self with nature, biological reproductivity, and the desiring female body in order to become what the feminist scholar of Romanticism, Margaret Homans, refers to as a bearer of the word.[3]

The transformation from associating personal identity with a natural embodied self to an ephemeral linguistic one that, as Diane Bonds shows, occurs in "All Hallows," illustrates Glück's theoretical understanding of what it means to become a lyric speaker. Glück has suggested that her poems should not be mistaken for "impressions" of life itself but rather as linguistic displacements of lived reality. She comments that her poems imply the author's detachment from life as necessary for the sake of her art: "What seems at issue is the discrepancy between the impression of exposure and the fact of distance" (PT 25). In Glück's terms, therefore, the nature poems in

3. Homans, *Bearing the Word.*

The House on Marshland create "the impression of exposure" to an environment that is figurative as well as immanent. Discussing John Berryman's illusive autobiographical "self" as it appears through the notorious mask of Henry in *The Dream Songs,* Glück appreciates a male poet associated with the "confessional" movement of intimate self-disclosure that she has repudiated in essays such as "The Idea of Courage" (PT). Her reading of the "self" in Berryman nonetheless seems especially sensitive to the relationship between the entrance into language and a state of personal absence, or detachment from nature, that Homans and Bonds have regarded as a deeply feminist concern. As Glück writes in her essay "Disruption, Hesitation, Silence": "A reader encountering the first person tends to identify that pronoun with a poem's central intelligence. But the problem in *The Dream Songs,* the drama of the poems, is the absence of a firm self. The proliferating selves dramatize, they do not disguise, this absence" (PT 76).

The theme of a woman entering into language at the cost of dissociation from nature, examined by Bonds in her important essay on *The House on Marshland,* lends itself to the discussion of Glück's poetry as a form of commentary. It seems that, in the nature poems of this work, Glück revises Romanticism in order to establish her lyric personae, in opposition to nature as well as in opposition to such prior masters as Wordsworth, Keats, and Yeats. Although Glück will attempt to distance herself from Romanticism in her anti-nature poems from *The House on Marshland,* James Chandler argues that late-twentieth-century practices of cultural-history writing have roots in the peculiar Romantic historicism in post-Waterloo Britain, and especially in the political views implicit in Wordsworth's transforming of nature in his major work.[4]

Glück's antinaturalism, ironically, turns out to have roots in a preeminent Romantic "nature" poet, Wordsworth. Glück, like Wordsworth, offers a subjective and politicized response to nature, a figurative space she does not so much inhabit as announce as different from her lyric persona. Chandler shows that Wordsworth had turned away from the Rousseau idea of nature to become a poet of what Edmund Burke calls "second nature," by which Burke means human nature cultivated by custom, habit, and tradition. In "Poem" (an ars poetica), "For Jane Myers," "Flowering Plum," and "The School Children" (a poem I read as a revision of "Among School Children" by Yeats, himself a modern inheritor of a romantic ideology on education), Glück turns to the figurative or "second" version of nature writing.[5]

4. Bonds, "Entering Language"; James Chandler, *Wordsworth's Second Nature: A Study of the Poetry and Politics* (Chicago: University of Chicago Press, 1984).

5. Burke cited from ibid., xviii.

In *Bearing the Word,* Homans offers a political reading of Romanticism in her examination of a "cultural myth of language's process and structure" that situates women as the "silent and absent objects of representation" with men controlling the symbolic domain.[6] She goes on to evaluate the logic of Jacques Lacan's theory of language, in which "language and culture depend on the death or absence of the mother and on the quest for substitutes for her." She further claims that the authors she has studied anticipated Lacan by disavowing their status as mothers and as physical beings in order to write.[7] Following Homans and Bonds, I argue that Glück's "second nature writing" is inflected with her experience as a female author who in *The House on Marshland* attempts to disassociate her speaker from the silence of nature. Her revisionary romanticism rejects nature as a site for personal appearance because she feels condemned to occupy it by other, male figures of linguistic power, who act to systematize and codify nature through rigid systems of division and classification.

Crossing into Language in "All Hallows"

The autobiographical Glück persona was cast as powerless victim of men, trapped in her own desiring body, in *Firstborn.* The woman-as-mother is represented rather differently in poems such as "All Hallows" that emphasize in sound and sense the representational nature of experience. Glück has chosen October twilight for the setting of "All Hallows," a moment of disequilibrium in terms of the external climate.[8]

> Even now this landscape is assembling.
> The hills darken. The Oxen
> sleep in their blue yoke,
> the fields having been
> picked clean, the sheaves
> bound evenly and piled at the roadside
> among cinquefoil, as the toothed moon rises. (FFB 61)

6. Homans, *Bearing the Word,* xi.
7. Ibid., 4.
8. "All Hallows" (also known as All Saints Day) is traditionally celebrated on November 1 and is observed in churches as a Christian feast in honor of all the saints. Saints are important personae in Glück poetry and represent a liminal experience that pivots in between this world

October twilight is, quite literally, a moment of crossing. It marks a transition from fall to winter, from day to night, from the period of harvest that brings to fruition what was planted in the spring to a harbinger of winter when the land lies fallow and covered with snow, effacing marks of human endeavor. Glück has made an appropriate, if conventional, decision by opening "All Hallows" at the climactic moment of temporal crossing in the outside world of weather and the changing quality of light. The in-between situation in nature, however, is important not for itself but because "October twilight" symbolizes nature as a site of initiation into language and ritual. It also indicates the speaker's concern with internal transformation. Her poem will go on in stanza 2 to describe how it feels to cross a border zone from one sphere of psychic awareness or emotional experience to another.

The first stanza of "All Hallows" offers a panoramic, aerial perspective. It provides an overall account of the October landscape with "hills," "oxen," "fields," "shade," and finally, the "toothed moon." These aspects of nature seem to be agents of change; they are depicted in the process of constructing "this landscape" of darkness, sleep, and emptiness by "assembling" it. The second stanza, by contrast to the first, begins with a mid-range impression of dream activity—"the wife leaning out the window"—and then moves to a very close-up view of "the seeds":

> This is the barrenness
> of harvest or pestilence.
> And the wife leaning out the window
> with her hand extended, as in payment,
> and the seeds
> distinct, gold, calling
> *Come here*
> *Come here, little one.* (FFB 61)

Unlike the female victims of *Firstborn* (such as the mother who feels violated by the male obstetrician in "The Egg"), Glück represents "the wife" as a figure of creative power. Her "hand extended, as in payment," the wife is calling to her little one, her "soul," or linguistic self. The child she bears through

and the next one. They have traveled the border between earth and heaven, and their exceptionally holy lives have enabled them to be capable of interceding for sinners, establishing them as on the edge between the sacred and the profane. Glück lauds her aunt's "true spiritual nature" in "Saints" from *Ararat.* She goes on to identify with the aunt's life of violence and sacrifice because she believes that suffering accompanies a life that has attracted the attention of the Fates (AR 50).

"seeds" denotes a figure of natural growth but now also connotes the words that are rendered via a speech act.

In order to be in a position to distinguish not mere seeds but "distinct" seeds, and then to be able to notice their colors, the viewer must perceive them from very close range. Clearly, the speaker's perspective has switched from the generalized, wide-angle "landscape" point of view in stanza 1. We are made aware of the speaker's altogether different relationship to her material. She has taken charge of the scene by defining what she sees—"This is the barrenness . . ."—and by hypothesizing about its meaning. The speaker's point of view shifts from objective reportage to subjective impression. The figure of a "wife" (absent from view in the landscape depicted in part 1) now emerges. The appearance of a human characterization in the visionary portion of the poem suggests a relationship between the speaker's verbal ability to make a "calling" and her visual entrance into a lyric space.

A lyric is a subgenre of poetry that expresses an individual point of view, but what of the lyric author, for whom there is no immediate sense of "I" to recover outside the textual sphere? What if—to paraphrase Gertrude Stein's comment about her native Oakland and apply it to Glück's perceptions of Berryman, as well as to the situation of "All Hallows"—there is no "I there"? If no first-person pronoun can be figured in "All Hallows," then we can infer that the issue of how the absent or inchoate self that is constructed through the speaker's utterance will be at stake in the poem, as Glück has pointed out that it was at stake in Berryman's *Dream Songs*. The poem begins in the ongoing present tense of "now," but persons are absent, as in a landscape painting. The agents—the human or nonhuman principals who act in the poem—suggest a landscape brimming with signs of life, even as the space is empty of human actors. In the first seven lines that comprise stanza 1, there are six different agents: landscape, hills, oxen, fields, shade, and the "toothed moon." When so many agents appear in a single stanza, a poem becomes invested with dynamic properties because the world described seems animated with lives and with perspectives. A poem with so many agents seems the verbal equivalent of a cubist painting, rather than a traditional landscape in realistic mode with a one-point perspective. Glück thus extends the monologic nature of the genre through her dynamic, often unusual versions of the persona poem.

The anonymous speaker—who, not characterized in stanza 1, "appears" only as a disembodied voice—interprets the landscape scene ambiguously at the start of stanza 2. "This is the barrenness / of harvest or pestilence." The speaker can interpret the unpopulated, relatively empty field as signifying the abundance that follows successful human endeavor (harvest). Nature could also be read as exhibiting the aftermath to blight, upon what humans have tried to achieve through a natural impediment (pestilence). With its description of "seeds," implying birth as well as an organic cycle of natural renewal, and its defining the female as "wife," "All Hallows," Vendler has suggested, is a veiled account of the author's ambivalent response to motherhood. As Bonds notes, images of birth and maternity are central themes in Glück's poetry, informing her approach to cultural issues of reproduction through language acquisition in poems such as "The School Children." Maternity also influences her reading of theological mystery, as in "Pietà" (DF).[9]

The shifting perspective in "All Hallows" pivots from the general landscape imagery in stanza 1, to the mid-range perspective on "the wife leaning out the window," to the "distinct" seeds in stanza 2. The perspectival shift concludes with the surrealistic image in stanza 3 of "the soul" as it "creeps out of the tree." The three-pronged transition from outer to inner to occult landscape corresponds to the speaker's movement from a perception of nature to a revision of personal experience through the entrance into a visionary mode in which a speech act occurs. Instead of organizing her poem according to established measures, stanzas, and line lengths, Glück has organized a series of modified perspectives, which parallel her speaker's different levels of engagement with the same scene. Her approaches range from a natural encounter, to a psychological encounter, to a visionary encounter with elements of the animal world and nature that all point toward her final poetic calling.

The mystical setting and ritual linguistic activity of "All Hallows," stanza 2, correspond to the speaker's felt need to detach from nature if she is to achieve power over her environment through language. This scene of detachment does not come about without a cost—the speaker must extend her hand "as in payment." But the speaker is the agent of a transformation that involves access to insight as well as dissociation from external nature. In this poem Glück identifies the task of receiving language as juxtaposed to nature. The transformation of identity from nature to culture lacks the sense of shock and terror that accompanied maternity in "The Egg" or sexual relationships in poems such as "The Edge" or "Labor Day" (F). Thoroughly in charge of her own experience through a language that is itself mediated by myth and legend, the speaker's linguistic calling in "All Hallows" becomes connected to the Garden myth of female expulsion from nature.[10]

9. Bonds, "Entering Language," 68–69.

10. For more on the relationship between nature and the Garden myth, see Miklitsch, "Assembling a Landscape," 2; Matson, "Without Relation," 96.

Whereas "October twilight" is a quintessential moment of crossing over, in the external realm of an agricultural cycle, Glück's title, which concerns canonized persons, suggests that nature will serve emblematic purposes as the poet describes other types of liminal experience. The poem in fact will concern the costs of literary empowerment in the form of estrangement from nature. On one level, as Deno Trakas has observed, the harvest theme in "All Hallows" marks a transition from innocence to experience, involving loss as well as gain:

> We pay for harvest, for experience—this is the business of living. Just as spring can symbolize death, so can autumn symbolize birth: the fruit, "the absolute knowledge of the unborn," is harvested and lost at birth in exchange for experience.[11]

His comment pertains as well to other poems from ***The House on Marshland*** such as "The Apple Trees" in which Glück expresses a mother's fear that her child, like her husband, will eventually leave her side. "All Hallows" and "The Apple Trees" may be read as following Blake in describing a psychological transition from innocence to experience that applies in general to the human condition. These two poems also emphasize the shift from nature to language in ways that speak more specifically to the experience of women and mothers. "All Hallows," for example, may be read as tracing the loss of the "absolute knowledge" that Diane Bonds (following feminist thinkers such as Nancy Chodorow) associates with the "gynocentric" or presymbolic type of communication that is said to exist between mother and unborn child.[12] We may read "All Hallows" as a parable of loss and gain with universal implications, or else as a story with a message specific to women and, especially, to mothers who believe they have communicated to their unborn children on a preverbal level. However we may interpret the meaning of the calling that takes place in "All Hallows," we can agree that it involves the speaker's entrance into a transformational space, in which her identity is figured for the first time in the poem. Where physical birth and expressions of personal independence were deeply at odds in ***Firstborn,*** images hovering between maternity and a symbolic rebirth of the self through language and ritual at once resemble and oppose each other in "All Hallows."

11. Deno Trakas, "Louise Glück," in ***American Poets since World War II,*** pt. 1, A–K, in ***Dictionary of Literary Biography,*** 290–95 (294).

12. Bonds, "Entering Language"; Nancy Chodorow, ***The Reproduction of Mothering: Psychoanalysis and the Sociology of Gender*** (Berkeley and Los Angeles: University of California Press, 1978).

Revisioning Wordsworth in "The Shad-blow Tree"

Wordsworth wrote, "I was often unable to think of external things as having external existence, and I communed with all that I saw as something not apart from, but inherent in, my own immaterial nature."[13] In "Tintern Abbey," the speaker notices how his perceptions of nature influence the appearance of the world outside the self. Certainly the speaker no longer experiences nature on the level of animalistic sensuality. That unself-conscious relationship to nature, which he believes was acquired in early childhood, has long since given way to the cultivated relationship that dominates the poem's reflections. The authorial vision of "my own immaterial nature" substitutes for a vanished sense of presence and immediacy in nature.

"Tintern Abbey" specifically explores how a mature male speaker construes the relationship between mutable life in "real time" and the "frozen forms" that the speaker goes on to associate with the consolations of art. "Tintern Abbey" becomes for M. H. Abrams a primary example of the "Greater Romantic Lyric":

> "Tintern Abbey" inaugurated the wonderfully functional device Wordsworth later called the "two consciousnesses": a scene is revisited, and the remembered landscape ("the picture of the mind") is superimposed on the picture before the eye; the two landscapes fail to match, and so set a problem ("a sad perplexity") which compels the meditation.

Abrams describes "Tintern Abbey" as a palimpsest. It is composed of "two consciousnesses" that chafe against one another, creating a productive tension in the speaker's psyche that "compels the meditation."[14]

A less supportive reading might describe the poem as a solipsistic manipulation of nature for the purpose of self-preservation. Anne K. Mellor argues that Wordsworth believed nature could be appropriated through his imagination in order to meet his desire for immortality, by way of recollections that would be transmitted within the poem and also through the perceptions of his sister.[15] Feminist interpretations of "Tintern Abbey" have called attention to how William appropriated Dorothy Wordsworth's Alfoxden Journal (1798) and Grasmere Journal (1800–1803) in compiling material he later used as

13. Wordsworth cited from M. H. Abrams, "Structure and Style in the Greater Romantic Lyric," in ***Romanticism and Consciousness: Essays in Criticism,*** ed. Harold Bloom (New York: Norton, 1970), 201–29 (224).

14. Ibid., 206.

15. Anne K. Mellor, ***Romanticism and Gender*** (New York: Routledge, 1993).

source material for the great poem. In "Tintern Abbey," the poet responds to his return to the British Lake District, but also to his relationship to his sister's relationship to the same place as it appeared in her journals. A jarring surprise in reading "Tintern Abbey" occurs when we realize the speaker is not alone. He is in fact with his sister, to whom he turns to speak in the final stanza:

> For thou art with me here upon the banks
> Of this fair river; thou, my dearest Friend,
> My dear, dear Friend, and in thy voice I catch
> The language of my former heart, and read
> My former pleasures in the shooting lights
> Of thy wild eyes. Oh! yet a little while
> May I behold in thee what I was once,
> My dear, dear Sister![16]

At the end of the poem, the speaker instructs Dorothy, his silent companion, to understand that her memory *of him* should take precedence over her own perspective of nature when, after he has died, she visits the abbey that reposes on a high bank over the River Wye.

In "The Shad-blow Tree," Glück joins Wordsworth in cultivating nature for symbolic purposes. She transforms a "tree" into a forum for self-exploration involving memory and creative revision of a "spot of time." Her poem, like "Tintern Abbey," is about the uncanny discovery of memory in the present tense of the lyric. Glück's poem, however, takes the association between gender, subjectivity, and nature into account in a way Wordsworth's poem does not. In fact, Glück reverses the gender politics implicit within "Tintern Abbey" (at the end of which Dorothy, the speaker's silent sister, is called upon to recover William's memory after his death). Glück's female speaker will come to possess a representation of nature, a photograph taken by a former lover. Through her commentary on his representation, she will come to own the experience.

"The Shad-blow Tree" is a short lyric divided into two numbered parts, "The Tree" and "The Latent Image." The binary structure clues us into how Glück engages an analytic shape, to transform her lived experience into an art form that moves readers away from the literal world of the biological given to a speaker's subjective response to life in a text. Especially in part 2,

16. William Wordsworth, "Lines Composed a Few Miles above Tintern Abbey, on Revisiting the Banks of the Wye During a Tour, July 13, 1798," in M. H. Abrams et al., eds., *Norton Anthology of English Literature,* vol. 2, 7th ed. (New York: Norton, 2000), 236–37.

she transforms her impression of nature into a psychological expression that casts a ghostly shadow over the initial image. At first, the speaker sees "the tree" but then imagines a latent—that is to say, potential, but hidden—image. Like the "Greater Romantic Lyric" (as Abrams has described it in his landmark essay on Wordsworth), the poem becomes a symbolic vehicle for the speaker to focus her attention on the belated significance of a place and time that can only be discovered through art.

Glück pays special attention to the significance of her speaker's interpretation of the tree. She focuses on its appearance, not in nature, and not even through the speaker's perspective or her own words, but through the way her ex-lover "focused on a tree" to capture the photograph she observes in part 1:

> It is all here,
> luminous water, the imprinted sapling
> matched, branch by branch,
> to the lengthened
> tree in the lens, as it was
> against the green, poisoned landscape. (FFB 67)

Through commentary on the photograph she asserts her desire to control a memory represented by her ex-lover. This is so especially in the last line of part 1, where the "poisoned" landscape connotes her negative response to an image she associates with a failed love affair.

In part 2, the photograph has become entangled with her memory of nature. Her access to the "real" place, or to an essential version of the self through memory of one's place in nature, becomes hopelessly entangled within a labyrinth of representations, interpretations, and recollections:

> One year he focused on a tree
> until, through sunlight pure as never afterward, he saw
> the season, early spring, work upon those limbs
> its white flower, which the eye
> retains: deep in the brain
> the shad-blow coins its leaf in this context,
> among monuments, continuous with such frozen forms
> as have become the trained vine,
> root, rock, and all things perishing. (FFB 67)

Apparently, the speaker is recalling nature, noting for example how the quality of sunlight in early spring was itself like a "white flower," transforming the tree into a metaphorical, yet memorable image. Apparently set in a natural environment, the poem's images are, ironically, characterized as artifacts whose interpretation is up for grabs.

Glück has commented that she designs her poetry less to give the "impression of exposure" than to signify the "fact of distance." In "The Shad-blow Tree" she figures nature as an "imprint." Nature is constructed out of an admixture of her speaker's memories of visits to the woods with her ex-lover, and the way his photograph has prompted her revision in the present tense of the narration. For her, as for Wordsworth, nature and the self are not static entities but compositions woven out of text matter. The various compositions of both nature and the self are subject to multiple meanings, metaphorical comparisons, and interpretations made over several time frames and in different circumstances, such as when the speaker is together with her lover, and when she is alone after the breakup. Nature and the self are fabricated out of visual images as well as words.

A feminist theorist of Romanticism such as Anne K. Mellor might well conclude that Glück's resistance to the body and to nature as immediate sites of presence signify her capitulation to a masculine ethos of English Romantic poetry—the dominant and dominating poetics of William rather than the receptive prose of Dorothy Wordsworth. Mellor writes that "Dorothy's Journals linguistically represent a self that is not only relational, formed in connection with the needs, moods and actions of other human beings, but also physically embodied. Dorothy is not only a 'mighty mind' but an organic body that feels heat and cold and hunger, that sees and hears and smells, that defecates and 'washes her head,' that suffers both psychosomatic and physical disease." By contrast to Dorothy's connection to the body, Mellor views William as attempting "to construct a permanent, even transcendental ego that endures beyond the limits of matter, time and space." Following Shirley Neuman, Mellor believes the main reason for William's emphasis on the transcendental ego that effaces the body is that he was abiding by two major strands of Western thought, in following "a Platonic and Christian tradition that identifies the self with the soul and hence the spiritual as opposed to the sensual, together with an Enlightenment definition of 'man' as the Cartesian ego which has only to think in order to be."[17]

By privileging language and commentary over body, nature, and immediacy, in "The Latent Image" as in "All Hallows" Glück struggles with the issue of a female poet's entry into the symbolic. For this reason it seems her poem

17. Mellor, *Romanticism and Gender,* 157.

is a feminist revision of the "Greater Romantic Lyric" as defined by Abrams, as well as a politically charged example of "second nature" writing as defined by Burke in Chandler's version of Wordsworth. "The Shad-blow Tree" implicitly challenges Wordsworth's attitude toward the male gaze as the predominant sensory apparatus for cultivating nature. Perceiving "luminous water, the imprinted sapling" where she once saw another person (perhaps "Tom," to whom the poem is dedicated) as he saw the world through a camera lens, the speaker takes possession of his photograph through her interpretation. The image, she now claims, resides "deep in the brain."

The photograph takes precedence over the immediate relationship to nature, and her commentary takes precedence over both, but the meaning of the picture remains ambiguous. In part 2, she describes the image as beautiful because mutable ("through sunlight pure as never afterward"), but it is difficult for the reader to know how that image has been transmitted to the speaker, and by whom, or through what medium.

> the eye
> retains: deep in the brain
> the shad-blow coins its leaf in this context,
> among monuments, continuous with such frozen forms. (FFB 67)

We expect the speaker to retain the image through the objective filter of a "camera eye," but instead she reports how the end of a love affair has altered her memory of the landscape that she now condemns as "poisoned."

Alluding to "A Slumber Did My Spirit Seal," another Wordsworth lyric in which a grieving speaker must in stanza 2 confront the mortality of a beloved whom he had willfully misbelieved was immortal in stanza 1, the image now exists for her, not through the photograph, but in her mind's eye, "among monuments . . . / as have become the trained vine, / root, rock, and all things perishing" (FFB 67). Since we do not ordinarily consider a rock to be something perishing, we are being persuaded to understand that the "things perishing" are images she has associated with the "season, early spring," when the couple was young and her boyfriend photographed nature. Her memory of his photograph has become "the latent image," or the one that lies hidden, but also the part that continues to haunt her in the present tense of the poem as a traumatic aftermath of loss. We associate representation with immutability, with a realm that does not perish, but here the "frozen forms" seem to be "continuous with," not other than, the things that perish.

As it was for Wordsworth in "Tintern Abbey" and "A Slumber Did My Spirit Seal," the speaker in "The Shad-blow Tree" establishes her will to control memory by commenting on a prior mediation of nature. At the same time, Glück dissolves the subjective quality of lyric as it is found in Romanticism. Nature appears through the work of a poet *and* a photographer, a creative self and another maker working in another idiom who has produced an artifact through which the author may find the residue of her identity. As the two-part structure implies, a dialogue exists between imagining "what is," the nature of the world outside the self, and "what does," what the individual viewer brings to the experience of "what is" through the imagination. In this sense, the poem recalls the following lines from "Tintern Abbey":

> Almost suspended, we are laid asleep
> In body, and become a living soul;
> While with an eye made quiet by the power
> Of harmony, and the deep power of joy,
> We see into the life of things.[18]

Wordsworth beholds "the mighty world / Of eye, and ear, both what they half-create, / And what perceive?" Similarly, Glück returns to a time when, and a place where, a crucial moment of observation occurred, but it is not a moment that originated within the speaker's perspective. With its distinctly antinatural features, Glück's cultivated version of Romanticism also permeates her reading of nature in "To Autumn," "Flowering Plum," "To Jane Myers," and "The School Children," four other poems from *The House on Marshland* that portray the author in an antagonistic relationship with nature.[19]

Against Romanticism: "To Autumn," "Flowering Plum," and "For Jane Myers"

A delightfully witty poem, "To Autumn" like "The Shad-blow Tree" uses Romanticism to meditate on the relationship between art, nature, and the speaker's awareness of a split between immanent world, aging body, and the introspective self that wishes to impose its will upon the world through

18. Wordsworth, "Tintern Abbey," 236.

19. In an interview with Ann Douglas, Glück suggested that the title of her book resonated with her perception of nature as an unstable environment for human dwelling: "Long Island where I grew up is marshy; the land is reclaimed. The knowledge that houses, these structures which are supposed to be consoling and stable, were being built on land that was itself profoundly unreliable seemed to me very moving." Douglas, "Descending Figure," 116.

language. "To Autumn," like "The Shad-blow Tree," foregrounds representation as an afterimage that, the speaker hopes, may compensate for the disturbing material that informs her poems about birth, aging, motherhood, and sexuality, but that is also associated with exile from the real world of mere being.

"To Autumn" illustrates revisionary Romanticism, in this case by referring back to an ode of the same title by John Keats, whose speaker invited us not to "think" of "the songs of Spring," but rather to celebrate the unacknowledged pleasures of the "season of mists and mellow fruitfulness."[20] Keats's poem calls to mind a time of natural overabundance with its images of ripe fruit, swelled gourds, and "full-grown lambs." But his poem also evokes a crepuscular moment that pivots on the threshold of decline, including unsettling images of the "winnowing wind," "maturing sun," and the ominous sound of "gathering swallows" that "twitter in the skies" in the final line. Although it is called a fall poem, Glück's "To Autumn," unlike its Romantic forebear, does not account for the nuanced beauty apparent to Keats. Her apostrophe offers a retrospective glance upon the archetypal seasons of youth and sexual awakening while altogether disassociating the speaker from natural cycles. Writing from a position of maturity, the speaker admits she is "no longer young," so she exists out of synch with nature, which, she fantasizes, bursts with erotic activity. Although separating herself from nature, her language seems infused with unusual vitality and an erotic charge—"the budded snowdrops / caked with dew like little virgins, the azalea bush / ejects its first leaves." Uniquely alienated from the seasonal rejuvenation, the speaker proclaims, not without a defiance that borders on pride, "Only I / do not collaborate, having / flowered earlier" (FFB 72).

Glück's "To Autumn" veers away from a lament over the conclusion to a life of youth and sexual passion. The speaker views nature from the perspective of an author who hopes—here, self-mockingly, but nonetheless announced—that symbolic accomplishment ("great poems") will compensate for experiential deprivation:

> What
> of it? Summer approaches, and the long
> decaying days of autumn when I shall begin
> the great poems of my middle period. (FFB 72)

20. John Keats, "To Autumn," *The Premier Book of Major Poets,* ed. Anita Dore (New York: Ballantine Books, 1991), 36.

The humorous touch concerning how literary judgments are often developed through the artificial grid of periodization reduces the painful quality of foresight into maturity. The poem bears little of the anxiety about the end of natural reproduction through childbirth exhibited by Glück in other poems about birth and nature.

In "Flowering Plum," for example, the mature female speaker observes the neighbor's daughter as the young girl "reads" significance into the singing of a woodthrush and matches it with her own song, as "the mild wind / floods her immaculate lap with blossoms / . . . leaving no mark" (FFB 70). The girl exists in between a sexual awakening and what is described as the painless because unself-conscious innocence of a prepubescent at play. The speaker also projects onto the scene another image of the female body when viewed from the perspective of a woman who is no longer so young, innocent, or at one with her surroundings. This time, however, female contact with nature suggests, not song, but the anguish of childbearing, as "the fruit that will inscribe / unraveling dark stains in heavier winds, in summer" (FFB 70).

In "To Autumn," the speaker expressed confidence in her career of literary productivity. Writing is cast as a way to come to terms with the waning of erotic fulfillment, the sting of aging, and the fear of creative decline. An author of "great poems," her career would have a shape—with delineated periods, that might rival those of Yeats, Stevens, or her main teacher at Columbia, Stanley Kunitz—in its final flourish on the road to canonization. Although parodic anticipation of her mature accomplishment in "To Autumn" replaced the anxiety over biological productivity expressed in "Flowering Plum," we may pair both poems to masculine Romanticism. Each offers a retrospective perception of nature as a metaphor for the self; neither poem identifies the speaker's experience with nature. Instead, as Matson observes, Glück severs the connection between language, the rhythmic mutations of nature, and the status of the female body, whether old or young:

> the speaker addresses the natural processes . . . but shows how time and art have made her immune to them. . . . From this perspective, the delicate balance of pre-fallen spring is not to be envied, for the very impending loss which makes it beautiful also creates a tumult to be endured . . . it seems that autumn is welcomed for restoring the privacy and interiority needed for the speaker's art.[21]

21. Matson, "Without Relation," 102.

Regarded as a pair, "To Autumn" and "Flowering Plum" express Glück's concern with questions of literary reproduction of the self as an alternative to biological reproduction in the form of maternity.

In "For Jane Myers," Glück explores the adversarial relationship between the ravaging forces of nature and the resources of art as a way to conserve the human image as a literary figure in the wake of aging and death. Like "The Shad-blow Tree," the speaker interprets the passage of time as a factor in how she interprets nature. As in "Flowering Plum," she is especially concerned with distinguishing her understanding of nature as a mature adult from the way a child—Jane Myers—views it.

> Look how the bluet falls apart, mud
> pockets the seed.
> Months, years, then the dull blade of the wind.
> It is spring! We are going to die! (FFB 74)

The mature speaker interprets the sound made by the breeze as "wearying, wearying." For her the seeds, associated in "All Hallows" with childbearing and poetic commissioning, are clogged with mud, implying an inability to grow flowers as a figurative way of speaking about menopause.

By contrast, the speaker observes the girl, Jane Myers, as so filled with the exuberance of youth that she seems oblivious to her own mortality. Jane Myers creates lively images out of the dead birch twigs and designs images of crocus flowers merely by "digging out" her "colored tennis shoes" from a "sodden ditch":

> Sap rises from the sodden ditch
> and glues two green ears to the dead
> birch twig. Perilous beauty—
> and already Jane is digging out
> her colored tennis shoes,
> one mauve, one yellow, like large crocuses. (FFB 74)

One might suspect the speaker would become depressed by comparing her own natural declension to such scenes of Jane's ability to create a "perilous beauty" out of nature. The tone, however, is flippant, exclamatory, and as in "To Autumn," surprisingly humorous: "It is spring! We are going to die!" Through the carefree and upbeat tone, Glück joins Wordsworth and Keats in subverting conventional attitudes toward nature. She refuses to give in to a sentimental view of youth as she celebrates the "second nature" of personal identity when understood as a linguistic construct.

Like Eliot in *The Waste Land,* Glück revises Chaucer by reading spring as a cruel season. Unlike Eliot or the Keats of "Seasons of the Mind" or "To Autumn," she refuses to make an analogy of correspondence between the seasons of the year and the speaker's emotional life or symbolic value. Instead, Glück limits associations between nature and the self to the mutable physical body. She concludes by setting up an adversarial relationship between nature and the human heart:

> And now April raises up her plaque of flowers
> and the heart
> expands to admit its adversary. (FFB 74)

Like Dickinson, who, in poem 632 proclaimed "The Brain—is wider than the Sky," the speaker at once transcends and consumes nature through her power to reconfigure the landscape.[22] She represents April as a female lover or defeated warrior who appears to offer the "plaque" of flowers to the speaker as a gift to the victor after combat or as a token of submission to a paramour.

In "For Jane Myers," Glück regards lyric poetry as an abstract expression of voice. It is an analytic shape that contradicts nature, imposing an artificial form upon the environment. Confident that her significant self—that is, the self performed in language—is not subject to the mutability of nature and time, the speaker may glibly interpret spring as a token. It stands as no match for her emotional contours and linguistic prowess. An ecofeminist theorist might well view Glück's resistance to identifying the self with the body in nature as a sign that she has capitulated to a masculine ethos of English Romantic poetry. "For Jane Myers" and "Poem" both illustrate Glück's poetics of revenge—against traditional associations of women with nature, silent parts of the world subject to representations designed by men. As in "All Hallows," Glück refuses what Matson calls the "economy of sacrifice or martyrdom"—in favor of "one of fruition; it is an economy over which the woman seems to have some creative control."[23]

22. Emily Dickinson, "The Brain—is wider than the Sky," in Ramazani et al., *Norton Anthology* 1:38.

23. Matson, "Without Relation," 96.

"Poem": Writing as Revenge

We must regard any lyric entitled "Poem" as a version of the author's ars poetica. Oddly, as in "The Shad-blow Tree," Glück does not cast the main speaker in "Poem" as the artist, but instead as a silent witness who comments upon a domestic scene in which another writer, a male, is at work "bending / over his writing table" (FFB 76). A woman (not the speaker) "appears, carrying roses," thus she is positioned as the traditional female subject of portraiture. Glück characterizes the male author's indifference to the woman's subjectivity by suggesting he is aware only of her image as a part of nature that is reflected through its traditional connotation in art. He observes her in a mirror where her reflection is "marked with the green spokes of rose stems," a striking image that connects her figure to the rose.

In the second stanza, Glück unravels the traditional associations of the woman as the silent figure of natural beauty, appearing as an image on a screen, reflecting a self made abject through representation. Instead of interpreting the female face ringed with "green spokes of rose stems" as embodying mysterious beauty, Glück emphasizes the violence done to the woman identified with the image that "marked" her face with the thorns of the rose stem. "It is a form / of suffering," she writes, going so far as to represent the male author as a kind of vampire, who breathes life into his creation by drawing the blood out of a victim-subject, and then by transforming the blood into ink:

> the transparent page
> raised to the window until its veins emerge
> as words finally filled with ink. (FFB 76)

To put it mildly, "Poem" responds to the sting of being a woman whose identity is concealed with an object of natural beauty, and who has been "reborn" in language by another maker.

In the second half of the poem, stanzas 3 and 4, it seems the speaker has been asked by someone else to comment on the rapport between the couple. The speaker seems perplexed, even put off, that she must try to comprehend a relationship that produces such misery:

> And I am meant to understand
> what binds them together
> or to the gray house held firmly in place by dusk. (FFB 76)

These lines sound ironic to my ear. It seems the speaker would find it perverse to assume that a relationship based on violence and misunderstanding could be understood in rational terms. Nevertheless, the final stanza suggests the speaker feels compelled to analyze the archetypal scenario of male artist and female object:

> because I must enter their lives:
> it is spring, the pear tree
> filming with weak, white blossoms. (FFB 76)

In "For Jane Myers" the speaker challenged the lyric associations of spring by connecting the season of natural rejuvenation with death, as well as with the sap-filled liveliness that the little girl found in the ditch along with her tennis shoes. In "To Autumn," the speaker admitted that although she was "no longer young" she would refuse to fetishize youth, by anticipating her mature years when she "shall begin / the great poems of my middle period." In "Poem," the speaker juxtaposes the command that she "must enter their lives" with the fact that "it is spring, the pear tree / filming with weak, white blossoms." The sense of urgency to "enter their lives" is informed by her awareness of the blossoming of a pear tree, suggesting the continuation of a natural cycle as well as the continuation of a cycle of violent representation. The final image is of the pear (a pun on the couple as a "pair") that is now "filming with weak, white blossoms." We recall that the woman in the first stanza was "marked" by the thorny "rose stems" as her image blurred with that of the flower in the mirror. Here, at the end of the poem, the flowering pear tree, and especially its "weak, white blossoms," take on a dangerous presence. Associations are suggested between a woman, a flower, a tradition of poetic affiliations between the two, and a cycle of violence and silence. Now it is the flower that is "filming"—in the sense of becoming opaque, but also surveying, recording.

Resisting Culture: "The School Children" and the Limits to Education as Entryway into the Symbolic

In "To Autumn" and "For Jane Myers," Glück inverted conventional meanings by associating spring with death, while reserving for the authorial self the right to a vital existence in language. "Summer approaches, and the long / decaying days of autumn when I shall begin / the great poems of my middle period" (FFB 72). In "The School Children," Glück critiques her own expectation that, by cultivating nature, she might preserve an element of her speaker's life through language. Revisioning "Among School Children" by Yeats, she also interrogates the value of the cultural arena that the speakers of "To Autumn" and "For Jane Myers" had wished to occupy, in an attempt to dissociate themselves from the sentimental concept of spring as the season of youth and biological productivity.

Unlike the High Modernist innovators, whose estrangement of the familiar was primarily a formal matter of prosodic style and not of radical political content, "The School Children" bitterly revises Yeats—from the perspective of an author grappling with the contradictory impulses of bearing children and bearing the word. Her poem takes into account the mother's elegiac perspective on the stereotypical version of the first day at school. The poem critiques reading that inauguration of formal education, the initiation into the symbolic realm, as an unambiguously cheerful event, when the mother is pleased to "offer" the child, complete with shiny red apple in hand, to the care of teachers. Entering school in "The School Children" is described as a contemporary version of ritual sacrifice in which children are given over to the control of the state.

James Longenbach has argued that Glück shares with Yeats an ambivalent reaction toward making myths out of personal experience. He claims that both are "poets repelled by their own impulse to transform experience into myth."[24] It is true that Yeats in "Among School Children" and Glück in "The School Children" both express ambivalence toward education as a form of cultural reproduction. Both represent education as an experience that alienates children from their parents, as well as parents from their own dreams and wishes. Unlike Yeats, Glück foregrounds gender conflicts in her conception of education. Where Yeats depicted nuns as the agents of state control, Glück pits the authority of maternity, and the preverbal language of apples that goes on between mother and child, against the socially conferred power of teachers, who, although of unassigned gender in the poem, nonetheless possess the symbolic power to influence children that has long been associated with the male domain of language in the public sphere.

Glück defines education in its etymological sense as a "rearing," a "leading forth" of the children. In her case the children are led away from the apple orchard, where the mothers once resided with their children. Stanza 1 depicts a scene that calls to mind the "gynocentric" or presymbolic type of communication that is said by Chodorow to exist between mother and unborn child:

24. James Longenbach, "Letter to the Editor," *PMLA* 115.7 (December 2000): 2058.

> The children go forward with their little satchels.
> And all morning the mothers have labored
> to gather the late apples, red and gold,
> like words of another language. (FFB 77)

The children go forward across a gap, to "the other shore" of the schoolroom, where the narrative of cultivation turns into a scene of distress for the mothers. The teachers wait to meet their pupils, like judges or priests, figures of unquestionable authority who sit "behind great desks / to receive these offerings" (FFB 77).[25]

Glück complements the poem's temporal dimension with a spatial arrangement. Shifts in space and time in this poem emphasize the environments that the children inhabit as they move from "presymbolic" communication with their mothers in the garden to become obedient disciples of the state. In the final stanza, the children enter a realm of silence removed from their mothers, who remain in the orchard, now exiled from their children as well as from the once-fertile orchard:

> And the teachers shall instruct them in silence
> and the mothers shall scour the orchards for a way out,
> drawing to themselves the gray limbs of the fruit trees
> bearing so little ammunition. (FFB 77)

Through spatial arrangement, each stanza traces how the image of the apples shifts in meaning when placed in the different environments of nature when inhabited by mothers and children (orchard in stanza 1), culture when inhabited by teacher and children (schoolroom in stanza 2), and nature when inhabited only by the mothers (in stanza 4).

In stanza 1, the mothers and children "gather the late apples, like red and gold, / like words of another language." The fact that they are described as "late" apples suggests that an agricultural season associated with maturation has come to an end. While the poem makes no direct allusions to the Garden myth, the images of fall, apples, mothers, and children must suggest Eden in Genesis. We are made aware of the injunction against Adam and Eve's eating from the Tree of Knowledge of Good and Evil that becomes associated with the pain of maternal labor, the responsibility of moral choice-making, the hardship of physical work to earn bread, and the exile from the garden. The mothers "have labored / to gather" the apples, but the apples as signi-

25. Chodorow cited in Bonds, "Entering Language," 60.

fiers of a presymbolic language become cultivated in stanza 2. The apples become synonymous with the children as ritual "offerings" to the teachers. In stanza 4, the apples are revised for a third time. Now, at the end of the poem, the apples are read as signs of absence, perhaps suggesting the end of the mother's role as childbearer. Finally, in the hands of the desperate mothers, who feel they have lost control of their children to the teachers, the apples become "ammunition." The mothers' attempt, without hope for success, to find a release from the pain of loss by reimagining apples—once cast as a preverbal form of language and exchange between mother and child—as a weapon of attack.

Glück connects education to a social regime that reduces differences among the children. In stanza 3, the speaker notices how upon entering the classroom each child must take off a coat, the garment encoded with signs of distinction through the variety of colors, that will "hang on nails" in a cloakroom.

> How orderly they are—the nails
> on which the children hang
> their overcoats of blue or yellow wool. (FFB 77)

Through enjambment, she also suggests "the children hang" in the metaphorical sense of being "offered" in a transfer of authority from parent to teacher. As well as maintaining the literal sense that "their overcoats" hang on nails in the cloakroom as the children move from the outside space of nature to the inside space of culture, education has the resonance of a sacrificial exchange.

Exiled from the apple orchard, the children must learn to forget the "mother tongue," signified by the apples, described in stanza 1 as being "like words of another language." Representing school instruction through martial images, which signify the teacher's disciplinary control over language and individual differences, Glück understands education as an initiation into a scene of cultural repression, rather than a scene of creative exploration, emancipation, and play. The speaker in stanza 3 observes "How orderly they are," while stanza 4 begins with a depiction of futurity that is spoken in a voice of prophecy. The "teachers shall instruct them in silence."

Glück troubles Yeats's vision of a potential union between nature and culture in her revisionary poem. If we look again at Yeats's "Among School Children," we see how Glück has taken into account the maternal point of view in a scene of education seeming to exemplify Lacan's theory that "language and culture depend on the death or absence of the mother and on the quest for substitutes for her."[26] In the first stanza of Yeats's poem, he appears as "[a] sixty-year-old smiling public man," in his public role as the inspector of schools in the newly formed Irish Free State. John Unterecker writes:

> "Among School Children" was written after a 1926 semi-official senatorial visit to Waterford, a progressive convent school, the poem is an effort to synthesize the "sixty-year-old smiling public man," the aged one-time lover, and the would be philosopher into something as organic as a chestnut-tree, as coherent as a dancer's movements.[27]

Yeats registers dismay over the instruction he sees on his semiofficial visit to Waterford, because he perceives a mechanical enterprise that breeds conformity and the passive learning of skills. Education robs the children of the "wonder" that Yeats associates with dream, nature, mythic vision, music, dance, and art.

In the first stanza, for example, Yeats mocks the way the nuns teach crafts. He uses words that represent the enlightenment method later characterized by Foucault as accumulating knowledge for the purposes of classifying, dividing, and ordering—"to cut and sew." Yeats notes that the children are taught to "be neat in everything / In the best modern way."[28] The things that cannot be explained are eliminated, so the modern way of thinking—through separation of the whole into parts—looks "neat in everything." The method of modern education, which sacrifices feelings and energy to achieve rational practice in the schoolroom, ignores the pleasure of process and valorizes the achievement and conquest.[29]

By contrast to education as a study in rationality and conformity, Yeats offers in stanza 2 an alternative journey, through the "long schoolroom" of personal, interpersonal, historical, and mythic versions of education, which includes a discussion of Maud Gonne as a child, and of how time has robbed her "Leadean body" of youth and beauty. In the faces of the schoolchildren, Yeats sees Maud's childhood through a compassionate re-creation of a time and place when, her feelings hurt in an unspecified but pivotal incident, she was "bent / Above a sinking fire, a tale that she / Told of a harsh reproof, or

26. Lacan cited in ibid.

27. John Unterecker, ***A Reader's Guide to William Butler Yeats*** (New York: Noonday, 1959), 191.

28. Yeats, "Among School Children," 124.

29. I am basing my reading of Yeats on education, in part, on the work of Bok-ki-Lee, a graduate student at Purdue who wrote a paper on "Romantic Visions of Education" in a seminar I taught on Modern British Poetry in the fall of 2000.

trivial event / That changed some childish day to tragedy" (9–12).[30] Yeats has crossed the threshold into the imagination of a little girl, who is no longer young, but the poem seems autobiographical, heartbreakingly so, as when he caricatures himself and wonders if his mother would have thought childbirth worthwhile if she were to see him today as "[o]ld clothes upon old sticks to scare a bird" (48).[31]

In spite of the psychic, temporal, and spatial fragmentation exhibited up to this point, Yeats retains in the monumental final stanza a utopian vision where beauty may be produced without the pain of bearing children. Similarly, he anticipates that wisdom can be gained without the hardship of the writing process, described as hard labor performed by a man late into the evening in a room lit by candle. In contrast to the physical pain of childbirth, or the emotional struggle involved with writing poems ("beauty born out of its own despair"), Yeats returns to images of wholeness, not division, in nature (the blossoming, rooted chestnut tree), and the graceful human body at creative play (the dancer). By stanza 8, Yeats has idealized the body at play by imagining it as no longer subject to the physical-mental split or nature-culture division that haunts his vision of the desiring self attached to the dying body. Observing the chestnut tree or the dancer dancing does not cause him pain, because neither image requires a separation from life's rich ongoingness to produce aesthetic pleasure or a feeling of rootedness in nature. Yeats has criticized how the nuns educate the children in mechanization and despair. Yet he also envisions a way out of culture, through images that associate art with organic growth. The lyric self is wildly imaginative, mythic, and yet bound to the body and nature as the locations of creativity and grace. In spite of the uncertainty and grief that animate the autobiographical elements of the poem, and however much "Among School Children" is composed like a patchwork quilt, his authorial persona remains intact as the controlling figure of metaphor, the master of all ceremonies.

Glück, on the other hand, begins her poem "The School Children" with images of mothers and children at one with nature and in harmony with each other. By poem's end, however, she undermines Yeats's imagined union between culture and nature by interpreting education from the perspective of an invisible speaker who empathizes with the isolated mothers who have "offered" their child to the state, rather than from the perspective of the Irish Senator and School Inspector, a statesman making an official visit in the guise of the "sixty-year-old smiling public man." From the maternal point of view,

30. Yeats, "Among School Children," 124.
31. Ibid., 125.

nature, the self, and the female body take on qualities of desperation, vulnerability, and hostility toward educational authority. Instead of invoking the chestnut-tree image and the dancer (who conjoins with nature when making art out of the body) as images of organic form, Glück in the end views nature, the apples in the orchard, as ineffective ammunition to combat the teachers' control and the symbolic order they have the power to convene.

In contrast to the dancers in Yeats, the mothers in Glück cannot imagine a future when they can resolve the conflict with the teachers holding sway over the children. The poem registers a terrible defeat suffered by the mothers at the hands of the teachers, because the speaker cannot find any resource—no artistic production or biological reproduction—to counteract the loss of the children. Like the mothers, Glück's speaker witnesses the outcome to an example of cultural work that involves irreparable loss and exclusion from both the immanent and figurative realms that she elsewhere desires to negotiate. Gender inflects the act of seeing nature—as a contest for interpretations of the past in "The Shad-blow Tree" and of the future in "The School Children." In each case she imagines nature and comments on what others—teachers, ex-lovers—have made of it, as a form of power relations involving a disturbance of the sense of being at home in the world around her. "The School Children" represents Glück's dilemma as an author who feels she is in a double bind, neither at home in nature without a relationship to a symbol system in which she can assert her power nor safe in the cultural setting she hopes to enter through her writing, but which alienates her from the realms of nature and maternity that in part define her identity.

In an essay devoted to T. S. Eliot, "The Idea of Courage," Glück questions confessional authors who claim "a capacity for facing down the dark forces" through the act of writing poems, which allegedly reveal their hidden wishes and prove their life experiences are indeed painful (PT 24). By contrast, she understands her compositions to be part of a revisionary process of detached analysis, which contradicts natural life forces through the shape her commentary has imposed on memory and experience. "A powerful re-seeing of family life animates many of the poems," Vendler writes.[32] Like Wordsworth, Glück reverses the agency of experience by transferring to the author the power to compose memory into words:

> No matter what the materials, the act of composition remains, for the poet, an act, or condition, of ecstatic detachment. . . . personal

32. Vendler, "Louise Glück," 304.

> circumstance may prompt art, but the actual making of art is a revenge on circumstance. For a brief period, the natural arrangement is reversed: the artist no longer acted upon but acting; the last word, for the moment, seized back from fate or chance. . . . No process I can name so completely defeats the authority of event. (PT 25)

Glück has also stated that poetry's "agenda [is] not simply to record the actual but to continuously create the sensation of immersion in the actual" (PT 92).

Critics refer to her tone as "mythic" or "visionary," and Glück has herself cast her poetry as an "ancient text" (in a poem of that title from *The Seven Ages*). Her speaker's placement in relation to the mysterious experiences she describes, after her moment of life crisis, influences our sense of a speaker who views her life as a text subject to emendation through commentary, a view that suggests language and experience are incommensurate phenomena. In her more pessimistic moments, Glück's perception of her life as a text that can be performed, and then reformed in subsequent writings, alienates her from nature. It also, however, enables her female speaker to possess symbolic authority over the meaning of her experience—in the act of remembering her past and defining the meaning of her life. Thus Glück's antinatural naturalism suggests a feminist subversion of the inherited myth that associates symbolic power with masculinity. In truth, as Bonds points out in her reading of *The House on Marshland,* Glück's poems concerning nature and maternity express the poet's uncertainty about her own position, regarding her placement as a woman, a mother, and a poet who attempts to enter the symbolic order by translating literal terms such as nature and child into figurative displays of linguistic power.

Chapter Seven

Should I Say It with Flowers?

Ararat and the Work of Mourning through Nature Poetry

In nature poems such as "All Hallows" (HM), Glück expressed her debt to Romanticism by registering the cost of converting a literal association with nature into a figurative one. A nature poet, she nonetheless regards the environment as a malevolent trap and represents it as an adversary. Nature, she fears, will diminish her symbolic accomplishment achieved in writing designed to convey her independence from the embodied life. *The House on Marshland* marked an advance over *Firstborn* because it depicted the main speaker after she had "left a skin there," thus allowing Glück to perceive identity as a part of language.

In the 1990s, Glück complicates her reading of nature as an impediment to linguistic mastery. In *Ararat* and *The Wild Iris,* she challenges the benefits of her hard-won linguistic victory over her environment. She regards flowers as a commemorative language, but she finds the language of flowers to be an inadequate container for her grief and yearnings. In *Ararat,* Glück evokes flowers to perform various speech acts. In "Birthday," she describes flowers as one way to memorialize her mother's legendary beauty. In "Brown Circle," through the image of an overzealous botanist, she examines the impact of her personality on the development of her son, Noah. At the same time, in "Yellow Dahlia," "Lover of Flowers," and "Paradise," she competes with her sister for her father's legacy, by refusing to lay flowers upon his grave because this is her sister's practice. By invoking the Noah story through the title of her book, Glück links a proof text involving an environmental disaster to her interpretation of family history.

In *Ararat,* Glück anticipates *The Wild Iris* by attaching nature to the spirit world through metaphor. In "Celestial Music," she imagines the connection between elements of nature, music, and the desire to return to a lost connection with God, and this is an association made throughout *The Wild Iris.* She combines images of birth and death, flowering in spring and the commemorative act of laying flowers for the father at Mount Ararat Cemetery, a place name that recalls the story of God's apocalyptic condemnation of human behavior in Genesis 6–9 through His performance of a natural disaster. In *Ararat,* a son named Noah survives God's anger, but a father is cast as God's sacrificial victim. Glück, then, makes use of nature and its biblical resonance to produce a conflicted portrait of the daughter's relationship to her father. The father-daughter relationship mirrors the author's ambivalence toward figures of literary authority in her commentary poems on biblical and Homeric themes. Nature becomes a contested ground that involves literary authority. Who in the Glück family "owns" nature as a meaningful symbol system?

Ararat revises nature, but in doing so, it is also a work of personal revision. In effect tearing down the authorial persona, the pyrotechnical stylist evident in *Firstborn,* Glück depicts herself in a reticent tone of voice. Because the laconic tone mirrors her father's silence and renunciation of floral gifts, as these elements of his personality are discussed, the speaker's voice and her relationship to nature also reflect the experience of trauma. Glück's deadpan tone suggests the impact on her psyche of the father's emotional sterility and his consequent distaste for all natural things. Although she is engaged in a struggle with his authority, the father has influenced the type of writer the daughter has become. The language of *Ararat* reveals that the author continues to act out and potentially work through the father's death.

The Wild Iris is Glück's foremost nature study from the 1990s. What is less obvious to most readers is that she sowed the literal and figurative seeds to that volume in *Ararat,* itself primarily a series of elegiac poems set in the cramped quarters of a home of suburban mourners in Long Island. In poems such as "Confession" and "Widows," *Ararat* documents how the emotionally benumbed speaker has learned from an older generation of Glück women how to survive the death of loved ones. She learns the lesson that one way to protect oneself from further despair is by renouncing the desire to forge compelling relationships with persons other than the grieving widows. Absence becomes the metaphysical status quo for the widows. They display a stoic disposition that seems to have influenced the pared-down rhetoric of this, Glück's most controversial volume.[1]

1. David Mason has denounced the book as "dull" and as a "disaster." Calvin Bedient celebrated it as an example of "English in its most purified form." See David Mason's review of *The Wild Iris* in the *Hudson Review* 46.1 (Spring 1993): 266; Calvin Bedient, "'Man Is Altogether Desire'?" *Salmagundi* 90–91 (1991): 218.

Describing the volume as "articulated depression," Calvin Bedient has suggested that *Ararat* exhibits "stripped-down desire—desire without transcendental dignities." Melissa Brown has stated that the poems are "bereft of the metaphysical, mythical and symbolic richness of Glück's previous books [as] meaning swirls and blows across the dry surface of these poems.[2] I clearly disagree with their analysis. In my view, *Ararat* offers a kind of "symbolic richness" that points back in her career to *The House on Marshland* and forward to *The Wild Iris.* Glück's nature poetry in *Ararat* accrues "symbolic richness," among other ways, through its resonance with Greek and Jewish narrative formats.

Along with the grim focus on a family in mourning over the death of the patriarch, *Ararat* has "Celestial Music" as its penultimate poem. Anticipating the gardener-poet's ambivalent relationship to God in *The Wild Iris,* Glück contrasts herself to "a friend who still believes in heaven" (AR 66). Unlike the skeptical bereft speaker, who is "moved by weakness, by disaster," the friend—of Christian, not Jewish faith, and based on the poet Ellen Voigt—"literally talks to god" because "she thinks someone listens in heaven." The speaker and the friend are described as "at ease with death, with solitude," but the friend expresses a desire for the peace that accompanies faith. The friend's desire for transcendence, the speaker argues, requires that she renounce the wish for control over her surroundings in the face of a divine source of creative power. The speaker interprets the friend's act of drawing a circle in the dirt with a stick to surround a dying caterpillar as an attempt "to make something whole, something / beautiful, an image / capable of life apart from her" (AR 67). The poem calls to mind *Ararat*'s epigraph taken from Plato's *Symposium,* which states that "human nature was originally one and we were a whole, and the desire and pursuit of the whole is called love."[3]

The mystical friend also instructs the despondent speaker to abandon what Brown calls her "secular fatalism" by hearing "celestial music." The intuition of theological mystery may be an anomaly in *Ararat.* The poem certainly takes readers away from attending to how a group of women keep up "appearances" of normality (the title of one poem). "Celestial Music" is not about coming to terms with domestic tensions, sibling rivalries, or reversions to a preadolescent disposition in which the main speaker abhors change and growth. The poem's expression of an aspiration toward transcendence, for example, contrasts sharply with the sentiment expressed in "Children Coming Home from School," where the speaker recalls: "The year I started school . .

2. Bedient, "'Man Is Altogether Desire'?" 215, 212; Brown, "Love of Form," 33.
3. Plato cited as unpaginated epigraph by Glück in *Ararat.*

. / I continued, in pathetic ways, / to covet the stroller" of the younger sister who "couldn't walk long distances" (AR 64). Perhaps "Celestial Music" is an anomaly when placed beside "Children Coming Home from School," but the poem nonetheless anticipates the dominant theme of *The Wild Iris.* The speaker responds to religious yearnings that imply the possibility of transcendence, but these yearnings are intolerable to her, for they require a loss of control. "Celestial Music" nonetheless previews the context of nature as a site for theological speculation most evident in *The Wild Iris.*

In *The Wild Iris,* floral personae direct their speech upward. Flowers such as Scilla ascend from the earth to critique the narcissistic strains of the gardener-poet, who, yearning for connection to a personal God, exists in relation to the flowers as Yahweh exists in relation to her. In *Ararat,* by contrast, Glück primarily writes about flowers and nature to discuss a kind of emotional descent into depression, and the literal descent of human burial. Flower and nature poems in *Ararat* focus on the speaker's mother ("Birthday"), father ("Paradise"), sister ("Lover of Flowers" and "Yellow Dahlia"), son ("Brown Circle"), and their connections. Glück's flower poems reveal the deep-seated tensions and repressed anxieties of familial life. These poems concern matters of the heart, not eschatological mystery. In some cases connected to biblical and Hellenic sources, the "second nature" poems from *Ararat* involve the speaker's ambivalent relationship to her family and to nature as the sources of consolation and of conflict.

In "To Autumn" (HM), Glück celebrated the linguistic prowess of an aging female speaker. Distinguishing the significance of the self from its physical presence, her accomplishment was not subject to the ravages of time, and her decline as an erotic being did not predict a loss of literary power. Similarly, "Birthday" detaches language from phenomenal experience by exploring how "bulletins of flowers" exist as a representation of affection that survives the admirer's death. The poem describes a gift of flowers to the speaker's mother, on whose doorstep a dozen roses "from an old admirer" appear at her birthday every year. The sender, however, has since died and the receiver is no longer so young or beautiful that she could possibly expect to curry such gifts in her present condition. In the face of death and aging, flowers communicate "the legend of my mother's beauty" in the same way that a poem may be said to endure as a figurative substitution for its author (AR 40). Glück shapes an analogy between flowers and poetry that commemorates the gift's giver as well as its receiver, thereby connecting the two in a social bond that reflects the relationship between reader and writer. Both flowers and poetry are sent as messages to defer the pain of forgetfulness and the mutability of existence through the language of sentiment.

In the second part of "Birthday," Glück questions the idea of flowers as a form of lyrical communication that stands in the way of death and forgetfulness. In fact, she wishes to challenge the initial reading of flowers as a symbolic vehicle that may commemorate the dead or express affection for the living. She distances herself from the process of converting flowers into a metaphor for art as a stay against mortality, or the metaphorical "seasons" of human life described by sonneteers from Shakespeare to Keats. For one thing, she bluntly states, "[a]fter ten years, the roses stopped." For another, the possibility that the "dead could minister to the living" through tokens that create social obligations requiring mutual displays of affection turns out to be an anomaly in the family history. The admirer's flowers contrast sharply with the father's silence and puritanical opposition to theatricality. The influence of the father's aesthetic on the author daughter may be construed through the poem's laconic voice and deflated tone: "for the most part / the dead were like my father" (AR 40).

Observing how the mother pays homage to her late husband, the speaker retreats from an optimistic conception of flowers as a posthumous expression of love.

> Her birthday comes and goes; she spends it
> sitting by a grave.
>
> She's showing him she understands,
> that she accepts his silence.
> He hates deception: she doesn't want him making
> signs of affection when he can't feel. (AR 40–41)

The speaker has ceased interpreting flowers as a gift that defers forgetfulness at death through the creation of a legend. Instead of flowers, Glück's speaker now validates silence as a testimony to the profundity of her grief, associated with her father's terse disposition, and she adopts his suspicion that beauty conceals a cold heart. On the surface, "Birthday" tells an anecdote about a man who continues to honor his passion by paying tribute to a woman's beauty through flowers. Formally, however, "Birthday" expresses the daughter's tribute to the father's aesthetic. In its spare outlines and distaste for artifice, the poem anticipates the Herbert-like association of grace with a spare style that is meant to convey sincerity in the supplication poems to Yahweh in *The Wild Iris.*

By perceiving flowers as a gift that conceals a deficiency of real feeling, Glück suggests the speaker's distance from an immanent perspective on nature. The poker-faced style of "Birthday," then, may be regarded as a paradoxical expression of emotional depth, one that resonates with an insight from "Children Coming Home from School," where the speaker recalls that her sister "envied me," because "I walked very slowly, to appear to need nothing," but the sister "didn't know / you can lie with your face, your body" (AR 64). Imitating her father's attitude toward gift exchange, and recalling the way she hid feelings as a child, the speaker condemns a type of rhetorical gift-giving through her tone. She challenges the exchange of flowers, a part of nature, for a cultural sign of affection. At first courting the turn of nature into a medium of communication through the story of her mother's admirer, she resists her own efforts to do so. Such a transformation of nature into artifact, she believes, would betray her father's best judgment.

The father's personality differs markedly from that of the mother's late admirer, but the issue of how to commemorate the father through natural symbols recurs in the ironically entitled "Paradise." This is one of several poems from throughout Glück's career in which she invokes the Garden myth to explore the problem of language as a by-product of alienation from nature and detachment from the body. "Lamentations" (DF) is another. In "Paradise," the speaker's sister has brought a bouquet of flowers from the city to the suburban household. The fact that these flowers were purchased from a flower shop suggests the cultivated nature of the memorial gift. The sister behaves as if the home on Long Island were no longer a place where a family resided in the wake of a recent death. Instead, she treats the home as if it had already become transformed into a kind of mausoleum, the parents' grave site.

Glück contemplates the pain of love and of childbirth in this poem, but she also complicates her interpretation of the meaning of planting flowers as a commemorative gift. In a nod to Whitman's famous elegy for Lincoln, the speaker denounces her sister for linking memories of the father to lilacs that now bloom around the house.

> More and more
> my sister comes from the city,
> weeds, tidies the garden. My mother
> lets her take over: she's the one
> who cares, the one who does the work.
> To her, it looks like country—
> the clipped lawns, strips of colored flowers.
> She doesn't know what it once was. (AR 55)

The speaker claims that her own disinterest in maintaining the garden memorial illustrates her cold, honest appraisal of the father. As in "Birthday," the father frowned upon anyone else who showed their emotion by showering gifts, an exchange that upsets the solitary nature of love when understood as an extreme emotion that cannot be contained through flowers or words.

From Glück's point of view, natural gifts upset the distinction between the kind of recognition that language may confer upon the person and the recovery of lived experience:

> They always said
> I was like my father, the way he showed
> contempt for emotion.
> They're the emotional ones,
> my sister and my mother. (AR 55)

Of course the statement is ironic. The speaker believes that she, not the sister from the city who fastidiously tends the garden, is the "emotional one." She, and not the sister who has managed to escape the emotional confines of the home for an independent life in the city, has most deeply identified with the father.

The sister in "Paradise" and in "Lover of Flowers" regards the cultivation of nature as a legitimate way to ritualize grief through acts of mourning. In "Lover of Flowers," the sister "plants bulbs by the brick stoop" in the autumn and then "every spring, waits for flowers" (AR 21). The sister's behavior makes her an outcast in the family, however, at least according to Glück's autobiographical persona. The group that Glück's speaker defines as "our family" decides to forgo placing the flowers that "everyone loves" on the father's grave site. The speaker wants the "terse" inscriptions on "plaques of granite" to speak for themselves:

> In our family, everyone loves flowers.
> That's why the graves are so odd:
> no flowers, just padlocks of grass,
> and in the center, plaques of granite,
> the inscriptions terse, the shallow letters
> sometimes filling with dirt.
> To clean them out, you use your handkerchief. (AR 21)

A by-product of the emotional space that her father has evacuated, the speaker in "Paradise" and "The Lover of Flowers" inherits in her own "terse" lyrics the aftermath to his painful lack of expression. His denial of the significance of nature may be read as a sign of his obsessive awareness of mortality. The speaker in "Celestial Music" defined herself as one who, through the "love of form," was expressing "a love of endings." The father too, with his morbid fascination with death and fear of life, seems to have been a lover of endings.

Agonistic toward nature, the speaker regards flowers as if they were a battlefield upon which to compete with the sister from the city for access to the father's legacy in "Paradise" and "Lover of Flowers." The speaker claims her sister has deluded herself about the physical setting of the household. Worse, she has denied the psychologically deadened landscape, the ironically named "Paradise," in which the sisters were raised. The speaker claims her sister has refused to acknowledge how their parents fostered distaste for the expression of strong feelings toward other family members. "To her, it looks like country— / the clipped lawns, strips of colored flowers. / She doesn't know what it once was" (AR 55). One of the gray houses now grown closer together as subdivisions that have expanded the neighborhood, with its television sets and kitschy streets "named after sweethearts or girl children," the "country" house in Long Island is cast as another instance of aesthetic deception (AR 54). Besides the cultural criticism of suburbia as an ersatz setting for communion with nature, the speaker insists that her sister's flourish on what amounts to the father's grave displays her refusal to acknowledge how the house resounds with the aftershocks of a childhood trauma. By contrast, the speaker's frozen rhetoric embodies childhood trauma. It is the speaker (and especially her words), not her sister bringing flowers from the city, who is the living witness to a father who in life was unapproachable and now represents absence.

Glück seems to rebuke her laconic personality by chastising her speaker's ineptitude at displaying signs of affection such as planting flowers. In the last stanza of "Paradise," which connects the poem to its title through the Garden narrative (and especially to the story from Genesis 2 of Adam's rib as the antinatural source of Eve's creation), Glück changes her tune. She argues that, by refraining from commemorating the father with flowers, and by refusing to accept flowers as a way to mediate the profundity of her loss, she has in fact established herself as the father's heir:

> Believe me, you never heal,
> you never forget the ache in your side,
> the place where something was taken away
> to make another person. (AR 55)

The speaker has claimed her priority in remembering with accuracy the father's personality. She is "the firstborn." She dons the mantle of emotional realist, truth-teller, and most of all, sacrificial victim to the father's memory. By deadening her own language—what, after all, could be more of a personal sacrifice for a poet?—she becomes, through the erasure of ornament in her work, a "gift" to the father.

Like the rib removed from Adam's side to create Eve, the speaker's memories of her youth and family life have in a sense become a wound on the body written into the style of her text. Her words register the tone of a mourner in the grip of inconsolable loss. If the father's memory is to be conserved, the speaker must endure a type of psychological distress so profound that she can perform old wounds on the level of rhetoric. To her way of thinking, verbal restraint approximates the sacrifice of the firstborn. It also calls to mind the physical pain of childbirth, the splitting of the self into two parts, as would be required by the story of Adam becoming both Adam and Eve. The speaker has reproached her sister's garden memorial for being too much like the flowers sent by the mother's old admirer in "Birthday." She has interpreted the sister's flowers as a form of concealment, not revelation, as a kind of natural wallpaper, "strips of colored flowers" (AR 55).

By contrast to the sister's flowers, the speaker's wounded body, masculine persona (she is, after all, the Adam figure who creates Eve), and damaged spirit—"you never heal"—become revised into stigmata. She interprets her voice as an authentic sign of another kind of "Paradise." Her voice corresponds to a genuine commemorative language that is itself related to the Garden narrative when interpreted as a story about exile from nature and alienation from the body. Her version of the Fall myth involves personal sacrifice as well as the male (Adam) story of generation through the artifice of naming, rather than the female (Eve) story of generation of life through maternity. Reading the Fall myth as alienation from nature, Glück supplies an origin for the present-tense narration that prioritizes her antinaturalism over her sister's natural display. She offers a source for the author's psychological condition and linguistic disposition—the lingering sorrow of a family life that was dominated by a detached and uncommunicative patriarch. Her focus on absence—"the place where something was taken away"—becomes her way to reproduce the father's presence in her text.

In "The Lover of Flowers," Glück described a family after her own heart. They refused to plant flowers, not because everyone disliked flowers but because that is what "everyone loves." In "Paradise," the speaker, a "firstborn," similarly believes that the best way to honor the father and then to fill the gap he left is to sacrifice her expressions of feeling for him. In effect, Glück honors him by shutting down the literary shop that had successfully cultivated nature in *The House on Marshland.* As in "Paradise," in "Lover of Flowers" the speaker contrasts her type of mourning with that of the sister, who comes from the city to plant bulbs and then returns "every spring, [and] waits for flowers" (AR 21). The father's grave site at Mount Ararat Cemetery is a memorial without flowers, but because the mother and the sister "see / the house as his true grave," their garden has been converted into a tribute with "every flower / planted for my father" (AR 21). In "Paradise," "Lover of Flowers," and "Yellow Dahlia," the speaker discredits flowers as an elegiac lexicon associated with a female version of mourning. They are the sister's terms for remembering a father who prefers the strong, silent type of his firstborn.

In "Paradise," Glück connects her personal suffering with images from Genesis (2:22–24). The biblical reference augments her theory of love as a scarce resource that involves splitting the self in half to make room for the life of the other. Referring to how Adam created Eve ("bone from my bones / flesh from my flesh!"), she explores the link between suffering and the conception of "another person." Her antinatural birth image features a male progenitor and a female creation of his own independent generation.

Birth and maternity are further developed in another flower poem, "Brown Circle." Set at the midpoint of *Ararat,* at the book's emotional center, "Brown Circle" connects a botanist's examination of a flower to the mother's concerns. She has transmitted her distress to the next generation through an excessive degree of attention for his safety:

> I thought I'd be
> the lover of orchids who finds
> red trillium growing
> in the pine shade, and doesn't
> touch it, doesn't need
> to possess it. What I am
> is the scientist,
> who comes to that flower
> with a magnifying glass
> and doesn't leave, though
> the sun burns a brown
> circle of grass around
> the flower. (AR 42)

Glück revises prior versions of her persona in this poem. First, she replaces an affection for something that is bold, showy, and extravagant (the orchids) for something that is relatively commonplace and yet hidden in the darkness (the trillium in the pine shade). Then the typical Glück persona is figured in "Brown Circle" through the scientist's resistance to "touch" or "possess" the flower. Here, however, she is no longer that remote individual who can express love through detachment. In this poem she claims that the metaphor of the self as clinician is a mask, but one with too many openings for it to contain the intensity of her expression. The veneer of professional scrutiny can hardly be said to veil the speaker's wish to hold onto the object of affection and never let go. Through a poem about clinical relationships to nature, Glück recasts her own image as a daughter, a parent, and a poet whose work has been defined (by Robert Shaw) as "classically severe."[4]

Far from being one who can resist the desire to possess her discovery, the scientist's fascination with nature proves destructive to the object of affection. She burns the flowers she so admired, by illuminating them through the distortion of a microscopic amplification. Glück is offering a confession. The veil of indifference to life and her expressed affection for "endings" (she is, if nothing else, the poet of comprehension, of conclusions) masks her love of life and hatred of endings. In this case she is confessing her unwillingness to let Noah grow up, change, become part of the great circle of life. She is also expressing a fear. Her refusal to relinquish possession of him will do damage to him. We must remember that we have been reading poems such as "Paradise" in which a daughter has not found it so easy to declare her independence from her father's legacy.

In these poems Glück is trying to define her own "human nature" as much as she is exploring her relationship to a natural setting. In the volume's final poem, "First Memory," the speaker in effect lifts the mask of her typical persona and admits that her "human nature" involves the capacity to love. Her admission suggests she has remained vulnerable to the losses characterizing this volume, in which mortality is highlighted. "Brown Circle" expresses her awareness that converting a part of nature into a cultural artifact may prove a dangerous act of conservation, both for the author and for her subject. Her exploitation of nature as a literary symbol destroys the object of attention by rendering it inert. Glück suggests in *Ararat* that a literary reading of nature is inadequate and even dangerous.

Ararat connects planting flowers and sowing seeds to a symbolic landscape that includes burying family members at a cemetery named Mount Ararat. The cemetery name suggests human rebirth through a covenant forged between God and the Jews. In the poem "Mount Ararat," the speaker

4. Robert B. Shaw, "Review of *The Triumph of Achilles,*" in *Poetry* 148.1 (April 1986): 42.

anticipates the primary speech act of *The Wild Iris.* She prays that Yahweh will preserve the son's life, a theme she has already connected to the language of flowers in "Brown Circle." Speaking of her father, she writes that God "doesn't hesitate to take / a son from a mother," but she also calls upon God to conclude a cycle of sacrificial violence by sparing her son (AR 30). A nature poem with theological implications, "Mount Ararat" turns the organic image of burying the speaker's father into an exploration of the ancient belief in blood sacrifice as a sign of faithfulness to God. In the Akedah (Genesis 22), Abraham avoids sacrificing his son when he notices out of the corner of his eye the ram caught in the thicket. A scapegoat, a non-human part of nature, may serve as a substitute victim. In "Mount Ararat," Glück imagines human death as a sacrifice, but no part of nature may stand in the way of a cycle of violence perpetrated by a ruthless god.

"Mount Ararat" describes a daughter's grief over her father, a sister's grief over the death of a sibling, and a mother's anguish for the safety of her son. Foreshadowing *The Wild Iris,* "Mount Ararat" is a prayer to the Jewish God, who the speaker believes exacts death in exchange for allegiance. Admitting her ambivalence, the speaker states quite openly that it was "a relief to bury an adult, / someone remote, like my father." She hopes that his death, associated with God's vengeance and the organic cycle of life her father found intolerable, could be interpreted as "a sign that maybe the debt's finally been paid" (AR 30). The image recalls "All Hallows," where the speaker must extend her hand as if "in payment" to become a singer with a soul. It also recalls her attitude toward writing as an unending scene of unfulfilled yearning because on further reflection, she does not "believe" that "the debt" will ever be paid. Her "relief" connects her interpretation of her father as an emotional invalid to her image of God as a silent and remote figure in *The Wild Iris.* In "Snow" she presents the father holding his daughter on top of his shoulders "so he couldn't see me" (AR 58).

As in her response to the sister's language of flowers in *Ararat,* Glück's speaker in *The Wild Iris* will announce an intimate, yet remote connection to the father through nature imagery. In effect, the flowers that address the world to which they have awakened after burial speak both to the father and from the father's position. A polyvalent meditation on doubt and prayer comparable to religious lyrics in the English tradition (exemplified by George Herbert), *The Wild Iris* continues to enact Glück's quest for control over her father's memory through the language of flowers. She ambivalently turns a part of nature into a cultural sign of yearning, in order to communicate with her father through the language of the distressed supplicant. By vocalizing flowers in *The Wild Iris,* Glück once again attempts to assert control over the flowers her sister planted as a form of commemorative language in "Yellow Dahlia" and "Lover of Flowers." Instead of confronting the loss of her father directly, as she does in *Ararat,* however, in *The Wild Iris* the speaker sublimates her grief over his death. She turns her attention to a nature study with religious implications. Primarily composed as a series of morning and evening prayers, often spoken by floral personae, Glück displaces her desire to communicate with her father by trying to address God, a symbolic father. In *The Wild Iris,* she links the seasonal changes evident in the garden to the ebb and flow of the speaker's hope to communicate with the real or imagined father, whom she tried to mourn in *Ararat* by denying the language of flowers its power.

Chapter Eight

Errand in the Spiritual Wilderness

The Wild Iris as Contemporary Prayer Sequence

Recalling the nature lyrics in *The House on Marshland* as well as the mourning of a daughter for her father in *Ararat* while also anticipating the "high-low" experiment of *Meadowlands,* Glück in *The Wild Iris* coordinates an eclectic grab bag of multicultural resources. She transforms these resources into a series of meditative religious poems, in which (following Wordsworth) the main human speaker experiences intimations of immortality, not a profound overwhelming vision. *The Wild Iris* marks a structural advance in Glück's career, as the author transforms the sequential gathering of related lyrics into a polyphonic theater.

She achieves this by allowing the author's persona to become assembled, disassembled, and reassembled into parts, thus fragmenting the speaker's "self" into three distinct categories. Her lyricists include a Yahweh-type God, who often speaks as a phenomenon of natural force through the "voice of nature" in poems such as "Retreating Wind"; the poet-gardener and religious suppliant; and the unusually vocal set of roses, daisies, violets, irises, poppies, ground cover, and one flowering tree, which represent the vegetative natural world. Although *The Wild Iris* is a heteroglossic text, Linda Gregerson rightly notes that the three main personae each "speak with the voice of the human; the human writer has no other voice to give them."[1] Glück divides the lyric self into parts, but each of these parts speaks in the same voice, as the author fashions different masks to open up reflections on mortality in the context of individuality.

From a Bloomian perspective, *The Wild Iris* concerns Glück's struggle to assert the independence of her voice and vision, in a context that depends on

1. Linda Gregerson, "The Sower against Gardens," *Kenyon Review* 23.1 (Winter 2001): 115–33 (117).

maintaining a conversation with God—the greater creative force that exists outside the domain of self and that, as in the Old Testament tradition, is characterized mostly through voice. In "Retreating Wind," this divine voice chastises the human speaker for what He considers her unreasonable demand, her desire for "the one gift / reserved for another creation" (WI 15). What could this "one gift" be? Immortality? A cyclical rebirth, like the rhizomatic iris with its bulb that grows, pollinates until a seed falls, and then appears to the human speaker to regenerate from the same bulb, giving the impression of the same flower? The speaker's agon with the divine force—that speaks (as in Job) as a wind—is especially prominent in her desire to set herself free from a domineering Jewish God, but only by invoking His covering powers, only by revealing her dependence on God as the object of her desires for recognition and rebirth through the apostrophic addresses to the "You," or "Dear Father." Her critical dialog with God at once critiques and affirms the influence of what Bloom calls *The Book of J* (or portions of the Old Testament authored by the "J" writer who refers to God as Yahweh), by putting Yahweh on trial. The gardener-supplicant indicts the sacred as "insufficient, limiting, or oppressive" (as Margaret Ann Gordon put it).[2] He is "limiting," but in the sense that Bloom associates with the "Covering Cherub," or figure of creative anxiety who blocks "a new voice from entering the Poet's Paradise," in part by making "writings into Scriptures."[3]

Glück's Yahweh is a paternalistic and yet creative force whose grand but perishable natural display competes for attention with the gardener-poet's "bouquet" of lyrics. Yahweh seems to cover "everything that nature itself covers" from the "richness of the earth" to "the Way to the Tree of Life."[4] At times "jealous" (or zealous of divine sovereignty), Glück's God displays "anger" at the foibles and narcissism of His human creation. He exists as a kind of remote, aloof, first mover in the tradition of Maimonides. Lacking compassion for the uniqueness of the suffering and yearning for affection experienced by the supplicant, Yahweh blocks the speaker from experiencing the realm of the spirit. "The language of the Judeo-Christian tradition in fact prevents her from communicating with the immanent sacred," writes Gordon.[5] The strained attempts at dialog between gardener-supplicant and divine figure in *The Wild Iris* testify to Glück's struggle for the text, her expression of a desire to base her authorial self on commentary that challenges her felt need to maintain distinctiveness.

2. Gordon, "Reconceiving the Sacred," 110.
3. Bloom, *Anxiety of Influence,* 35.
4. Ibid., 38.
5. Gordon, "Reconceiving the Sacred," 110.

Besides imagining Yahweh, Glück enacts narrative motifs, themes, and characters found in the Jewish Bible. The fact that Glück's human speaker is cast as a gardener as well as a religious supplicant suggests she has chosen to imitate God's first act after Creation—planting the Garden of Eden (Genesis 2.8). In flower poems such as "The Gold Lily," the gardener is addressed as if she were a masculine paternal God, by a speaker whose color is associated with beauty, rarity, monetary value, and durability. A poem that exists on the knife edge between a nakedly autobiographical utterance, by a speaker facing death, and a clever conceit, "The Gold Lily" represents the lily's experience in a way that mirrors on the earthly plane the conflicts and confusions that arise between the human speaker, who seems vividly aware that one's mortality is inescapable, and the ineffable sky God, accused of being a failed creator:

> I call you,
> father and master: all around,
> my companions are failing, thinking
> you do not see. How
> can they know you see
> unless you save us?
> In the summer twilight, are you
> close enough to hear
> your child's terror? Or
> are you not my father,
> you who raised me? (WI 62)

In its morning and evening prayer poems, *The Wild Iris* resonates with the Jewish Bible through the Garden story of paradise and expulsion in Genesis, the suffering of Job, the comparisons that can be made with the Psalms of David, and the allusions to Moses and the story of the Burning Bush. But Glück's struggle for control of her text is especially apparent in the way she imagines Yahweh's rhetoric, as when He speaks to the supplicant in "Harvest" in a blunt tone mixing contempt and pity:

> Look at you, blindly clinging to earth
> as though it were the vineyards of heaven
> while the fields go up in flames around you—
> . . . .
> how many times must I destroy my own creation
> to teach you
> this is your punishment:

with one gesture I established
in time and in paradise. (WI 46)

This deity calls to mind Yahweh, whom Brown rightly characterizes as "the voice of the master creator, the First Poet, whose disappointment in his vision, his flawed creation suggests, moreover, his own failings, omniscient creative power having been mistakenly equated in the poet's mind with perfection."[6]

God in *The Wild Iris* at times resembles Yahweh's more primitive aspects, but here again we should be careful to observe Glück's ecumenical relationship to religious discourse, even to differing Jewish conceptions of God. The personal God in "Harvest" is precisely the one rejected by Spinoza, and replaced with the numinist idea of God as identical with the totality of nature. Throughout *The Wild Iris* numinism will compete for Glück's attention with the strident tones of the personal God who chastises her alter ego in poems such as "Harvest." Discussing the Renaissance tradition of "accommodation," in which divinity is "clothed in earthly garments" (as in poems such as "Clear Morning" and "End of Winter"), Gregerson points out that "the God-voiced poems take their titles from the saturating conditions of nature: weather, season, the qualities of wind or light."[7] Although the titles of the poems connect God to nature, Glück's speakers seek to rise above the material world to experience a sense of permanence.

In "a lady's garden," the long-stemmed free-standing flower with fernlike leaves known as Jacob's Ladder reaches from outside the "porch window" to address the gardener-poet, figured here as a lovesick lady inside her bedroom crying. A love poem that one critic has associated with the troubadour tradition, "The Jacob's Ladder" also illustrates the larger religious theme of *The Wild Iris,* which is how an earthbound speaker wishes for transcendence, even as she wants to partake of what the Jacob's Ladder flower refers to as another kind of "knowledge of paradise," the fleshly realm, in which "men and women seem / to desire each other" as much as this flower desires to arrest the attention of the sad lady in the bedroom:

6. Brown, "Love of Form," 83. Brown continues: "The harvest recalls every year the story of the expulsion from the Garden, a myth that has long fascinated the poet. Trapped both in time and in paradise, those who inhabit and tend the garden participate in its yearly rituals, mistaking eternal recurrence for timeless eternity. But the poet-gardener knows better, she knows that the condition of being human is expulsion—from the womb, from continuity, from wholeness" (90).

7. Gregerson, "The Sower against Gardens," 116.

Trapped in the earth,
wouldn't you too want to go
to heaven? I live
in a lady's garden. Forgive me, lady;
longing has taken my grace. I am
not what you wanted. But
as men and women seem
to desire each other, I too desire
knowledge of paradise—and now
your grief, a naked stem
reaching the porch window.
And at the end, what? A small blue flower
like a star. Never
to leave the world! Is this
not what your tears mean? (WI 24)

"Trapped in the earth," the Jacob's Ladder experiences a longing to "want to go / to heaven," where it would seek "knowledge of paradise" (WI 24), but paradise turns out to be a form of erotic desire located in the lady's bedroom.

The fact that the flower is granted consciousness, possesses a voice, and displays an emotional range that includes the wish for transcendence—as well as an awareness of the gardener's paradoxical urge both to experience human love and to transcend her body—suggests how freely Glück mixes immanent and transcendent conceptions of divinity. The flower's namesake recalls the ladder, with angels trafficking both up and down its rungs, that Jacob imagined in a dream when he slept with his head on a rock on his journey toward Haran at Bethel, "the house of God" (Genesis 28:10–22). In Genesis, Jacob hears the voice of a Personal God who agrees to be "with you" and who "will protect you wherever you go." Jacob's God, who establishes a covenant, mirrors Glück ambivalent relationship to the values of earth and sky, of body and spirit, in *The Wild Iris.*

Other poems with flower-speakers, such as "Scilla" (WI 14), mock the poet-gardener for fantasizing about an exclusive relationship to a Personal God. The flowers believe that nature is all of holiness, and that claims to uniqueness suggest the sin of pride:

Not I, you idiot, not self, but we, we—waves
of sky blue like
a critique of heaven: why
do you treasure your voice
when to be one thing

is to be next to nothing?
Why do you look up? To hear
an echo like the voice
of god? You are all the same to us,
solitary, standing about us, planning
your silly lives: you go
where you are sent, like all things,
where the wind plants you,
one or another of you forever
looking down and seeing some image
of water, and hearing what? Waves,
and over waves, birds singing. (WI 14)

One of fourteen flower-speakers that appear throughout the volume, as if the wind had scattered them into various positions, Scilla, which speaks as if it were part of the chorus in a Greek tragic theater, represents a pagan perspective in which the spirits or gods are believed to inhabit places or things.

We may also associate "the wind" with the symbolic expression of God's agency. In the Pentecostal tradition, for example, the Holy Spirit comes down on the Holy Disciple in tongues of fire and with the sound of a rushing mighty wind. In Genesis, God speaks to Moses in a tempest that breaks up the rocks, appearing as a "still, small voice." Scilla speaks on behalf of the collective existence of all natural things, manifesting the will of a divine force that dictates, as does the wind, where the seeds will be planted and where the flowers will emerge in the spring. The poet-gardener's desire for individuality, for a unique presence, for some signal from God that her suffering is meaningful, seems ludicrous from the communal perspective voiced by Scilla.

In "Witchgrass," Glück imagines an unsung part of uncultivated nature. A weedy field, the witchgrass endures—without reference to God's "wind," to infuse its lowly being with spirit, or to the gardener's "praise," as a figure for the author's words, which cultivate nature for her own purposes throughout the volume:

I don't need your praise
to survive. I was here first,
before you were here, before
you ever planted a garden.
And I'll be here when only the sun and moon
are left, and the sea, and the wide field.

I will constitute the field. (WI 23)

In "Witchgrass," Glück offers priority to, as well as a kind of immortality to, the grass that bears a name associated with the excluded—because feminist, immanent, and pagan—tradition that classical Judaism wished to supplant. In Gordon's terms, she "explicitly indicts patriarchal religious discourse as conflating women and nature, demonizing them both."[8]

While Glück may yearn to invoke a female-centered pagan tradition, and by so doing to lay claim to a source of religious power that preceded Judaism, she nonetheless associates the field with the tribe of Jews:

> If you hate me so much
> don't bother to give me
> a name: do you need
> one more slur
> in your language, another
> way to blame
> one tribe for everything— (WI 22)

Instead of associating the covenantal relationship between Yahweh and the Israelites as a source of protection from foreign adversaries, Glück interprets Yahweh as the dangerous adversary and the Jewish tribe as His special victims. God's power to name becomes an exertion of control through what Althusser refers to as "interpellation." God's covenant involves scapegoating and sacrifice, not a recognition of the significance of His creation. From a Bloomian perspective, Glück is swerving, reducing, and correcting Judaism through daemonization, surpassing the master text through a return to other, earlier sources of inspiration.

Although I join many other readers in identifying the "you" to whom the supplicant offers her apostrophes as Yahweh, *The Wild Iris* draws upon a mosaic of sources as diverse and yet related as Puritanism, Catholicism, Judaism, Romanticism, and Modernism. As Ann Townsend argues, Glück's plain style alludes to the Puritan idiom of George Herbert. In poems such as "Jordan (II)" and "Love (III)," the plain style teaches us that the poet has been "touched by the direct hand (or voice) of God: Herbert is one of the chosen, the elect, and the clarity . . . seeks to erase all that came before, all the rampant language that 'sprout[s] and swell[s]' in a kind of poetic pride."[9] We may go along with Townsend and connect in a rough sense Glück's lan-

8. Gordon, "Reconceiving the Sacred," 137.

9. Ann Townsend, "The Problem of Sincerity: The Lyric Plain Style of George Herbert and Louise Glück," *Shenandoah* 46.4 (Winter 1996): 47.

guage to the yearning for salvation expressed within the sixteenth-century English religious lyric. Glück, however, does not narrate the story of her election as one chosen for salvation, as does Herbert in "Love (III)."

Glück shows her debt to Catholicism through the sequencing of prayer poems in *The Wild Iris.* She does not follow in the poetic tradition of invoking the "aubade," or dawn poem, in which, as John Drury reminds us, "the lover—Romeo, for example—bids farewell to his beloved," and "nocturne," a musical form belonging to the evening. Instead, Glück announces the repetition of the temporal occasions for the gardener-poet's utterances through the arrangement of public worship laid down by the Catholic Church. The titles of seventeen of the poems in this book follow the liturgical setup of the Hours, that is Roman Catholic morning and evening prayer rituals—or Matins (seven poems) and Vespers (ten poems).

In its spare diction, Protestant; in its overall prayer, format Catholic; in its representations of God as immanent and transcendent, personal and numinous, and in its speaker's alienation from the garden setting, Jewish, *The Wild Iris* also resonates on a narrative level with the Eleusian mystery cult through the story of descent and return via the Homeric Hymn of Persephone and Demeter, which Glück also commented upon in "Pomegranate" (HM). In *The Wild Iris,* the overall account of flowers is infused by the grain goddess Persephone's cycle of descent to Hades and ascent for two-thirds of the year back to Earth to ameliorate the suffering of her grieving mother, Demeter, and so to allow the crops to grow again. As was the case with "The Jacob's Ladder," the flowers experience a kind of death-in-life, upon burial as seeds or bulbs in the soil; then they express a yearning for an emergence as flowers, in a transcendence of the horrendous situation of being conscious of one's burial. As Brown points out, the initial lyric, "The Wild Iris," suggests the Persephone myth. It describes a soul that recalls the terror of surviving its harrowing journey to the underworld as a "consciousness / buried in the dark earth" that will then raise itself up to speak as a soul that has found its embodiment, in the final stanza when, in a sublime flourish, "from the center of my life came / a great fountain, deep blue / shadows on azure seawater" (WI 1).

To this eccentric blend of religious and mythic combinations, I must add to the list Glück's debt to Romanticism, especially the invocation of God via a celebration of natural cycles, and the meditative strain of modernism, as found in lyrics by Wallace Stevens. Like poems from Glück's cycle such as "Heaven and Earth" (WI 32) and the fourth "Vespers," Stevens's "Sunday Morning" represents a meditative and solitary female speaker who ponders the relative merits of an emphasis on the limited pleasures of this world against the potentially limitless but possibly fallacious merits of the next.[10] A prayerlike book, *The Wild Iris* at the same time expresses a greater confidence in the creative powers of the lyric speaker than it does in God's omnipotence—suggesting a debt to Milton's Satan in *Paradise Lost,* which Bloom reads "as an allegory of the dilemma of the modern poet, at his strongest."[11]

Given its hybridity, *The Wild Iris* may be read as a contemporary manifestation of the Jewish American dilemma of betweenness, of being neither here nor there in terms of cultural indebtedness and affiliation. Stephen Fredman in a recent study has demonstrated that liminality creates both tension and poignancy in the poetry of Charles Reznikoff, the influential Jewish American objectivist, with debts to both Hellenic and Hebraic culture.[12] The anxious condition of being what the poet Carol Muske in her reading of Glück calls "human, split, dichotomized" may in part be a judgment on the poet's station as commentator, who draws, like a postmodern pastiche artist, from diametrically opposed or clashing cultural, aesthetic, and religious traditions.[13] The position of cultural and philosophical magpie makes the lyric speaker in *The Wild Iris* seem frustratingly insecure about her stance on metaphysical and ontological issues. Her ecumenical theology makes the volume as a whole seem off-kilter in terms of its tripartite lyric posture. At the same time, the multiple perspectives on the speaker's condition, pivoting between skepticism, dread, and faith, lend to the volume its dynamic texture as a meditative debate focusing on the unsolvable mysteries of ultimate meaning.

Glück's polyvalence in *The Wild Iris* provides a response to the Scilla flower critique of the gardener-poet's emphasis on individuality—"why / do you treasure your voice / when to be one thing / is to be next to nothing?" (WI 14). Through dialogism and the fragmentation of the self into parts, Glück, ironically, maintains a degree of subjectivity and aesthetic control over her composition. At the same time, she avoids being trapped into placing her main speaker within a specific religious discourse, and she also avoids the self's being limited and contained within the discourse of identity politics. Loosely borrowing frames of reference from so many traditions, the book registers the contours of a representative spiritual struggle undertaken by an unstable self whose voice remains apparent throughout the sequence. The

10. Wallace Stevens, "Sunday Morning," in Ramazani et al., *Norton Anthology* 1:239.

11. In *Anxiety of Influence,* 20, Bloom wrote: "Satan is that modern poet, while God is his dead but still embarrassingly potent and present ancestor. . . . The incarnation of the Poetic Character in Satan begins when Milton's story truly begins, with the Incarnation of God's Son and Satan's rejection of that incarnation. Modern poetry begins in two declarations of Satan: 'We know no time when we were not as now' and 'To be weak is miserable, doing or suffering.'

12. Fredman, *Menorah for Athena.*

13. Carol Muske, "The Wild Iris," *American Poetry Review* 22.1 (January–February 1993): 54.

desire for salvation seems elusive, because the gardener-poet is determined to distinguish herself from her interlocutor, Yahweh, and because she also rejects an association with the common lot of flowers, which recognize their vulnerability as mutable beings subject to the whim of the wind, or God's seed planting (as in "Scilla").

Glück as lyricist abandons the confessional ethos of the individual voice as stable, univocal, transparent.[14] Instead of a unified subjectivity, her speaker becomes in *The Wild Iris* a ventriloquist with a range of subject positions, including her invocation of both the spiritual and material elements of what is nonhuman. Like a contemporary queer theorist such as Judith Butler, Glück in *The Wild Iris* does not wish to stabilize or consolidate the self into a single category of being. In fact, her lyric sequence comes to question the idea of a stable identity category for the speaker. Instead, she imagines the self as unruly, as crossing the border between the human and the not human, as under construction, and in a state of becoming.[15]

As the title indicates, *The Wild Iris* concerns uncultivated flowers. The iris is also a religious symbol that by itself suggests the author's figurative interpretation of nature as a medium for self-reflection and metaphysical speculation. Muske reminds us that "iris" in Latin means "rainbow"; it is also the rainbow goddess "whose prism-bridge connects sky and earth."[16] Brown reminds us that Jung notes how the iris (also known as "the messenger of God") is particularly important for an understanding of the alchemical process, "since the integration of all colours points, as it were, to a coming of God, or even to his presence."[17]

The iris is also the colorful part of the eye, which is integral to focusing and seeing. Iris as eye-focus is a symbol for how the speaker constructs meaning by reflecting on nature (the wild) through the instruments of imagination the iris represents: theology, language, and the subjective experience of human vision. Brown hypothesizes that, because the iris of the eye controls the amount of light passing through the pupil, we may connect voice and iris as mediators between image and thought. Discussing "The Wild Iris," the first flower-speaker of the volume, Brown describes the growth of the wild iris (Blue Flag), which flourishes without human cultivation, as an "allegory of renewed poetic vision, and of the liberation of a voice."[18]

14. Townsend, "Problem of Sincerity," 51.
15. I would like to thank Minrose Gwin for helping me to understand the intricacies of queer theory.
16. Muske, "Wild Iris," 52.
17. Brown, "Love of Form," 8, citing Jung, 288.
18. Brown, "Love of Form," 78.

In Exodus the Jews must journey into the wilderness to enter a covenant with Yahweh, who is responsible for their liberation from slavery in Egypt under Pharaoh. Since the wild zone that exists in between the sites of persecution and freedom is where the Torah was given to Moses, can we not link part of Glück's Jewishness in *The Wild Iris* to her association of meaningful prayer with being in the wild, or the wilderness? We could say that the "I" and the "eye" of this poet's "iris" are related in sound and sense to the adjective "wild." The speaker exists in a state of nature, but she could also be called wild because her vision is turbulent, passionate, and transgressive. She goes beyond the normal bounds of social constraint that ordinarily demarcate the realms of the human, the natural, and the divine.

A Reading of *The Wild Iris* as a Fragmented Prayer Sequence

Glück amplifies, complicates, and destabilizes the lyric form by interweaving poems spoken from the perspective of a single human speaker with other poems that offer her replies from the perspectives of flowers and a version of God. These alternative voices perform their own commentaries on the speaker's lyric project. They critique the ambitions of an authorial self who wants to transcend the mutability of embodied life.[19] Glück also expands the lyric form by tracing the gardener-poet's morning and evening prayers as these apostrophes take place at different times of the day and in the course of a gardening season. She negotiates lyrical intensity with a narrative sweep through intriguing vignettes grouped under the stable headings of Matins and Vespers.

Close readings of the seven morning poems and then the ten evening poems show how various lyrics within the sequence focus on the speaker's faith. They self-critique her hubristic desires for absolute knowledge of divine power, existential fear, anger, and sense of creative liberation (as these mixed emotions follow God's silence when she calls to her Maker and does not receive an answer), and confidence in her own creative endeavor in the face of radical doubts about God's existence, except in an unfathomable realm that exists beyond language, difference, figuration, nature, and human understanding.

19. As Gordon notes: "The poems alternate between the voices, as we see in the cycle that begins the collection: first a flower speaker ('The Wild Iris'), followed by two prayer poems (titled 'Matins,' as are all the prayers of the first half of the collection), then three flower speakers ('Trillium,' 'Lamium,' and 'Snowdrops'), followed by three 'replies' to the prayers ('Clear Morning,' 'Spring Snow,' and 'End of Winter')." Gordon, "Reconceiving the Sacred," 120.

Through the restricted yet malleable format of a morning and evening prayer cycle, Glück can focus on the gardener-poet's unfulfilled spiritual desires, her yearning for affection, as her moods shift during the day, and in the gardener's different seasons of cultivation, fruition, aftermath, and desire for renewal after her withering garden has, metaphorically, suggested the limits to any human endeavor. Through the stability afforded by the conventional format, she can address a mysterious, possibly fictive, and yet at times intimate figure of divinity known variously as "you," as "Father," or as "Dear Friend." The "you" could refer to Yahweh, to the author's father (whose death, burial, and commemoration as flowers was chronicled in *Ararat*), to the reader, or to the authorial self (if the series is taken to be an extended interior monologue).

Ironically, Glück achieves a poignant tone and narrative dynamism in "Matins" and "Vespers" through the solid-state format, which replaces an established prosodic form, a linear plot line, and a consistent system of allusions to classical literature and myth as a disciplined idiom for identity construction. Her prayer-poems instead correspond to her varying perceptions of nature and to the changes of her moods. Her petitions to God pivot from tones of exultation to tones of desolation and collapse, sometimes within the limited space of a single lyric. The consistent but shifting format enables readers to chart a speaker's volatile emotional course—in the same way a photograph would if taken of the same person standing in the same place but at different times of the day and over several months. Like snapshots of internal states of mind and emotion, or (as in Dickinson's Master Letters) like entries from a diary of religious yearning, the poems intimate the paradoxical appearance of God as silent, invisible, and, just possibly, as immanent through the dynamic contours of nature as it changes from periods of growth to fruition to diminution to potential renewal.[20]

Matins

The first "Matins" begins the sequence of morning prayers on an awkward note.[21] The speaker must defend her project to herself, because her

20. Glück implies that God appears as a fleeting aspect of nature, through the titles of the poems in which God "replies": "Clear Morning," "Spring Snow," "End of Winter," "Retreating Wind," "The Garden," "April," "Midsummer," "End of Summer," "Early Darkness," "Harvest," "Retreating Light," "Sunset," and "September Twilight." Ibid.

21. For the sake of argumentational clarity, I will be numbering the matins and the vespers, but Glück does not do so, suggesting that she is encouraging readers to understand the prayers as occurring at once simultaneously and also existing in narrative time. We might consider her

son has offered a psychological interpretation of her motives even before the book has begun to take shape:

> Noah says
> depressives hate the spring, imbalance
> between the inner and the outer world. I make
> another case—being depressed, yes, but in a sense
> passionately
> attached to the living tree, my body
> actually curled in the split trunk, almost at peace,
> in the evening rain
> almost able to feel
> sap frothing and rising: Noah says this is
> an error of depressives, identifying
> with a tree, whereas the happy heart
> wanders the garden like a falling leaf, a figure for
> the part, not the whole. (WI 2)

If read generously, as it is by Gordon, the speaker's aspiration for connectedness to a part of nature could be viewed as demonstrating the "I-Thou" relationship described by the Jewish theologian Martin Buber.

> If will and grace are joined . . . as I contemplate the tree I am drawn into a relation, and the tree ceases to be an It. The power of exclusiveness has seized me.[22]

But Noah is not reading generously. A study in the contrasting perspectives of youth and age, Noah reads his mother's wish to find God in nature, not as an example of numinism but as a sign of her insecurity, a sign of the fact that unlike her he's comfortable merely being a part of the whole picture, comfortable going with the flow. For Noah, the mother's projection onto the tree stems from the depressive's aspiration to connect to a complete and rooted part of nature, to not let go. He argues that she cannot accept comparisons with an aspect of nature that is partial, shifting, and subject to constant change, such as a floating leaf. Noah abhors her failure to accept

---

combination of temporal movement and structural repetition to be an example of "Jewish" time, in which the contemporary Jew repeats in the present tense the archetypal experiences narrated in the Torah.

22. Gordon, "Reconceiving the Sacred," 128.

mortality, because she refuses to embrace natural declension in a seasonal cycle in exchange for the privilege of being alive, but Glück's main speaker sees her attachment to nature differently. She is depressed, yes, and as a meditative poet, obsessively preoccupied with mortality, but at the same time she is "passionately / attached to the living tree," which in the poem rhymes with "my body" (WI 2). Like a figure from Ovid, she reacts to nature in such an intense way that when it does speak to her, she imagines her body "actually curled in the split [tree] trunk, almost at peace, in the evening rain / almost able to feel / sap frothing and rising" (WI 2). Like the rebukes of the flowers and God in subsequent lyrics, her son's words suggest the speaker's isolation from those around her, as well as the combative environment in which she must defend herself. Noah, like God and the flowers, seems to want to control her actions by labeling her. Like Yahweh, Noah seems insensitive to her struggle to find meaning in nature through a kind of radical intensity. Recalling his psychological interpretation of her "identifying / with a tree," the gardener-poet expresses reservations about her invocation of the affective fallacy.

Perhaps responding to Noah's doubts about her task of establishing personal stability through natural metaphors emphasizing divinity rather than mortality, the second "Matins" expresses the speaker's own uncertainty about her figurative conception of nature. She approaches God through prayers based on natural imagery, which at first sounds like numinism, but when addressing the "Unreachable father" she invokes the Garden narrative of alienation from Yahweh and expulsion from nature, where God "drove out the man; and He placed at the east of the Garden of Eden the cheribum, and the flaming sword which turned every which way, to keep the way to the tree of life" (Genesis 3:24):

> Unreachable father, when we were first
> exiled from heaven, you made
> a replica, a place in one sense
> different from heaven, being
> designed to teach a lesson:
> . . . .
>   Left alone,
> we exhausted each other. Years
> of darkness followed. (WI 3)

Speaking as "We," the gardener-poet states that human beings "were learning to worship" God in absentia, but this merely replicates on another level the scarce economy of affection, foiled desires, and tight-lipped attitudes that Glück has chronicled in her personal books. Her comment "We never thought of you / whom we were learning to worship. / We merely knew it wasn't human nature to love / only what returns love" (WI 3) suggests a connection between this speaker and God as "Unreachable father" and the daughter-father relationship set up in *Ararat.*

In spite of the son's criticism, and her own reservations about projecting symbolic meaning onto nature in the second "Matins," Glück's tone gains assurance in the two prayer poems that follow. She accepts the manyness and the oneness in nature as a divine paradox. She addresses God as a personal figure, but at the same time reconvenes her focus on nature as illustrative of God's appearance in various guises, in the third and fourth "Matins."

The third "Matins" begins with the speaker's declaration of love for the powerful "you." With self-abasement, she addresses her listener as if her religious drive were connected to her being in a state of protracted childhood, in need of parental comfort. Driven by fear, weakness, and panic at the unimaginable character but influential stature of Yahweh, the gardener-poet asserts her willingness to exchange freedom for comfort. At the same time, she expresses her desire for authority over her text, by interrogating her love for a God that she cannot "conceive" (in the sense of giving birth to, but also of imagining) as subject to her own linguistic domain: "I cannot love / what I can't conceive, and you disclose / virtually nothing" (WI 12). The complex tone resembles a strained love lyric between the speaker and the beloved, a God, parent, or unreachable lover—whom she criticizes for being coy, for failing to appear without various floral masks as the vehicle for sincere expression. (We may recall that in "Birthday" [AR], the speaker aligned herself with her father's criticism of the gift of flowers to the mother, as a gaudy display of emotion that masks insincerity.)

> You must see
> it is useless to us, this silence that promotes belief
> you must be all things, the foxglove and the hawthorn tree,
> the vulnerable rose and tough daisy—we are left to think
> you couldn't possibly exist. (WI 12)

The gardener-poet may be teasingly playful about God's infusion in nature, but she interprets His silence as obfuscation: "inconsistent, first springing up / a pink spike on the slope behind the daisies, / and the next year, purple in the rose garden" (WI 12).

Impatient, the speaker concludes with more questions than answers about the proof of God's existence, as it is either illustrated in or covered over by nature's silence and variety:

> Is this
> what you mean us to think, does this explain
> the silence of the morning,
> the crickets not yet rubbing their wings, the cats
> not fighting in the yard? (WI 12)

The poem ends with a question mark, even as she interprets God's silence as a meaningful absence—or a sign, as in Levinasian theology—of God's absolute unlikeness from anything as perishable as a human being. For Levinas, God's resistance to any attempt by human beings to conceive of Him in totality is the mark of God's infinity. In "Clear Morning," one of God's "reply" poems, the divine speaker seems to assert God's incomprehensibility, what Levinas would call His "infinite" and untotalizable otherness, as signs of the difference between human and sacred:

> I've submitted to your preferences, observing
> patiently
> the things you love, speaking
>
> through vehicles only, in
> details of earth, as you prefer,
>
> . . . .
> you would never accept
>
> a voice like mine, indifferent
> to the objects you busily name,
>
> . . . .
> I cannot go on
> restricting myself to images
>
> because you think it is your right
> to dispute my meaning. (WI 7–8)

Descending to a quotidian realm from the steep and icy peak of metaphysical interrogation, in the third "Matins," she settles down to admire the momentary tranquility discoverable in the suburban setting with its cats at peace in the yard. Even here she cannot resist upping the ontological stakes, especially when she reads the lack of conflict in the domesticated version of the animal world as signs that may be interpreted as figures of a higher order of peace.

Building upon her observation in the third "Matins" that divinity is imbued in the variety and particularity of nature, in the foxgloves and the hawthorn tree, the gardener-poet steps out of her role as supplicant to summarize her confusion about the function of prayer thus far—and to continue to speculate about the nature of God as an absent presence who is desirable because not forthcoming. "I see it is with you as with the birches: / I am not to speak to you / in the personal way." She wonders. How can her language be at once an act of communication, dependent upon the response of a presumed listener, and also an independent monologue, performed without a specific audience in mind? Is there in fact an audience beyond the self to respond to her doubts? Is her doubt about God's existence necessary for her to prove how genuine is a supplicant's faith? If so, the unfulfilled desire to know God seems a necessary posture for an author trying to fashion her self through her relationship to God in the form of prayer. "Much / has passed between us. Or / was it always only / on the one side?" (WI 13). *The Wild Iris* is not meant to answer such questions, but to allow the reader to witness an account of a speaker wrestling with issues of ultimate meaning with a seriousness that some contemporary readers might find hopelessly old-fashioned.

Frustrated by God's "absence / of all feeling, of the least / concern for me," the gardener becomes self-conscious about her wish to transform the literal environment into a symbolic location that would affirm her creative prowess. She considers abandoning her sequence and returning to her "former life" as a secular nature poet (perhaps one in the tradition of Frost, the author of a famous poem about birches): "I might as well go on / addressing the birches, / as in my former life" (WI 13). We recall that Glück has described her writing process in *Proofs & Theories* as part of an agonizing conversation with literary masters, whom she considers to be part of her familial inheritance, but whose voices she fears have muffled her own. A return to conventional nature poetry reminds Glück in the fourth "Matins" that the moment has gotten rather late for such a project of what Abrams called naturalism/supernaturalism, considering the saturated tradition of nineteenth-century and early twentieth-century poets (from Keats to Dickinson to Rilke) who developed a language of flowers.[23]

More concerned at this point about her literary reputation than about speaking to God, the speaker expresses second thoughts about letting go of her theological framework:

23. Brown, "Love of Form," 119.

let them
do their worst, let them
bury me with the Romantics,
their pointed yellow leaves
falling and covering me. (WI 13)

As in *Meadowlands,* with her invocation of *The Odyssey* to depict a contemporary marriage on the rocks, Glück's daring as well as her vulnerability to criticism in *The Wild Iris* resides in her attempt to express her originality through a conventional repertoire. How can she assert her independence by trying to sustain the inherited values of nineteenth-century conceptions of God, prayer, the human voice, the lyric poem, and of how nature can be understood as an interpretable language that reflects on meanings pertaining to the isolated self? Aware that her belated return to a Romantic ethos in which spirit is projected onto nature might be interpreted as a sign of her submission to the outmoded paradigm, of dependence rather than independence, Glück nonetheless controls the interpretation of her process by drawing a conclusion about her own efforts. She speaks in bold, comical tones reminiscent of "To Autumn" (HM), where she dismissed concerns that "[s]ummer approaches" because it will be in "the long / decaying days of autumn when I shall begin / the great poems of my middle period" (FFB 72). Now, by contrast, the gardener-poet dares readers—addressed scornfully as "them" rather than intimately as "you"—to perceive her relationship to Romanticism as being anything other than an indication that she has become a canonical author through her dependency on prior literary models. Her identity becomes conserved, rather than concealed, by being covered with the fallen remains ("yellow leaves") of forebears whose dead work illuminates her own living witness to religious mystery.

Something of the speaker's anxiety—that her readers might be onto something in assuming her philosophy is out of touch with her current life—follows her into the fifth "Matins." Her concern is evident when the gardener applies the metaphor of weeding clumps of unwanted plants to her symbolic act of "looking for courage" to believe it worthwhile to try to communicate with God through nature in the unpromising context of postmodern American suburbia. Set in the modest landscape of a "front lawn," and with the distracted and depressed speaker "pretending to be weeding" the flower beds, the poem purports to express the speaker's flickering perception of divinity in an ordinary setting, but the gardener seems to be going through the motions, continuing to perform tasks that have lost their ritual function (WI 25).

Annoyed to the point of outrage by an inquiry that presumes the reply should be self-evident to the questioner—"You want to know how I spend my time?"—the perplexed speaker becomes enraged at Yahweh, who seems to know about everything, except how she feels and what she wants:

> I'm looking for courage, for some evidence
> my life will change, though
> it takes forever, checking
> each clump for the symbolic
> leaf. (WI 25)

A poem that began with the speaker's critique of the Creator's lack of insight into how mood influences behavior and perception concludes when the gardener-poet inspects her own struggle to accept that faith must exist without proof. Suggesting a circular rather than developmental model for the sequence, the speaker ends with her hands "[a]s empty now as at the first note." Although circularity may suggest a frustrating lack of progress toward salvation, she also expresses confidence in her project by imagining her search for courage in "each clump" of weeds as the condition necessary for faith. And perhaps more important, from an author's perspective, circularity suggests the continuation of her illusive project of transforming literal garden into symbolic creation: "Or was the point always / to continue without a sign?" (WI 25). Understanding prayer as a paradoxically detached form of intimacy, Glück imagines a speech act in line with Žižek's theory of desire as a libidinal current that registers a fantasy of a conclusion to yearning but that is not destined to reach the horizon of access to the beloved. The supplicant assumes that Yahweh requires the suspension of contact in order to perpetuate the state of yearning for a change in one's condition from despair to peace.

Glück sets up *The Wild Iris* sequence as a triangulated conversation, in which the authorial self comes to know herself by pitting her impressions against the reflections of others beneath her (flowers) and above her (God) who think they know better. In spite of the attempt she has made to stretch lyric poetry into the novelistic or dramatic realm of heteroglossia, the sixth "Matins" continues to express disappointment, even despair, at the one-sided "love relationship" that has been building up over several lyrics between the speaker and the "you," addressed here as "Father." "Father" here refers to God, but we are encouraged to recall her biological father, Daniel, whose life and death infused the pages of *Ararat*. God's distance from and silence toward the speaker repeats the parent-child relationship as it was construed in poems such as "Snow" (AR).

By collating images from each volume, we notice another dimension to how Glück transforms nature into the "second nature" of personal testimony. This is especially so when we link the speaker's grief for and emotional identification with her father, described in "A Novel" (AR) as the distant patriarch, "sitting at the head of the table, / where the figurehead is most needed" (AR 18), with her ambivalent and quixotic (hoping, doubting, fearing, loving, pitying, identifying) relationship to God in *The Wild Iris.* Like her father's, God's voice in "End of Winter" is the "persistent echoing / in all sound that means good-bye, good-bye— / the one continuous line / that binds us to each other" (WI 10–11).

Autobiographical lyrics set in a domestic sphere from *Ararat* include the bathetic "A Novel," where the once domineering father has become transformed into a frail and dying mortal, "his wife holding a mirror / under his mouth" (AR 18) to detect if he is still breathing. "A Novel" expands in meaning when placed next to *The Wild Iris,* where the speaker addresses a symbolic "Father." Both the father-daughter relationship in *Ararat* and the Father-gardener relationship in *The Wild Iris* discuss personal as well as theological issues involving identification and separation, closeness and distance, power and helplessness, and oneness and manyness. In both cases the speaker must face the difficulty of saying good-bye to a childhood of parental protection. The gardener-poet suspects that the object of her apostrophe, Yahweh, may exist only as an illusory projection of the speaker's longing for the father whose burial was announced in *Ararat.*

Similarly, the relatively abstract and impersonal prayers that take the form of speaking trilliums, red poppies, and irises in *The Wild Iris* reappear as personal meditations on the burial of the speaker's father and sister when placed in relationship to *Ararat.* A belated example of liturgical poetry in the Protestant tradition found in Herbert, *The Wild Iris* becomes Glück's medium to discuss her relationship to literary power and religious traditions. She tries to connect the late father's voice to the significance of her own authorship through the mobilizing force of absence, or "the one continuous line / that binds us to each other" (WI 11). Giving voice to flowers in *The Wild Iris,* Glück certainly does not follow the instructions from the third "Matins" to "go on / addressing the birches, / as in my former life." Instead, she acts out and, potentially, works through a complicated network of familial, psychic, literary, historical, and spiritual associations by, perhaps hubristically and atavistically, transforming prayers into acts of personal mourning. Her work also corresponds to an ambitious author's contest with traditional invocations of nature as a place of sublime meaning in Romanticism.

More so than any before, the speaker in the sixth "Matins" resembles Job, the prototypical figure of illness from the Jewish Bible, whom René Girard has characterized as a scapegoat, the "victim of his people."[24] Like Job at the most despairing points in his argument with God and with the "comforters," whose platitudes and pieties so annoy him, Glück's speaker wishes to detach herself from a God who she feels has singled her out for punishment by, ironically, paying excessive attention to her. At the same time she is like Job in that she has turned to God for solace, and as with Job, it is to God that she states her case about His mistreatment. Job complains about God's surveillance of his every action at a time when he would simply like a few moments alone to catch his breath ("time to swallow my spit") before he perishes. "What is man, that you notice him, / turn your glare upon him, examine him every morning, / test him at every instant?"[25] Glück's speaker expresses outrage at being manipulated by Yahweh, who treats her "heart" as if it were an experimental plant being tested by a scientist in a horticultural laboratory:

> What is my heart to you
> that you must break it over and over
> like a plantsman testing
> his new species? Practice
> on something else. (WI 26)

As in Job's reply to Bildad, where he wishes he had never been born because he feels he has become little more than God's plaything, a toy being mauled by a cat, we have reached the speaker's emotional nadir, especially when the sixth "Matins" is assessed from the perspective of the sequence of morning prayers. "Brown Circle" (AR) described the speaker's overbearing relationship to her son, Noah, casting the mother as a botanist, who burned the objects of desire through excessive scrutiny of their details. Now, in the sixth "Matins," the speaker claims that God has imagined her as a "new species" of plant, isolated from the spirit world but also quarantined from other people.

In her isolation from God and from a human community, as well as in her yearning for understanding from them, Glück's speaker reminds us of Job: "All my friends have forgotten me; / my neighbors have thrown me away. / My relatives look through me / as though I didn't exist."[26] Like Job, she carries a disease (of incurable melancholy? or of excessive pride in the unique-

24. René Girard, *Job: The Victim of His People,* trans. Yvonne Freccero (London: Athlone Press, 1987).
25. Stephen Mitchell, trans., *The Book of Job* (New York: HarperCollins, 1992), 24.
26. Ibid., 48.

ness of one's own suffering?)—"dividing me / from healthy members of / my own tribe." Imagining herself as a "new species" of sick plant, she differs from the "sick rose," which may, through "the tiny aphids / [that] leap from plant to plant," contaminate other members of its species by "wav[ing] its sociable / infested leaves in / the faces of the other roses" (WI 26). By contrast to the "sick rose," Glück's speaker is cut off from the analogy between flowers and self. Associating herself with the impatient Job of the first and second rounds of his dispute with the "comforters," rather than with the Job who becomes "speechless" before the "Unnamable" who answered Job from within the whirlwind, the gardener-poet continues to dispute Scilla by imagining her predicament as uniquely horrific. She defines herself as "the lowest of your creatures" with the "Father" as the punitive authority figure, the "agent of my solitude" (WI 26).

The tone drifts away from the edge of despair to epiphany, however. She transforms her loss of confidence in a beneficent God, and in ever hoping to make connections with other human beings because of the stigma God has cast upon her, into a renewed version of a childhood fantasy. In her fantasy, the speaker connects immortality to isolation, the state Glück has long associated with the social sacrifices an artist must make to perform her literary commission:

> Father,
> as agent of my solitude, alleviate
> at least my guilt; lift
> the stigma of isolation, unless
> it is your plan to make me
> sound forever again, as I was
> sound and whole in my mistaken childhood,
> or if not then, under the light weight
> of my mother's heart, or if not then,
> in dream, first
> being that would never die. (WI 26)

At first the speaker requests that the Father alleviate the stigma of isolation, not the creative state of isolation itself, a brand or mark that sometimes is said to accompany the experience of religious ecstasy in martyrs. The speaker then complicates her understanding by interpreting the stigma as a mark that is at once constructive and destructive. The stigma is associated with the guilt she wants removed. This mark also enables her to return to a "mistaken childhood" sense of being "sound and whole," the prenatal intimation of immortality, or the constructive side of the stigma. The stigma is especially constructive because it is related to the speaker's creativity; the possession of the stigma transforms the self into a "sound" being (read: into a permanent literary voice) that is the positive valence of isolation, emotional wounding, and a relationship with the Father as agent of her suffering.

If the speaker encourages a return to a childhood perception of her autonomy, with God imagined as a limiting figure of consolation who nonetheless restricts human freedom, Glück also ironizes her experience. She characterizes her speaker's return to a naive vision of wholeness as an example of what Wallace Stevens defined as a "supreme fiction." However mistaken, the childhood fantasy of being the "first / being that would never die" may alleviate the despair she experiences in the present tense of her speech act, where the gardener-poet fears she has spoken out to a void. As Gordon has noted, "given how *The Wild Iris* so overtly takes spiritual experience as its theme, the speaker cannot seem to trust her experience."[27]

At the end of the sixth "Matins," Glück's confident tone suggests a reversal of feeling. She downplays the oppressive stature of a personal God, admires a sublime example of natural splendor, and emphasizes the value of her own creative endeavor as an approximation of god's grandeur.

> Not the sun merely but the earth
> itself shines, white fire
> leaping from the showy mountains
> and the flat road
> shimmering in early morning. (WI 31)

Where the portrayal of the sun's rays as a "white fire" would in other poems signify God's destructive strength, in the sixth "Matins" Glück portrays illumination that originates from earth, not sky: "Not the sun merely but the earth / itself shines" (WI 31).

In the seventh "Matins," the gardener-poet interprets her words as if they were part of a divinely inspired performance, which verges on Hierogamic marriage, or sexual union between supplicant and God. Trading notes in an off-hand manner with the deity about the pleasurable surprises that occur during her own act of lyric composition, the speaker interprets her creative effort as being equivalent to God's natural displays. She addresses God as "Dear friend," rather than as "Father." In the time interval that has passed

27. Wallace Stevens, *Letters of Wallace Stevens,* ed. Holly Stevens (New York: Knopf, 1966), 820; Gordon, "Reconceiving the Sacred," 134.

between the sixth "Matins" and the seventh, the speaker's position has shifted from the Job-like image of the diseased plant and "lowest of all creatures" in the sixth: "I am ashamed / at what I thought you were, / distant from us, regarding us / as an experiment" (WI 31). Far from Job's speechless acquiescence in the face of God, the ungraspable figure of infinity, Glück's speaker subverts the understanding of power dynamics between God and the speaker as a form of parent-child relations.[28] She conceives of God, not as an unfathomable whirlwind, but as the masturbatory adolescent who is "helpless / to control yourself / in earth's presence." She regards the gaudy natural display—"white fire / leaping from the showy mountains"—as a sign of Yahweh's need to prove his power to human beings, and as distraction from boredom. Less angry than bemused and even empathetic at Yahweh's isolation, helplessness, and consequent need to display signs of authority that verge on autoeroticism, Glück writes that it is "a bitter thing to be / the disposable animal" (WI 31). The "disposable animal" here could as easily be applied to God as to the human gardener-poet.

Comparing herself to God in terms of creative drive, erotic longing, and isolation from the world she puts forth in words but whose meaning she cannot control once published, the gardener has imagined authorship as a partnership between two authors, a human writer and a God. Her warm conversational tones celebrate a coupling that on another level occurs as a love affair between the poet and her "Dear friend, / dear trembling partner":

> what
> surprises you most in what you feel,
> earth's radiance or your own delight?
> For me, always
> the delight is the surprise. (WI 31)

Examining the human author's relationship with God, a relationship that combines a divine perspective with an erotic charge, the gardener's imagining of God's perspective mediates the characteristic strains of bitterness and vulnerability at God's force and human mutability found in the sixth "Matins."

One of the divine "reply" poems—"Retreating Light," which appears very late in the sequence—develops Glück's insight into the dialogic nature of creativity described in the seventh "Matins." This poem imagines God's

28. Mitchell, *The Book of Job,* 88.

side of the dialogue in a way that will inform subsequent prayer poems. In "Retreating Light," God grew "tired of telling stories" and so directed persons such as the author to "write your own story." Returning to the image of God escaping from the earth to the sky as the Garden narrative was recast in "The Clearing," the fourth section of "Lamentations" (DF), Glück's speaker imagines the Earth as an uncompleted text, which she holds the power to develop through commentary. In "Retreating Light," eschatological mystery lends itself to narrative suspense. Cast as a kind of literary critic, God "realized you couldn't think / with any real boldness or passion; / you hadn't had your own lives yet, / your own tragedies" (WI 50). As is the case throughout Glück's career, poetry compensates for the speaker's theological doubts, experiential deprivations, and erotic disappointment. Perhaps alluding to the conclusion of Milton's *Paradise Lost,* God's "retreating light" becomes, as it was for Adam and Eve, a source of anguish for the speaker, but also a license for literary entitlement.

It is not a surprise that the seventh and last "Matins" occurs midway through the cycle. The next three poems in the sequence—"Heaven and Earth," "The Doorway," and "Midsummer"—chart the psychological, seasonal, and artistic midpoint of the speaker's efforts to come to terms with the fragile epicenter of human happiness, and the "I Thou" aspect of the relationship between a person and her God, which Glück had celebrated in the seventh "Matins." At times in *The Wild Iris* sequence, the speaker judges her life to be terribly finite, and therefore insignificant, and her search for God to be futile—but not in "Heaven and Earth," when the resurrected speaker declares: "everything is possible. / Meaning: never again will life end" (WI 32).

"The Doorway" places the speaker in a liminal zone between accepting life as a process involving change and eventually termination and a desire for stasis in the form of the midsummer fantasy of heaven where "never again will life end." Brown refers to the poem as a nostalgic look back to "our first world," to "the pre-analytic condition of the child," and to a time before the pressures of public reception might lead the author to fear loss of control over the interpretation of a text once disseminated. I read "The Doorway" as an expression of Glück's ongoing struggle with the creative powers of God—through the speaker's desire for immortality without loss of subjectivity: "to stay as I was / still as the world is never still" (WI 33).

Interrogating the husband's daydream of stopping time, found in "Heaven and Earth," the speaker imagines surviving the gift of literary empowerment without succumbing to time, or engaging in her husband's fantasy of endless presence, in a garden that represents the constancy of change. She wishes to "stall" her growth the way the sun "truly does stall" above the woods in "Heaven and Earth" (WI 32). In "The Doorway" she says:

> I wanted to stay as I was
> still as the world is never still,
> not in midsummer but the moment before
> the first flower forms, the moment
> nothing is as yet past— (WI 33)

Casting the gardener-poet as merely on the cusp of appearance, and so not subject to erasure as a part of nature or as a graphic inscription (the self as an effect of writing), Glück imagines the paradoxical form of survival through disappearance that characterizes her poetics of desire. Wanting to be like "the grass not yet / high at the edge of the garden," she describes herself as like "a child hovering in a doorway, watching the others, / the ones who go first" (WI 33). A poet who has described her own periods of intense creative effort as comparable to a state of "wild possession," her poem "The Doorway" addresses the moment "prior to flowering," the time "before the appearance of the gift, / before possession" (WI 33). The gift of appearance, at once desirable and repulsive, implies the speaker's self-control, but also her being subsumed by someone or absorbed into something other than the self, "both the act of possessing and of being possessed."[29]

The gardener's desire to cheat death by stopping time resonates with how the mother in "A Fantasy" (AR) wanted to make time go backward in order to forestall her husband's death:

> In her heart, she wants them to go away.
> She wants to be back in the cemetery,
> back in the sickroom, the hospital. She knows
> it isn't possible. But it's her only hope,
> the wish to move backward. And just a little,
> not so far as the marriage, the first kiss. (AR 16–17)[30]

29. Brown, "Love of Form," 102.

30. In "Fable" (SA), Glück's speaker at once embraces and transcends the sentiment of "The Doorway" (WI) and "A Fantasy" (AR). She observes that while "[w]e had, each of us, a set of wishes," the one consistent yearning was "the wish to go back" (9). While "Fable" continues to express the speaker's uneasiness with embracing life and the biological given of the body and its sensual needs, ultimately subject to time and erasure, the speaker at the end seems to come to some degree of acceptance of the preciousness of life, once she acknowledges that "we knew in our bodies / it [freedom from time] was never granted." Once "the wish released us," the night becomes "sweet" but "utterly silent" (9).

As with the mother, the gardener-poet wants to turn clock time back—as if personal history were a film strip that could be rewound, a motif employed most famously in the Delmore Schwartz short story "In Dreams Begin Responsibilities."[31] In terms of family dynamics, the speaker has modeled her account of time and change on the mother's example, but in terms of literary forebears, we may recall the late lyrics of Wallace Stevens. In "The Solitude of Cataracts," Stevens abandoned the poetics of process that had characterized his position in "Sunday Morning":

> He wanted to feel the same way over and over.
>
> He wanted the river to go on flowing the same way,
> To keep on flowing. He wanted to walk beside it,
>
> Under the buttonwoods, beneath a moon nailed fast.
> He wanted his heart to stop beating and his mind to rest
>
> In a permanent realization.[32]

Glück's gardener-poet accepts theological doubt and emotional instability as the personal cost for a life of solitary contemplation and symbolic achievement. But "Heaven and Earth," following the late poetry of Stevens, critiques the analogy between cyclical nature and mutable human life that drives *The Wild Iris.* This critique is from the perspective of a gardener-poet who does not want to face the consequences of her own design, as it veers toward conclusion.

"Midsummer" takes part in the analogy between persons and different species of flowers, all of which may appear distinct when seen from the garden level, but which are in many respects comparable when seen from a higher level. "Midsummer" offers God's indictment of the speaker's conceiving of human relationships as based in scarcity, difference, and conflict rather than in abundance, sameness, and cooperation: "You were / my embodiment, all diversity" (WI 34). To Yahweh, the gardener-poet's Job-like insistence on the uniqueness of her struggle merely reflects the narcissism of all persons who are "strangling each other" to be distinguished:

31. Delmore Schwartz, "In Dreams Begin Responsibilities," in *Jewish American Literature: A Norton Anthology,* ed. Hilene Flanzbaum et al. (New York: Norton, 2001), 540–45.

32. Wallace Stevens, "The Solitude of Cataracts," *The Palm at the End of the Mind: Selected Poems and a Play,* ed. Holly Stevens (New York: Vintage, 1990), 320–21.

How can I help you when you all want
different things—sunlight and shadow,
moist darkness, dry heat—

Listen to yourselves, vying with one another— (WI 34)

Moving from sowing seeds in early spring to the epicenter of human and natural abundance in midsummer, then shifting to assess the gardener-poet's yearning for recognition from God's perspective, "Midsummer" marks a major structural transition in *The Wild Iris*—away from morning prayers. The next three poems, all entitled "Vespers" (evening prayers), report the speaker's shift from ascent toward emotional descent, from anticipation of physical growth or enhanced understanding of her condition to an acknowledgment of the suffering that goes with change, when assessed through the variable contexts of nature, time, and the vulnerable human body of which the seasonal flowers are signs.

Vespers

The gardener has expressed her misgivings about the outcome to her project in "Heaven and Earth." She has imagined God's reprimand of her desire to distinguish herself in "Midsummer." In the first of ten "Vespers" in the second part of *The Wild Iris,* she answers God's critique. Where, in the sixth "Matins," God was shown to be experimenting on her, as if He were a botanist and she a diseased plant, here, in the first "Vespers," the speaker defies God's omnipotence by performing a rather humorous, if childishly literal, experiment to determine if God really does exist in nature. Planting a fig tree in the inhospitable climate of Vermont, she reasons that, if it survives, "it would mean you existed," but "[b]y this logic, you do not exist. Or you exist / exclusively in warmer climates, in fervent Sicily and Mexico and California" (WI 36). In the fifth "Matins," the speaker at first sought courage in the form a four-leaf clover but then wondered if "the point [was] always / to continue without a sign?" In the fifth "Matins," Glück interpreted paradox and irrationality as if these breaks with logic were necessary for religious faith and poetic understanding (WI 25).

By contrast, the gardener in the first "Vespers" is a skeptic whose empiricism puts in question the necessity for belief. This three-stanza poem should not be read as a definitive testimony to the gardener's loss of faith. Evidence that the gardener is reacting to God's condemnation of her egocentrism in

"Midsummer" appears in stanza 2, where she no longer requires proof of God's existence to go on:

> If there is justice in some other world, those
> like myself, whom nature forces
> into lives of abstinence, should get
> the lion's share of all things, all
> objects of hunger, greed being
> praise of you. (WI 36)

Valuing absence and silence as codes of sacred meaning, the gardener asserts her willingness to endure hunger as an expression of her desire for recognition.[33] She has imagined herself a monastic figure of the Christian tradition such as Julian of Norwich, or Joan of Arc, or more recently, Simone Weil. She hopes a final reward will come to "lives of abstinence" when she argues (in a conditional format that ironizes her allegiance to God) that "[i]f there is justice in some other world," her "praises" and her "painfully checked desire" will merit the privilege to "sit at your right hand," in a space that joins elements of earth and heaven: "partaking / of the perishable, the immortal fig / which does not travel" (WI 36).

The first "Vespers" may be read as commentary on the radical humanism defined by Stevens in "Sunday Morning." Glück attempts to infuse a secular position that promotes the adequacy of the human imagination with a theological dimension, what Stevens in "Sunday Morning" dismisses as "some imperishable bliss." Her position embraces mutability but allows room for what Glück calls "the immortal fig, / which does not travel," that is, the always abundant but emotionally static realm of God. In "The Doorway," Glück dismissed the position from "Sunday Morning" by referring to Stevens' rejection of it in "The Solitude of Cataracts." Although the speaker of "Heaven and Earth" criticized her husband for wanting "everything," when he perceived the garden as a numinous site, the first "Vespers" suggests that, as she approaches the conclusion to her cycle, the speaker has vacillated between embracing the fleeting pleasures of this world and hoping for permanent safety in the next.

33. Glück's speaker engages in what Hegel called the "struggle for recognition," which animates heroic behavior when the warrior pursues abstract values above his desire to preserve his life. For Hegel, history began with the test of the first man's humanity, which occurred when he agreed to a fight that would leave the victor in the role of master, and the loser, who feared death and so was willing to capitulate, in the role of slave.

In reading the second "Vespers," one might suspect "the cold nights that come / so often here" and that blight her tomato plants, as well as the signs of seasonal beauty that also indicate decline ("the spotted leaf, / the red leaves of the maple falling"), would discourage the gardener-poet from believing prayer or gardening might continue to function as meaningful rituals. Instead, she perseveres in spite of or because of the "terror we bear" in facing the conclusion of a cycle: "I planted the seeds, I watched the first shoots / like wings tearing the soil" (WI 37). Acknowledging the contingency of inclement weather on the success of her project ("the heavy rains, the cold nights"), the speaker makes it clear that "[a]ll this / belongs to you [God]." Such an admission might suggest she will submit to God's will and admit that her attempt to plant the seeds for a garden so late in the season is prone to fail because she lacks control over her surroundings. Ironically, the disjunction between her decision to plant tomatoes and the inauspicious moment at which she chooses to do so convinces her she is "responsible / for these vines." With the "vines" as a figure for "these lines," and failure to produce fruit the likely outcome of her efforts, Glück asserts control over a sublimely figurative domain, in which the tomato seeds shoot up as if with "wings." As in "For Jane Myers" and "To Autumn" (HM), her tone now is liberated and defiant, because failure to succeed in the realm of nature (planting a successful tomato garden) signifies difference, and therefore poetic authority over her "vines," which recall the praise of maturity in Keats's "To Autumn": "With fruit the vines that round the thatch-eves run."

The speaker has distinguished her practices from God's flawed creations. She has dissociated herself from the nature represented at times by divinity, when assessing her moods as well as the success or failure of her ritual actions. She affirms the dignity of a rich emotional life that, she boasts, Yahweh could never appreciate, from a remote perspective where He does "not discriminate / between the dead and the living."

> I doubt
> you have a heart, in our understanding of
> that term. You who do not discriminate
> between the dead and the living, who are, in consequence,
> immune to foreshadowing . . .
> I am responsible
> for these vines. (WI 37)

As Gregerson points out, pain and suffering may be what distinguishes humans from God.[34] Her ritual efforts at planting and praying may well be flawed, atavistic, and in the end subject to erasure, but the gardener-poet celebrates her determination to continue to make an analogy between constructing the self in words and cultivating nature in a garden. A lyric that is structured as a prayer, that is, as a vertical speech act that imagines God as its direct audience but that must not be answered by the figure of apostrophic address if the prayer cycle is to continue, the second "Vespers" remains in a Stevensian mode of humanistic affirmation.

As in "Sunday Morning," in which Stevens declares that "Death is the mother of beauty," the gardener suggests that, unlike God, her mortality, her fallenness or loss of connection to the biblical Paradise represented by the garden, is necessary for the expression of symbolic achievement, because the passage of time is a narrative requirement. The quality of suspense in life as well as in narrative art, the speaker argues, is a by-product of the suspension of time described through the formal plot device of foreshadowing. The success of human endeavors that involve cultivation such as gardening may be contingent upon unpredictable weather conditions or, perhaps, the capriciousness of God, but a lyric sequence is distinguishable from God's designations because of its time-bound and therefore narrative dimension. Existing outside of time, Glück's speaker argues, Yahweh is condemned to exist outside of the narrative domain and, therefore, must remain (as in the Levinasian theory of God as untotalizable Other) in an abyss beyond representation. Yahweh exists outside of the textual compensations of story and lyric drama that demand temporality.

Set in August, the third "Vespers" exudes an elegiac quality as it describes a late point in the gardening season, as well as, by analogy, lateness in the sequence of lyric meditations. A commentary on her ambition to transform the literal environment into a symbolic landscape throughout *The Wild Iris,* the poem takes a retrospective glance at the volume's overarching metaphor of the self when imagined as a speaking flower. Unlike the Shakespearean sonneteer who refused to compare his beloved to a summer's day, the speaker proclaims that she "compared myself / to those flowers" of August (WI 38). We would suspect that, because the speaker acknowledges she has accepted "perishable bliss" as the necessary sign of human difference from God, she would be celebrating the creation of a lyric opening and the temporal interval necessary for storytelling through "foreshadowing," but not here. Instead, the speaker laments her suspicion that by "study[ing] the hawkweed, / the buttercup," her representations of nature are redundant and superfluous, because nature is already a symbolic representation of God's grandeur. "You

34. Gregerson quoted in Diehl, *On Louise Glück,* 35.

[God] already know / how like your raiment it [nature] is" (WI 38). Lines such as, "I am uniquely / suited to praise you. Then why / torment me?" and "is pain / your gift to make me / conscious in my need of you[?]" register the persona of Job at his lowest points, a scapegoat whose pain is unredeemed. This "Vespers" refers back to the sixth "Matins," which portrayed the gardener as isolated from other human beings and, therefore, as worse off than the "sick rose," which could at least share its misery by spreading contagion to other members of the species.

Comparable to "Heaven and Earth," and at twelve lines one of the shortest lyrics in the sequence, the fourth "Vespers" documents a fleeting incident in the speaker's life. Living in suburbia, the speaker compares her attitude toward gardening with her husband's attitude toward thinning the lettuce patch with his green trowel. Unlike the speaker, who is so preoccupied by metaphysical concerns that she cannot focus on the simple pleasure of performing physical tasks, John seems childlike in his unself-conscious contentment, but he also takes breaks to interpret his activity: "fifteen minutes of intense effort, / fifteen minutes of ecstatic contemplation" (WI 42). Answering her own question of "where you [God] are" by declaring that "You're in the garden; you're where John is," her numinism does not satisfy her desire for consolation from a personal god. As in the Garden narrative, her self-consciousness implies separation from God, nature, and husband. Where "peace never leaves" her husband, the gardener compares herself, not to the flower that finds nourishment by absorbing the sunlight, but to the "bare tree" through which the "bright light" rushes, a figure for an alienated individual and emotional minimalist not unlike the father in *Ararat*. "Peace," in the speaker's reading, is anathema to the character who possesses a spiritual drive and creative struggle that must resist a "bright light" coming from outside the self in order to appear as an essential being, the "bare tree."

As much as this image asserts her independence from God through the image of the "bare tree," the speaker in the fifth "Vespers" expresses what Gordon calls a "desire for communion with the sacred" in a poem in which "the speaker feels she may have had the sacred encounter for which she prayed."[35]

> I climbed
> the small hill above the wild blueberries, metaphysically
> descending, as on all my walks: did I go deep enough
> for you to pity me, as you have sometimes pitied

35. Gordon, "Reconceiving the Sacred," 134.

> others who suffer, favoring those
> with theological gifts? As you anticipated,
> I did not look up. So you came down to me:
> at my feet, not the wax
> leaves of the wild blueberry but your fiery self, a whole
> pasture of fire, and beyond, the red sun neither falling
> nor rising— (WI 43)

The poem links her "need" to keep faith in God's appearance to her acute response to "the slightest brightening" of hope for an epiphany in an existence that is now characterized primarily by metaphysical darkness. Because "I need you, you appear to me," she writes of God's presence, an example of a necessary fiction in which desire precedes belief. In terms of the speaker's agon with the Jewish Bible and its God, Glück's speaker has asserted her authority over God by casting Him as her fictional construct.

The poem refers back to Stevens and his theory of the Supreme Fiction to discuss the gardener's yearnings, but it also confronts motifs from the Jewish Bible by connecting the gardener's struggle to find God in nature with the appearance of Yahweh to Moses as a burning bush on Mount Sinai (Exodus 3). Blending natural and supernatural imagery and permanent and fleeting elements together as "your fiery self, a whole / pasture of fire, and beyond, the red sun neither falling / nor rising," the gardener's vision transcends the scene of natural beauty, "the wax / leaves of the wild blueberry" that the speaker discovers as she walks on a small hill. Positioned at one of the lowest ebbs in the sequence, this depressive speaker nonetheless records a vision comparable to the revelation in Exodus 3, but she suggests that this image, too, is part of the Supreme Fiction: "[e]ven as you appeared to Moses, because / I need you, you appear to me." Through irony she releases herself from any confidence that the mystical "pasture of fire" has occurred in the literal world outside herself. She steps away from believing she has witnessed anything other than a fictional event, which she must create, must also know that she has created, but must nonetheless believe in, as a way to ward off nihilism and despair. In "Midsummer," a desire for stasis—in the form of the fantasy that "never again will life end"—represented the speaker's nostalgic wish to return to the innocence of childhood. Here, the gardener states specifically that she knows what she is doing by creating a divine fantasy: "I was not a child; I could take advantage of illusions" (WI 43).

The sixth "Vespers"—paired with the next poem in the sequence, "Early Darkness"—records an argument between the speaker and God. The latter poem repudiates the gardener's charge that God has taken "advantage of illusions" by turning humans' attention toward the heavens, and so against each other, and turns toward an embrace of nature as a stand-in for something more sublime. The speaker goes so far as to accuse God of emotional blackmail. He has fostered mistrust among siblings in order to lead the speaker into a "solitude" that requires the consolation of a divine compensation from which God, cast as some kind of cosmic insurance salesman, would "profit" by providing.

Lamenting a loss of the bond between a brother and a sister, Glück returns to explore her guilt at engaging in sibling rivalry. We should read the poem in the context of the speaker's memories of intimacy between children that was a major theme in *The House on Marshland* and *Ararat.* In "Magnet" (AR), the sister's death returns as a source of trauma for the speaker, but also as an event in the sibling rivalry for the mother's attention. In "Midsummer," Yahweh condemned human beings for their misguided attraction to individual striving—"strangling each other" (WI 34). Here, in the sixth "Vespers," Glück revises her opinion of God's critique of human independence. Claiming that God was jealous of the sister's affection for her sibling ("lying in a field, touching my brother's body"), God "had reason to create / mistrust between a brother and sister" (WI 44). The reason, she argues, was God's "envy" of human solidarity and erotic pleasure; the punishment is her solitude, and the victory is God's achievement of the separation of the brother and sister. Sibling separation occurs through a metaphysical "lie" (punning on the "lying in a field" with the brother). According to the speaker, God's "lie" was His threat to exclude the speaker from heaven as the cost for a transgression (in this case the physical intimacy between brother and sister). God's "lie" was to represent the pleasure and closeness between two human beings as a costly sin. Since Glück has established her speaker's belief in God as a necessary fiction to avoid the narcissism of metaphysical despair, the "lie" God told the children was that "it was not earth / but heaven we were losing" (WI 44).

The speaker's address to God in *The Wild Iris* resembles the daughter's ambivalent relationship to her laconic father in *Ararat.* "Early Darkness" represents God as an annoyed and annoying father who cannot take pleasure in His "children" (WI 45). He feels burdened by the responsibility of succeeding "with all of you," and God is put off by the arrogance of a child, such as the speaker in the sixth "Vespers," who "would like to dictate to me," and who "would like to tell me / who among you is most valuable, / who most resembles me" (WI 45). Dismayed by the speaker's conceit in the sixth "Vespers," the father answers her accusation that He is to blame for the speaker's disappointments in life. He argues that her lack of respect for His authority has caused her despair.

Never forget you are my children.
You are not suffering because you touched each other
but because you were born,
because you required life
separate from me. (WI 45)

The seventh "Vespers" continues to wrestle with the fundamental relationship between desire and mutability. The speaker feels caught in a dilemma—of loving the world that she knows she must eventually leave and of representing a world that she knows is already a manifestation of another creator, God. Instructed by God "to love the world, making it impossible / to turn away completely," she regards nature as something "you mean to take . . . away, each flower, each connection / with earth" (WI 52). The lines echo Glück's comment to Ann Douglas on her own extraordinary affection for life in an interview conducted after *Descending Figure* was published:

> I feel that human life is tragic. . . . It's our attachment to the world that makes our departure from it and change within it so terribly painful. It's like the anorexic myth: people don't realize you're not anorexic if you don't love pleasure, because pleasure doesn't have that hold on you. If you feel that sensory experience is so powerful that you could be undone by it, that fear can take a number of forms, anorexia being one. . . . Happiness in time is the most tragic thing there is. Its loss will be felt.[36]

A tension emerges between devoting herself to nature for the sake of its beauty and adjusting to the truth of its mutability and, therefore, to the reality of her mortality and her separateness from other persons, as well as from the impressive physical world that surrounds her. At first the speaker tentatively faces the problem of death by accepting life in the present tense, but then she engages in an experiment with sensory deprivation, which only magnifies the paradoxical relationship between absence and desire Glück has been exploring throughout her book:

impossible
to turn away completely, to shut it out completely
ever again—
it is everywhere; when I close my eyes,

36. Douglas, "Descending Figure," 121–22.

> birdsong, scent of lilac in early spring, scent of summer
> roses. (WI 52)

The gardener's attempt to negate the influence of the world on her psyche—her wish to refrain from absorbing the sights, sounds, and scents of nature—only seems to deepen the problem of her absorption in the phenomenal world. The experiment confirms a theme that Glück has stressed throughout her writings: to prove her worthiness to the beloved, be it the mother (AR), the wayward husband (M), or God (WI), an experiential deprivation must take place.

The long relaxed lines of the seventh "Vespers" break off with a dash about two-thirds of the way through. The sudden dash marks a shift from a tone of confidence in her understanding of God's design ("I know what you planned, what you meant to do") to a tone of outraged interrogation as the speaker unravels God's plot to foster belief: "why would you wound me, why would you want me / desolate in the end[?]" The poem ends when the speaker answers her own question about God's purposes, but her reply is hardly comforting:

> you wanted me so starved for hope
> I would refuse to see that finally
> nothing was left to me, and would believe instead
> in the end you were left to me. (WI 52)

These pain-filled lyrics are the cries of a wounded daughter. Her testimony suggests a child mourning a parent.

The eighth, "Vespers: Parousia" (a Greek term referring to the return of the Son of God, or the Second Coming), may be interpreted as an updated version of the metaphysical poetry written by Herbert, whose work remains compelling today because he infused sacred longings with the libidinal energy of modern secular love poetry. Combining the religious imagery associated with the appearance of Christ at the apocalypse with the speaker's yearnings to behold her lover, Glück leaves deliberately vague the nominal referent to the beloved, the "you," as she laments the "love of my life" who is "gone forever." The "you" could refer to a lover, whom the speaker remembers when she was a girl, or to her desire for a return of her father, or to the God who speaks, and then turns silent: "I try to win you back, / that is the point / of the writing." The speaker also invokes the image of fading flowers at the end of summer as a traditional symbol for lost youth. Instead of her flashback in stanza 2 to "the apple tree . . . studded with blossoms," the world-weary speaker now watches "the blossoms shatter, / no longer pink, / but old, old, a yellowish white" (WI 53). On various levels, the speaker is bringing a cycle to a close. It is the end of a gardening season, but also the closing stages of the speaker's confidence that her prayers will enable her to maintain her identity while also coming to terms with a God that throughout the sequence has renounced human subjectivity as hubristic folly.

The speaker finds a God reflected in the flowers to be wanting, especially when compared with the permanence of art. Examples of the divine creation such as the fig tree that could exist only in southern climates seem less durable than the author's lyric poetry:

> What a nothing you were,
> to be changed so quickly
> into an image, an odor—
> you are everywhere, source
> of wisdom and anguish. (WI 53–54)

The speaker, whose angry tone barely conceals her vulnerability, concludes by criticizing God's natural creations as subject to conversion into "an image," part of the speaker's lyric domain. The poem calls to mind Cordelia's reply of "nothing" to her father after she has found herself unable to "heave / my heart into my mouth" when asked to express her love for him in the first act of Shakespeare's *King Lear.* Stressing the imperfections of nature by pointing to mutability, rather than to endurance through the repetitive cycle of the planting seasons, she also returns to her observation that, like Stevens in the "Snow Man," the lover she is addressing remains "the nothing that is."[37]

In the seventh "Vespers," the speaker tried unsuccessfully to "turn away completely" from the world that reflected God's creative powers. When she closed her eyes, the sounds of birdsong and the "scent of summer roses" (WI 52) filled the air anyway, reminding her of a world that was not of her making. Nature remained a place she loved, but that death would eventually force her to relinquish it in favor of a faith in the "nothing . . . left to me" (which is synonymous with God, when imagined from the Levinasian perspective as an Other whose presence may never be breached). In the eighth "Vespers," the speaker's repudiation of God results from her frustration at remaining in the world of sensation. It is in effect an ironic statement of her continuing affection for the world that she associates with divine creativity: "How lush

37. Wallace Stevens, "The Snow Man," in Ramazani et al., *Norton Anthology* 1:247.

the world is, / how full of things that don't belong to me" (WI 53). As much as these concluding remarks evoke signs of God in nature, they also express the speaker's liberation from the paternal authority of God even as they lament her maturation. The lyricist points toward the speaker's inevitable confrontation with death as the ultimate horizon to her own creative aspirations, but she has also affirmed her distinctiveness when compared to God or to the nature that reflects God's creative powers.

If these last two "Vespers" express the mystery and disillusionment of finding God in nature—"you are everywhere, source / of wisdom and anguish" (WI 54)—then the ninth "Vespers" offers a negative theology in which God's silence becomes a paradoxical trace of unimaginable divinity. As we saw in Glück's understanding of the nature of desire in poems such as "A Fable" (AR), however, absence and hunger may paradoxically indicate the speaker's intense need for God's existence. Relinquishing possession of the beloved may, from this point of view, become rewritten as a sign of affection. With no access to God ("Your voice is gone now . . . / I have no access to you; / I do not exist for you, you have drawn / a line through my name"), the speaker's faith in absence and loss as signs of divine presence must suffice, must lead her through the fear that if God does exist then she does not exist for God (WI 55). Glück here takes a perspective on the relationship between God and human beings that is reminiscent of the theology of the modern Jewish thinker Abraham Joshua Heschel. As in Heschel's "God in search of man,"[38] Glück understands that, although God is "deducting visible life from all things," her life remains necessary to God as the source of a voice to acknowledge Him through prayer or apostrophic address:

> When you go, you go absolutely,
> deducting visible life from all things
>
> but not all life,
> lest we turn from you. (WI 55)

Set at the "end of August," the final "Vespers" express the speaker's ambivalence toward closure, on several levels that include nature, prayer, and her own creative efforts, which, after all, constitute the text of her performance as a speaking subject. Commenting on the cessation of a gardening cycle, she refrains from accepting the end of her ritual activities. She notes

38. Abraham Joshua Heschel, *God in Search of Man: A Philosophy of Judaism* (New York: Farrar, Straus, and Giroux, 1976).

that "some things / have the nerve to be getting started, / clusters of tomatoes, stands / of late lilies," even as she acknowledges the "lilies / winter will kill, that won't / come back in spring" (WI 56). Perplexed and yet celebratory of the defiant "optimism / of the great stalks" that rise in late summer, she recounts varying degrees of optimism and despair about the endurance of her voice and of her faith in reaching her audience as the volume nears its conclusion. Like the blossoming lilies, her voice has flourished with the "glory / of the open throat" (WI 56). A poet who has understood desire for recognition as an abstinence from meeting the needs of the body, she worries about her survival, as in the poem "Midsummer," where she announced her poetic flowering and, therefore, foreshadowed her inevitable decline as a speaker. The season and the book of the seasons are nearing their conclusion, but Glück notes signs of growth that contradict the rhythms of natural life as she challenges the expectations for lyric closure. Writing late, in a saturated tradition of nature poets who have also invoked an intimation of the divine substance in the abundance of the world's riches, she expresses the folly, hubris, and cautious optimism that must have factored into her decision as an author to select the prayer format and to imagine nature as the vehicle to express her movement in time intervals as well as in the interior space of the mind and heart.

Everything that informs the speaker's sense of her relationship to the world around her and everything she is trying to resist or absorb into her own vision exist on the same plane in *The Wild Iris*: debts to the Protestant lyric, elements of Catholic liturgy, the invocation of the Jewish personal God as found in the Psalms of David, Spinoza's numinism, the Greek myth of Persephone, allusions to the secularism of Stevens in "Sunday Morning." All these elements of literary history and theological speculation enable the protagonist (masked as the poet-gardener and supplicant) at once to expose and to hide her contested relationship to philosophical and aesthetic vocabularies. Traces of a variety of once dominant versions of religious explanation for human suffering and philosophical understanding of cosmic mystery seem to produce her identity and to haunt her as aggressive threats to the stability and uniqueness of her self. Glück's commentary on these sources creates the dynamic give and take of the sequence as well as the painful fragmentation of the lyric self. The form of the sequence exhibits qualities of splitting, or detaching, or dissociating elements of one's past, of one's memories, of one's ideas characteristic of the traumatized self. The self that cannot quite piece itself together, but that wishes to detach itself from the source of pain, from the body, is certainly an element of *The Wild Iris.* Unresolved are the speaker's relationships to words, to the nature of transcendence, to paternal authority, to the issue of her singularity versus her nature as a representative figure, to her desire to embrace the realm of material life, of the body, of the moment, and to somehow cheat death by reaching for a permanence in God or through literary canonization. This array of factors is segmented into the Yahweh God, the poet-gardener, and the unruly flowers that speak back to the poet-gardener—chastising her for her desire to have her autonomy acknowledged, for her denying her status as merely another living being, planted on this earth and extinguished by a power greater than herself. The tonal similarity of these voices suggests that the dialogism of these grouped lyrics is really a foil for an internal conversation—the self attempting to exert a degree of control over the literary remains by acting as ventriloquist for each of them.

Chapter Nine

Mythic Fragment

Sequence, Commentary, and the Composition of the Lyric Self through *The Odyssey* in *Meadowlands*

In *A Menorah for Athena,* Stephen Fredman shows that Charles Reznikoff, a leading Jewish American poet from the first half of the twentieth century, was, like H.D. and Ezra Pound, fascinated with Greek poetry, but his relationship to the material differed from theirs even if his "objectivist" style was, like their "imagism," informed by *The Greek Anthology.* H.D. and Pound interpreted the Greek texts as examples of a purely aesthetic model from which to build a new kind of poetry, as a way to inform their Imagist goals. H.D. and Pound, in other words, adhered to Matthew Arnold's influential association of Hellenism with aestheticism, and Hebraism with a Puritanical strain of English culture that privileged "right doing" at the expense of a celebration of beauty for its own sake. For Reznikoff, the Greek materials registered what Fredman calls his "liminal position between cultures":

> Placing himself in a symbolic position of betweenness—between Hebraism and Hellenism, between Judaism and modernism, . . . Reznikoff joins not only the other Objectivist poets but also an entire generation of American Jewish intellectuals. Sensing an opportunity to overcome a two-thousand-year history of marginalization, these Jews are hungry to enter the mainstream of American culture. The most ready route that presents itself involves refiguring the authoritative dichotomy between Hebraism and Hellenism in such a way that it supports rather than impedes their entry.[1]

1. Fredman, *Menorah for Athena,* 2, 7.

Reznikoff held a law degree from New York University, worked as a script analyst for a major film producer in Hollywood, and was an influential poet and chronicler of American legal history and of the places where Jews had made an impact on colonial American life such as in Charleston, South Carolina, but his poetry suggests he could never quite overcome his feeling of inferiority, which stemmed from his humble beginnings in 1894 in the "Jewish Ghetto" of Brownsville, Brooklyn, New York, and with familial origins in Russia. Regardless of how learned he became in Greek culture, he viewed prestigious artifacts such as a sculpture of Athena in his poem entitled "Hellenist" from the position of "barbarian."

Writing at the end of the twentieth century, as a thoroughly assimilated American hailing from an economically comfortable background, Glück in her relationship to Hellenism shows none of the anxiety that so plagued Reznikoff. She seems as able to don the mask of Penelope or Persephone as Abishag or David. Like the midrashic application of biblical narratives to everyday life, *Meadowlands* is a "high-low experiment" in which bits of what Stephen Burt calls "almost kitchen-sink realist dialogue between the poet and her ex-husband" are juxtaposed to parables and other poems spoken through Homeric personae.[2]

The juxtaposition prompts the question: What exactly does *The Odyssey* represent to the speakers in *Meadowlands* as they move through the flimsy banalities of a stale marriage that is sputtering out in the context of American popular culture and suburban lawn parties? Dressing herself up as Penelope, Glück may not be able to contain the traumatic dissolution of the contemporary marriage, the confrontation with the fears of a poetic falling off and erotic decline, the fact of aging, and the contradictory and confusing impulses of a speaker who both cherishes her autonomy and yet is compelled to pursue a relationship with the disloyal beloved, all of which are central to the marital dynamics in *Meadowlands*. Nevertheless, precisely because her worries and wounds are not trivial, she yearns, and this yearning does make *The Odyssey*'s plot, structure, characterizations, and themes function for her speaker in ways that seem heartfelt and, therefore, too heavy with deep meaning for mere parody, which, at least according to Linda Hutcheon, represents the definitive cultural style in postmodernism.

How does this happen? I suggest that Glück's "high-low" structure, juxtaposing the Homeric personae and quotidian poems, foregrounds the issue described here, namely, how we as readers should receive the Homer we receive through *Meadowlands*. Glück allows us to perceive the appearance of *The Odyssey*

2. Burt, "'Dark Garage,'" 78.

from two opposite vantage points. One is external to the way the lyric personae experience Homer as a meaningful fantasy space through which they have felt free to assess their condition as it changes over time, and one is internal to the lyric speaker's fantasy world, a realm where Homer can and indeed does matter very much to them. The multiple "takes" on *The Odyssey* enable Glück simultaneously to objectify (and parody as overly ambitious and therefore hubristic) her drive to amplify her experience through myth in the public context of postmodern American suburbia. At the same time they enable her to retain the passionate aura of a subjective perspective on Homer, in which *The Odyssey* offers her speakers a chance to exert their interpretive powers. On a formal level, having her characters see their world through the Odyssean lens makes *Meadowlands* one of her most successful attempts to extend the resonance of the individual poem through a meaningful sequencing. The view toward and through Homer's *Odyssey* creates a productive tension that negotiates a space between what Bonnie Costello calls "the lyric's investment in the moment as an eternity, or rather, its elegiac sense of the present" and the concern of "the strictly narrative artist" with conclusions.[3] We could say that *Meadowlands* is a form of literary biography that exists in the gap between personal confession and transhistorical literary reflection on a classical theme.

No doubt *The Odyssey* at times seems terribly remote from and therefore fastened in a parody relationship to the emotionally numbing world described in "Void" (M), where the contemporary female speaker—or Penelope when she dons the mask—has so completely internalized her rage at her husband that he claims "the only time you're totally happy / is when you cut up a chicken" (M 49). The speaker has sublimated her desire for sensual experience, which is signified throughout the book by her interest in buying, preparing, and fear of eating meat. Equally far from a Homeric banquet is the state of affairs described in the final image of the final poem, "Heart's Desire," where she orders meat from a special grocery store, Lobel's, to serve at a patio party where "no one's / going to be hurt again" because "the passion / will all be in the music" (M 61). Whereas erotic desire, the quest for adventure, the reunion with family at home, and the more abstract social needs—for recognition, for the glorification of his name—propel the eponymous protagonist of the Homeric comedy toward a profound series of reconciliations, desire for Glück's main speaker, as Brown writes, "is dangerous in its devouring aspects, distanced from any healing or productive human contact."[4]

3. Bonnie Costello, "*Meadowlands*: Trustworthy Speakers," *Pn Review* 128 (July–August 1999): 19.

4. Brown, "Love of Form," 152.

As much as I want to challenge a parodic reading of the Homer we get in *Meadowlands,* evidence for the answer of postmodern parody can be found as soon as we glance at the title of the book, which refers to the location of the New York Giants football stadium in northeastern New Jersey. Such a bucolic designation for a field of artificial grass carpet where the ultimate postmodern spectacle of America's telemediated version of a titanic clash takes place on Sunday afternoons in the fall, but one surrounded with so much hype for light beer, disposable razors, and SUVs that we as readers have trouble taking seriously the comparison between the exploits of star Giants' players Phil Simms and Lawrence Taylor and those of Odysseus and Achilles. As the speaker herself glibly remarks in "Meadowlands 3":

> How could the Giants name
> that place the Meadowlands? It has
> about as much in common with a pasture
> as would the inside of an oven. (M 34)

Along with the speaker, we may mock the polluted environment and thoroughly consumerized venue of New Jersey as an infernal site more appropriate for a latter-day version of Dante than of Homer. We may also call into question how such a trivial entertainment and yet overbearing place name can legitimately recall the site of epic grandeur, which the very name Giants (a team once known as the Titans) would signify, let alone the distance between the urban detritus of the region with its pastoral namesake.

And yet, for all the obvious parody going on in *Meadowlands,* did not William Carlos Williams decide in 1946 to set an influential American epic in the context of working-class immigrant life in prosaic Paterson, New Jersey (an epic quest that he would continue to develop until his death in 1963)? Perhaps, then, we should reconsider whether parody is the only answer to my opening question: "What exactly does *The Odyssey* represent to the speakers in *Meadowlands* as they move through the flimsy banalities of a stale marriage that is sputtering out in the context of American popular culture and suburban lawn parties?" Perhaps instead of parody, Glück has engaged in a kind of transitional poetics that still bears the residue of her penchant for archetypes and myths in earlier work such as *The Triumph of Achilles*. Now, however, she is throwing garbage into the mix in order to bring her work down to earth, something that she has stated as an intention for her later work, even as she has acknowledged her struggle to embrace the pluralistic mess of American life that was the stock in trade of Williams, as well as an Objectivist poet such as Charles Reznikoff, who struggled with Hellenism from a Jewish perspective.

In *The Wild Iris,* Glück extends the lyric domain by exploring the various contours of a single speaker's contemplative life as her thoughts evolve and as she adjusts her feelings about God, nature, and her own creativity in changing atmospheric, seasonal, and psychological conditions. In *Meadowlands,* by contrast, she extends the border of the lyric, usually considered as the container for a single zone of consciousness, to incorporate a narrative dimension in a different way, by representing the main plot line (of a contemporary marriage at its conclusion and its imaginary reunion) from many viewpoints and through a variety of high and popular culture sources (Homer, Maria Callas, and Otis Redding among them). Her poetic practice suggests that the public record and private versions of a lyric self—the author's alter ego—may be composed from a verbal collage of many voices and texts speaking in different registers, but all about the closely related problem of identity formation. Each narrator's outlook on his or her own part in the lyric theater is thus a commentary on the power of commentary to help shape the self, in that each character interprets the words of other storytellers within the sequence, as the primary vehicle toward one's own identity formation.

Borrowing from *The Odyssey* to stage—as well as to conceal—the author's evolving sense of self as a construct subject to constant revision in and through a canonical text that itself focuses on Homer's foremost character of wandering and metamorphosis, Glück in *Meadowlands* chronicles the complex dynamics of a contemporary family in crisis and on the verge of dissolution. The sequence of poems maps out how the individual members of the family come to terms with their experience through a classical analogy that remains relevant to their most significant concerns. Penelope, who speaks in the voice of the author's alter ego, controls many of the lyrics in the sequence. But Glück, in a sense, lets up on her control of the volume by including seven poems (out of the volume's forty-six) spoken from the perspective of Telemachus (the son); three from the viewpoint of Circe, the witch who turned Odysseus's crew into animals and delayed him on his return voyage to Ithaca after the Trojan War; and one from the perspective of the Siren portraying the woman (also represented as Circe in *Meadowlands*) with whom the husband has had an affair. Glück thus extends the traditional lyrical emphasis on personal confession of fears and desires, to include other perspectives on her speaker's experience. This again suggests how she regards the Homeric frame as flexible enough to offer the simultaneity of internal and external prisms through which to view the self. She interprets her life through the eyes of characters such as "Siren" or "Circe," a hurt, frightened, angry woman who has nonetheless taken part in the affair that has hurt her, and the son "Telemachus," who at times seeks verbal revenge against his mother, claiming he has been scarred by Penelope's narcissistic desire to control the world around her through her interpretations of it.

Glück's compositional strategy in *Meadowlands*—which collates the ordinary and the oracular, the contemporary and the classical, the individual story and the collective response to it, the public reception and yet private significance of donning a mask to ventriloquize the self—is as much theatrical (or operatic, given the allusions to Callas's performance of Puccini's *Norma* in "Heart's Desire" [M 60]) as it is lyrical. By representing masked performances of a self in trouble through the different voices in a narrative sequence, she offers what the Joyce scholar Daniel R. Schwarz, following Mikhail Bakhtin and his theory of dialogism, refers to as "a complex chorus of voices showing us that history is composed not merely of the actions of the powerful but of the behavior of ordinary people and their retrospective views of it."[5]

Glück initially draws attention to how the narrative sequencing of lyrics—which accrue meaning through juxtaposition with other lyrics in the book, and with the classical text—relates to her own interest in revisiting her tone as an author, by imagining Penelope's widely variable responses to Odysseus's absence and betrayal through several poems that correspond to her ambivalent desire for his return home. Penelope, the weaver whose unraveling of a shroud for her husband's father, Laertes, defers the conclusion of *The Odyssey* by suspending the day when she must choose a suitor to marry, and so end the suspension of her story by accepting that her husband has died. Glück, like Penelope, is in a metaphorical sense both weaver and unweaver of her identity, as she challenges her characteristically hieratic and trancelike lyric voice by speaking in what had been for her until *Meadowlands* the unfamiliar tones of colloquialism and vulgarity. The book opens with "Penelope's Song," which temporally belongs later on in the sequence, as the speaker prepares to subjugate her demanding personality to accommodate Odysseus's wish for a more submissive partner. Through the Penelope persona, Glück then travels backward in narrative time to recall better moments in the marriage before Odysseus left home.

In "Quiet Evening" and "Departure," Glück folds still earlier memories into her "song," enabling the speaker to explore layers of experience and emotion, including how Penelope felt about her marriage when it was troubled but ongoing. Although they appear later in the sequence, these two poems retroactively create an emotional context in which to interpret Penelope's unappealing because self-lacerating behavior in "Penelope's Song." They shed light on, even if they do not excuse, her subsequent

5. Daniel R. Schwarz, *Imagining the Holocaust* (New York: St. Martin's Press, 1999), 24.

willingness to make at least an attempt to sublimate her demanding personality by placating her husband with the obsequious tone she takes toward him the first time we hear her voice.

The sequence of Penelope poems then moves forward in narrative time with "Ithaca," in which she abandons any serious hope that Odysseus will leave "Circe" to return to her bed, and then forward still further in time to "The Dream" and "Return," in which a period of real or, more likely, fantasy reconciliation occurs between husband and wife. Finally, in "Penelope's Stubbornness," the speaker revises her initial position of submission to her husband by accepting psychological detachment and the pain of physical isolation from the beloved as signs of her status as a maverick who must continue to be willing to endure a diminished existence in the literal realm, in order to be granted what is described in "The Wish," as the fundamental authorial desire, the longing "for another poem" (M 58).

In "Penelope's Song," Glück begins to diagram Penelope's shifting versions of her identity by noting changes in her relationship to her husband. The "song" conveys the evolving nature of her alter ego's contemplative life, representing the eponymous speaker in the unattractive emotional states of desperate longing; self-loathing at her desire for her estranged, narcissistic, and philandering husband; and such wild anticipation at ever seeing him again that she willingly agrees to refashion herself as a passive object of his desire so he can be free of challenges from a demanding partner.

> He will be home soon;
> it behooves you to be
> generous. You have not been completely
> perfect either; with your troublesome body
> you have done things you shouldn't
> discuss in poems. (M 3)

Addressing her "soul" while waiting for Odysseus to return "home soon," she reconstructs her identity, preparing herself to behave in a demure fashion, especially by warning herself not to do or say anything that might threaten, upset, or alienate her husband ("suntanned from his time away, wanting / his grilled chicken"), should he ever choose to be so kind as to return from his affair with the waitress known as "Siren." Deciding that it is not in her interest to interrogate him too closely about what happens "wherever he goes in the meantime," she has in a sense become a player in Odysseus's fiction by internalizing her husband's view of herself as the source of marital trouble: "[y]ou have not been completely / perfect either."

A soliloquy that is nonetheless informed by her husband's criticism, she deflects blame from Odysseus onto herself before imagining her "soul" as a songbird that can "climb / the shelf-like branches of the spruce tree" to "call out to him over the open water." "With your dark song" as another type of siren to instill in him a desire to return home from the waitress "Siren," Penelope seems at first glance to express her longing for erotic fulfillment, but she transforms her desire for sexual pleasure into an aesthetic replica of genuine feeling for the beloved—"passionate, / like Maria Callas." Brown is most helpful in her discussion of Callas, and especially on the plot of *Norma,* the operatic role most often played by Callas, and the one that the Penelope figure wants to play at the party in the final poem. Brown writes that "Bellini's opera about lost love, lost youth, mythical and mystical triumph and sacrifice as well as passionate revenge, offered Callas' intensity as singer and actor brilliant expression." Brown also summarizes the plot involving Norma, a druidic priestess in Roman occupied Gaul:

> Long ago, she had been seduced by the Roman proconsul, Pollione, and secretly had two children by him. Now, still obsessed with the Gallic priestesses, Pollione is in love with the young Adalgisa and tries to persuade her to follow him to Rome and become his wife. Adalgisa confides in Norma, and, siding with Norma, the two women declare their anger towards Pollione. After failing to persuade Pollione to give up Adalgisa, Norma announces that a priestess has betrayed her vows and will be a sacrificial victim. As Pollione waits for Norma to declare Adalgisa the victim, she gives her own name to her people. Moved by her nobility, Pollione feels his love revive and joins Norma on the pyre.[6]

Likening herself to Callas (1923–1977), the Greek American diva whose voice, legend has it, grew more expressive, even as her once plump body diminished into a shape resembling the anorexic self Glück occupied as a teenager, Penelope suggests her willingness to sublimate the yearning for her husband into the speaker's "dark song." A textual expression of desire, the song represents the strong feeling that has become detached from the speaker, like a bird that has flown away from the branches of a tree and into the air.[7]

6. Brown, "Love of Form," 129–30.

7. In "Ellen West," Frank Bidart develops this theme in a long dramatic poem based on the life of a suicidal anorexic who identifies her own struggles to come to terms with the mind-body split by evoking Callas. Frank Bidart, "Ellen West," in *In the Western Night: Collected Poems, 1965–1990* (New York: Farrar, Straus and Giroux, 1990).

Like "The Dream" and "Reunion" that appear toward the end of the volume, "Penelope's Song" expresses the power of sexual desire to override (or at least to compete with) Penelope's critique of her husband's behavior or her own self-regard. A strong narrative tension in that poem, however, distinguishes Penelope's desire for recognition from the beloved through "song," which language may be able to accomplish, from the elusive state of libidinal fulfillment, which language can only defer and so perpetually frustrate through linguistic sublimation. Rather than understanding the object of desire as preceding the subject's journey to love, Glück, like the theorists Žižek and Lacan, understands the object of desire as the after-effect of the subject's drive to create a pattern out of libidinal impulses.

Unlike "Penelope's Song," which is set after Odysseus has left home, "Departure," also from early in the volume, distorts the linear dimension of narrative time by flashing back to incidents from the marriage when it was, if not flourishing, then at least still in existence. Dealing with the period just prior to when he goes off on his escapades, "Departure" represents Penelope recalling with nostalgia images of "your [Odysseus's] hands on the back of the chair" and then "lightly stroking my shoulders." Penelope compares the way Odysseus, here figured as an Arnoldian aesthete of the Hellenist sort, stroked her shoulders to how he handled a possession—the smooth wood "on the back of the chair." Through this comparison, we begin to understand how memory of his aesthetic disposition and acquisitive nature has influenced the speaker's willingness in "Penelope's Song" to transform herself into a piece of art subject to his consumption by turning her "soul" into "dark song."

In "Departure," Penelope considers Odysseus an aesthetician who prizes things over persons, but also one "who prizes longing above all other emotion" (M 10). Interpreting his wanderlust as an illustration of the principle that desire can only be conducted by avoiding contact with the object toward which it flows, Penelope detects a tragic element to his nature that will have a grave impact on their relationship. Stating that Odysseus will always "need / distance to make plain its intensity," she believes, in a stunning remark, that he only trusts his wife's affection if he can "*see you* [Penelope] *grieve over me.*" Although Penelope is describing her husband, the poem seems especially self-referential at this moment, because for author, speaker, and the two main characters, desire turns out to be a negative or void emotion, a dynamic agent that cannot tolerate the making of a connection between self and other if it is to endure. "Departure" suggests that Odysseus's attitude toward desire remains contingent upon the characteristic Glückian postures of emotional detachment and physical departure. Perhaps more like Penelope than she would care to admit, Odysseus, himself a narcissist, mirrors her moods as "a man training himself to avoid the heart" (M 10).

In reading "Ithaca" we may do well to recall a late poem by Wallace Stevens, "The World as Meditation," which also characterizes Penelope's figuring of Odysseus "in the head" as superseding her need for his physical appearance in fact. As in Stevens's poem, which expresses Penelope's confusion about whether Odysseus has appeared before her in a literal or a figurative sense, Glück in "Ithaca" explores weighty metaphysical issues concerning the roles played by subjectivity, dream, and desire in constructing the idea of the beloved as a sufficient compensation for his desertion. Beginning with the claim that "The beloved doesn't / need to live. The beloved / lives in the head" (M 12), Penelope tries to convince herself that the figure Stevens referred to as the "interior paramour," or the imaginative creation of one's own libido, can fill the gap left behind after Odysseus's actual departure.

In "Ithaca," the speaker imagines two versions of Odysseus: one refers to "the body," or the literal self of her husband, and the other to "the voice," a figurative self or linguistic construct associated with the abstract realms of "idea" and "dream," and therefore held under the auspices of Penelope. She re-creates her wayward husband's voice to deal with real loss, as an "image / shaped by the woman working the loom" (M 12). If Penelope has re-created Odysseus's "voice" on the loom, we must also understand that Glück has linked representation of "voice" to the work of mourning through a text, as Penelope wove (and unraveled) a shroud designed for Odysseus's father, Laertes. Homer associates the covering on the loom with burial of the dead, but Penelope's decision to make and unmake that ceremonial garment is also associated in *The Odyssey* with deferring her decision to marry a suitor and so represents a way for the poet to delay her choice of a new husband, thereby granting the storyteller an extending narrative space to continue the wait for Odysseus. In "Ithaca," the "voice" Penelope constructs on the "loom" expresses Glück's emphasis on figuration rather than literalness as she associates the value of her husband's image with a symbol. As in Stevens's meditation, Penelope maintains confidence that the sea has only captured her "actual husband," an insignificant detail when compared to the superior figure of Odysseus that "lives in the head."

The poem ends with the shroud transformed into another ceremonial garment, a wedding dress, suggesting that the speaker's act of mourning enables her to connect herself to the husband in an emotional sense, rewriting desertion as marriage, and once again displaying the Odyssean—and, for that matter, Glückian—perspective on desire as loss-based. According to the logic of "Ithaca," Odysseus's abandonment of Penelope inaugurates a "marriage" that weds the speaker's creative imagination with her husband as a figure whose image remains under her jurisdiction, "shaped by the woman working the loom" (M 12). Husband and wife are paired together in love, desire, and textual pattern because, like Odysseus in "Departure," Penelope too "needs distance to make plain its intensity."

In *The Odyssey,* Homer delays the narrative time frame in which Odysseus and Penelope may be reunited in book 24 by devoting four books to the "Telemachiad," which records the son's journey from Ithaca to discover information about his father, even as the father is, ironically, traveling homeward to unite with his son to defeat the suitors. Similarly, Glück postpones the "Dream" and "Reunion" scene between husband and wife—the latter a poem in which Odysseus asks Telemachus to leave the room so the reunited couple can make love—by recalling the "Parable of the Hostages" (M) who do not want "to go home," and also by allotting seven poems to the impact that the parents' tempestuous relationship has had upon the son. In this delayed space, the son's identity evolves into that of an outwardly aloof but inwardly tortured artist-critic whose personality resembles that of his mother.[8] *Meadowlands* narrates the marriage conflict, but it is also a *kunstlerroman,* or "Portrait of the Artist as Young Man," because the book charts Telemachus's development as a storyteller and interpreter of stories about the self told by others. As Penelope does in her mutable responses to Odysseus's absence, Telemachus forms and reforms his identity through the shifting tones of his reactions to how his parents have shaped versions of their son, in texts that correspond to their own subjective impressions of who he is or who they think he ought to be.

The first poem spoken from his perspective, "Telemachus' Detachment," expresses the reticence of its title by being brief, only seven lines long. Although terse, it displays the emotional range and modulated tone that become more prevalent in subsequent lyrics associated with his name.

> When I was a child looking
> at my parents' lives, you know
> what I thought? I thought
> heartbreaking. Now I think
> heartbreaking, but also
> insane. Also
> very funny. (M 13)

8. The "Parable of the Hostages" represents the Greek warriors "sitting on the beach / wondering what to do when the war ends." Like Odysseus, who can only experience desire when he is away from his wife in Ithaca, here on the beachhead, "No one / wants to go home" because "everyone wants a little more / of what there is in Troy / more life on the edge" (M 14).

At first he regards his parents' relationship as "heartbreaking." But then, reconsidering his analysis, and complicating it, he adds to his admission of emotional distress a measure of ironic distance, describing the marriage as "insane" and, finally, "very funny." As with his mother's, we may interpret Telemachus's sardonic tone as a protective garment, designed to shield him from the pain of abandonment, in his case by parents who are cast as physically (Odysseus) and psychically (Penelope) remote.

In "Telemachus' Guilt," his second poem in the sequence, Glück explores how the parents' bickering and self-absorption, and final breakup, have contributed to the psychological turmoil that the son acts out. Telemachus's first poem thus reduces heartbreak to a source of mocking laughter.

> Patience of the sort my mother
> practiced on my father
> (which in his self-
> absorption he mistook
> for tribute though it was in fact
> a species of rage—didn't he
> ever wonder why he was
> so blocked in expressing
> his native abandon?): it infected
> my childhood. (M 19)

Like Penelope who struggles for control over her identity by analyzing the motivations of other characters, her son perceives his parents' activities as displaying a code with a latent content that only he has the power to decipher. For example, he identifies his mother's "patience" with his father's affairs as a passive aggressive sublimation of her anger toward him, "a species of rage," as he calls it. The son also ridicules his father's blindness to his mother's rage when Odysseus interprets Penelope's "patience" as a "tribute" of love for her husband.

Given the polyphonic texture of *Meadowlands,* we must suspect the accuracy of any of Telemachus's insights into the motivations behind his parents' behavior. As much as Odysseus's reading of Penelope may be narcissistic, Telemachus's refusal to imagine that his mother would be willing to pay "tribute" to her husband through her "patience" is equally based on subjective requirements, in this case the needs of an adolescent who wants to bolster his mother's stature by refusing to believe she could not rise above such irrational behavior as continuing to look the other way when his father goes off with the waitress. As "Penelope's Song" intimates, Telemachus cannot identify his mother's understanding of desire as fueled by absence, and so he cannot grasp the libidinal motivation behind her acceptance of her husband's affairs. Telemachus will not or cannot imagine that his mother remains attracted to Odysseus in spite (or because of) his infidelity.

Telemachus is engaged in his own wrestling match of interpretive prowess with his father, when coming to terms with his mother's decisions on how to behave toward her husband. He cannot accept her affection for a man who he believes has abused her, who has abandoned wife and son alike for "Circe," the witch who in Homer delayed Odysseus's return home to Ithaca. The son portrays himself with confidence as a sophisticated analyst of his parents' motives, but when "Telemachus' Guilt" is juxtaposed to other poems that reveal his perceptions of his parents, he often seems to lack self-knowledge, especially when the aloof veneer of the ironist comes apart, as if it were a flimsy mask that cannot hide the tears of a wounded boy.

In "Telemachus' Guilt," the son critiques Penelope by converting her tolerance for Odysseus's behavior into a sign, not of tribute or of rage, but of neglect that indicates her narcissism.

> It seemed clear to me
> that from her perspective
> I didn't exist, since
> my actions had
> no power to disturb her. (M 19)

To catch his mother's eye, Telemachus admits he has indulged in his own type of passive aggressive behavior, by "test[ing her] with increasing / violence," and how he would then "smile / when my mother wept." His claim to critical objectivity concerning his parents appears to be a cover for an adolescent anguish over Penelope's emotional impenetrability and Odysseus's physical abandonment. By the end of the poem, the son asks the mother to "forgive that cruelty" of smiling when she wept. His request may express genuine remorse at his "cruelty," but it may also convey his wish that Penelope would for once pay some attention to him. Either way, "Telemachus' Guilt" forces us to reconsider our impression of the son as the aloof but insightful teenager that we first met in "Telemachus' Detachment." What is clear is that the son has learned from his mother how to deal with unsatisfying relationships with other family members by casting himself as an ironic person. Cool commentary has not enabled him to achieve the psychological distance from her that he says he craves, but that is psychologically impossible.

Poems such as "Telemachus' Detachment" suggest that the parents' behavior and their unsuitable personalities have permeated their child's outlook on life to the point where we could say that he has become a fiction of their mutual creation: an emotional by-product of their selfishness and the broken marriage. Telemachus's icy exterior, but also his tenderness and vulnerability, as well as his wish for forgiveness from the mother resonate with how guilt, affection, and forgiveness play out in the relationship between Odysseus and Penelope, especially as Glück explores these themes in "Penelope's Song" and in "Parable of Faith." In moments of genuine self-awareness, Telemachus does admit that he has designed an ironic self to protect himself from interpreting Penelope's distance as a personal rebuke. By maintaining the psychological distance from his mother, Telemachus mirrors in emotional terms his father's physical departure from Penelope. The son has repeated the father's belief that "remaining / separate from what / one loves deeply" (M 20) is a legitimate way to protect himself from the vulnerability that Glück associates in "The Triumph of Achilles" with the ability to love what is perishable.

"Telemachus' Kindness" represents the son at a later, but not necessarily more winning, stage in his emotional development, when, as an adult, he reflects on his childhood by telling secrets about his life story to friends who he knows in advance will approve of his interpretations.

> I found
> I could share these perceptions
> with my closest friends, as they shared
> theirs with me, to test them,
> to refine them: as a grown man
> I can look at my parents
> impartially and pity them both: I hope
> always to be able to pity them. (M 24)

With the distance afforded by time, he can translate parents into texts and don the mantle of a literary analyst with a psychological bent. Claiming to understand their behavior better than they have understood themselves, Telemachus pities his father, perceiving Odysseus's absence from home and erotic questing as reactions to Penelope's inability, due to her isolated nature, to express empathy for his physicality and adventurous nature.

> what
> a life my mother had, without
> compassion for my father's

suffering, for a soul
ardent by nature, thus
ravaged by choice. (M 24)

Observing familial conflict from a steep and icy peak reminiscent of his mother's analytical posture in her lyrics, the son who had once felt "sorry for myself" because "in practical terms, I had no father," now claims with pride that he can "look at my parents / impartially and pity them both" (M 24). By transforming his parents into characters in a twisted drama composed of almost comically mismatched partners, and then by analyzing them as specimens with his friends as supportive chorus, Telemachus may claim to have arrived at a formula for healing old family grievances and the pain of abandonment. When viewed from another perspective, his commentary and willingness to abstract his autobiography by turning it into a specimen may also be read as a mask of sympathy that veils contempt for parents who have hurt him so deeply that he cannot forgive the ache.

Like Glück, who engages in a veiled form of personal mythmaking as well as an analysis of her domestic life and family relationships through the revision of Homer, Telemachus has transformed his private testimony of familial strife into an abstraction by treating his parents as if they were characters in a case study: "my trials / were the general rule, common / to all of us" (M 24). Performing the role of analyst, and then exposing his therapeutic findings to friends, Telemachus creates a community of interpretation that will be sympathetic to his point of view, while establishing an emotional distance from his childhood, but more important, he gains an upper hand in the competition with his parents to control the interpretation of family history. Certainly the ability to work through misery by analyzing childhood memories with an audience of friends has its merits. As commentary, it allows Telemachus to assert his common humanity with his peers and at the same time to feel "pity" for his parents. More than a little hostility lurks, however, behind the ironically named "kindness." His sympathy hardly masks a wish for a patronizing form of domination over his parents, reversing the role of parent and child. Interpreting Penelope and Odysseus as emotional cripples, he absolves himself from entanglement with their strife by testifying to the guilt he experienced after smiling at his mother's sadness in "Telemachus' Guilt." His final pronouncement, "I hope / always to be able to pity them," suggests that he may not look forward to the day when the parents will no longer require his pity.

If "Telemachus' Kindness" suggested a sublimated form of aggression toward the parents by commenting on their lives as if they were public stories that only the son could truly understand, then "Telemachus' Dilemma" takes belligerence through interpretation one step further. It portrays the young man imagining a future when his parents are already dead, depicting the grave as a text that contains the definitive meaning of his parents' sayings according to their son's perspective. By his claim that he "can never decide / what to write on / my parents' tomb" (M 33), we realize that Telemachus's thinking about the parents' death and burial have been habitual preoccupations. As in "Telemachus' Kindness," the son places himself in a position of authority over his parents by imagining what they would like to have written on their gravestones, and then by critiquing his speculation about his version of their words.

Telemachus knows the father "wants ***beloved***," which the son rather glibly thinks apt, "particularly / if we count all / the women." Telemachus remains the mother's son in terms of his writing style, insisting that his own "taste dictates / accuracy without / garrulousness." Through Telemachus, Glück addresses the question of who controls the family history as part of the individual characters' struggle for acknowledgment in a combative atmosphere where recognition of one's experience is a scarce resource. Here, the son and the mother discuss his plans for her epitaph. "[S]he prefers / to be represented by / her own achievement" (M 33). In control of the writing on the memorial for his mother, the son views her desire for self-inscription to be another form of vanity.

In the previous Telemachus poems, the son has asserted his power to represent his parents in perpetuity and, therefore, has imagined his ability to wrest authority away from them through his act of commemoration. "Telemachus' Fantasy" further reveals that his wish for literary power sublimates his feelings of sexual inadequacy when he compares himself to his father. "Telemachus' Fantasy" represents another side of Telemachus, that of an inexperienced adolescent who, although hurt, stands in awe of his father's erotic conquests, especially when the son construes Odysseus as an older man whose libido is "unthwarted" as he seduces appealing younger women. Wondering "why / was he so attractive / to women," Telemachus responds to his father's affairs with an ambivalence that mixes admiration, suppressed anger, and sadness over the infidelities that have destroyed the marriage and challenged what had remained of family harmony. Telemachus engages in his own erotic fantasy by imagining that the younger women have, like the speaker's mother, found his father attractive not in spite of Odysseus's emotional troubles, but because his "disintegration reminds them / of passion" (M 39).

The poem becomes especially intriguing when we consider how many layers of interpretation, and how many interpreters, Glück has combined in picturing Telemachus's fantasy. On one level, the author has transformed her own autobiographical experience of a contemporary marital conflict into a revised version of Homer's myth of abandonment and reconciliation, after a long period of detachment in which the woman must wait behind at home while an adventurous man engages in acts of love and war. The author has also relinquished her perspective as a mature woman and wife by speaking of her husband through the mask of Telemachus, who comments about how and why the young women have imagined his father as "disintegrating" and, because of their awareness of his vulnerability, have fallen in love with him. At the same time, the issue of "passion" and its relation to "disintegration" (of self, of relationships with the beloved, and to "music") has been on Glück's mind in more overtly autobiographical poems such as "Heart's Desire," which concludes ***Meadowlands*** with a meditation on the destructive nature of passion, and on the way music may sublimate or control it.

In "Brown Circle" (AR), Glück's alter ego feared that her intense scrutiny of her son, Noah, was a form of smothering, an image of the stereotypical Jewish mother's love for the son gone haywire as her affection transforms into the image of the overzealous botanist with a magnifying glass who burns the plant she adores by inspecting it too closely. In contrast, Telemachus's poems about his mother suggest a very different picture of her care. Taken together, his lyrics represent a cry for help from parents who literally (in Odysseus's case) and figuratively (in Penelope's case) had abandoned or ignored him to pursue their own desires—extramarital affairs for Odysseus and composing "dark songs" for Penelope. These songs attempt to attract the husband's attention, or to follow in the tradition of Maria Callas by approximating the feeling of an intense love affair in the abstract domain of the text. Telemachus's poems also serve as evidence that the mother's concern in "Brown Circle" that she has constricted her son was, from the son's point of view, unwarranted. As Glück addresses her author's struggle to represent herself in opposition to how she believes others perceive her, so "Telemachus' Confession" suggests that his parents impeded his ability to form his own identity independent of their versions of him. He has spent his youth trying to "fabricate the being / each required," so Telemachus has failed to develop a strong enough sense of self. He must, therefore, confess that he was "better off" when his father left home, because he could then develop "my own voice," and "my own perceptions," since he was no longer "having to be / two people" (M 48), an object to be contested by the parents in conflict, a someone or a something for them to fight over or for them to see as a reflection of themselves.

"Telemachus' Burden" offers the son's perspective on his father's decision to return home, however briefly, after the affairs, but the poem is especially compelling to read for the sharp observations it offers about Penelope, whom

Telemachus perceives as an isolate, who has become inconsolably depressed to the point where she rejects her son when he tries to "relieve her misery" (M 50). "Parable of Faith" and "Reunion" will represent the husband returning home to ask forgiveness when Odysseus "very delicately . . . signs to Telemachus to depart," but we must recall the "burden" of Telemachus's observations about his mother as inconsolable. We as readers must also relinquish the mythic level of the tale at this point and return to our earlier realization that Glück has enabled us to imagine her suffering from multiple perspectives, in this case from the point of view of the son who can feel things about his mother that may contradict Penelope's own expressions of pleasure at the dream "that we were married again."

In "Circe's Torment" and "Circe's Grief," Glück extends the lyric domain to include the perspective of a character—the waitress stereotyped as the seductive witch, but here presented as a complex admixture of rage and vulnerability—whom she could just as easily have cast aside for being responsible for the affairs, and so unworthy of recognition in the sequence. Instead of banishing Circe from her text, Glück includes her perspective and, by so doing, enables her readers to see beyond Penelope's pain to address the bitter, confused, and hurt perspectives of the other woman, for whom Odysseus will not soon leave his marriage. Taking the form of a curse spoken by Circe against Odysseus, "Circe's Torment" imagines her addressing him at the end of the affair:

> When
> you see her again, tell her
> this is how a god says goodbye:
> if I am in her head forever
> I am in your life forever. (M 46)

Mirroring Penelope's confidence in her ability to re-create Odysseus as a "voice" on her "loom" in "Ithaca," "Circe" recalls how she has disrupted Penelope from her work as a weaver but then suggests how she will continue to exist in Penelope's "head" as a living specter.

By representing the perspectives of the wife, the "Circe" figure, and the son, Glück reconfigures each lyric pronouncement as a commentary that is then subject to revision by other speakers. At various points, even the same speaker is willing to produce a fresh analysis of his or her own perceptions, suggesting what Frost would call a "momentary stay against confusion," or a provisional clarification of prior attitudes, beliefs, and judgments. As much as *Meadowlands* engages as a whole in the freewheeling attitude toward canons as common but adaptable reference points for identity construction (as we have observed in her idiosyncratic commentary on the Bible), the collection also exhibits in its formal structure a process of commentary that is internal to thc lyrics themselves, especially when they are considered as juxtaposed elements, parts of a whole that exist independently but also within the collection's narrative sweep. The final poem that includes Penelope as the title character, "Penelope's Stubbornness," illustrates how Glück alters her protagonist's attitudes toward prior events, by reinterpreting their meaning as she perceives them from a different place and time within the sequence.

The revision begins in the first line of "Penelope's Stubbornness," when the speaker observes that "[a] bird comes to the window," but she metaphorizes the bird into a messenger:

> It's a mistake
> to think of them
> as birds, they are so often
> messengers. (M 47)

Penelope's narcissistic tendency to read personal and emblematic significance into elements of nature continues when, isolated in her home, she interprets the bird's stillness as a deliberate attempt to "mock / patience." When she hears three notes of birdsong, she interprets these repetitive sounds as signifying pity: "***poor lady, poor lady.***" After transforming a random natural event such as birdsong into a message specific to her plight, in the first ten lines, the speaker then, in the final six lines, contests and in the end dismantles her prior reading strategy. She dismisses the birds' warbling sounds as signifying a language that mocks her "stubbornness"—or her willingness to believe that her desire for her husband's return from his affair and her ability to love her husband in his absence are folly.

Protesting her initial judgment upon her life as impoverished and subject to mockery, Penelope chooses to reimagine her situation as a person who asserts her freedom by existing apart from nature, in contrast to the birds whose songs express an unself-conscious harmony with their environment. At first she reasons that birds are free to fly away from the sill "to the olive grove," only because they are "weightless beings." She takes control of her metaphor of the birds as able to fly away because they are quite literally lightweight when she suggests an emotional dimension to her reading of nature, claiming that, although those (like her husband) with "the smallest hearts" have "the greatest freedom," her "humanity" (M 47), her grave yet courageous ability to remain in place while enduring the pain of abandonment, and the length of her memories of better times, all may compensate for the lack of worldly experience in the present tense as she records her story as a song. We recall that in the collection's initial poem, Penelope's "song" was imagined as a bird that could fly to Odysseus as a messenger, a harbinger of her desire for her husband's return. Her "soul" was likened to a songbird that could "climb / the shelf-like branches of the spruce tree" to "call out to him over the open water" (M 3). With her "dark song" as a siren, she would awaken in him a desire to return home.

"Penelope's Stubbornness" illustrates Glück's ability to alter her protagonist's attitudes toward her prior pronouncements through the Homeric framework by placing lyrics within a sequence of responses that occur over time. The songbird that initially represented her willingness to subjugate herself to her husband must in "Penelope's Stubbornness" be connected to her image of her husband. He has mobility, like the birds on the sill, but he lacks the gravitas associated with Penelope's stubbornness, or her ability to stay put, weaving and unweaving interpretations of the world around her.

In "Midnight" (M 26), the speaker watches herself acting, as if from the outside, by speaking to her "aching heart" in the second person and then asking her deep self, as if it were another being,

> what
> ridiculous errand are you inventing for yourself
> weeping in the dark garage
> with your sack of garbage: it is not your job
> to take out the garbage, it is your job
> to empty the dishwasher. (M 26)

The poem takes out Homer and plays seriously with his characters, as masks, rather than following the emphasis on emptying the meaning of established signifiers as in postmodern parody; when viewed objectively the poem seems to exemplify intellectual irresponsibility because it avoids a direct confrontation with current reality, a kind of trash talk that can only lead to parody. When viewed from the perspective of the "aching heart," however, or from within the lyricist's own fantasy space, the Homeric material can matter enormously.

Indeed, Glück regards *The Odyssey* as a theatrical device, a series of shifting zones of consciousness (to follow Judith Butler). The speaker reuses or redeploys a subject position in provisional and improvisatory ways that have not been previously authorized, but that serve the psychological function of at once distancing her from and enabling her to covertly discuss her failing marriage and other vital issues. Far from parody when looked at from the inside of the lyric's speaker subject position, Homer's text becomes an ideal forum in which to address, through the figure of Penelope as forlorn lover and lonely weaver, the author's interpretation of artistic prowess, as being contingent upon the sublimation of erotic longing and upon a dissociation from nature through the shift toward figuration.

Conclusion

In "Some Questions concerning Art and Suffering" another leading contemporary Jewish American poet, Alan Shapiro, explains the satisfactions he found in translating a Greek tragedy, *The Oresteia* by Aeschylus, during a period in his life when he experienced what he describes as a contemporary version of Job's sufferings.[9] In the fall of 1999, and in the midst of dealing with his own divorce, a brother who was dying of brain cancer, and life with a landlady who suffered from dementia, Shapiro found a peculiar kind of comfort and solace in working on a Greek tale that involves a chain of blood vengeance including the murder of Agamemnon by his wife, Clytemnestra, and the successful conspiracy of their children, Orestes and Electra, to kill their mother in the cause of justice.[10] His essay speculates about why such disturbing subject matter could have been for him "one of the great joys of my writing life." The answer: "in times of difficulty the objects of desire become a refuge as well as a passion."[11]

Shapiro has touched upon a paradoxical aspect of art-making: that involving oneself as an artist in materials dealing with extreme suffering can be a form of "refuge" from one's own personal struggles, especially if the materials concern terrors that are fictional, ancient, and come to us in another language. For Shapiro, the attention to the aesthetic dimension of the art—the bringing to life, as it were, of this representation of a totally "other" experience of suffering, through his linguistic and prosodic skills—became a task of such absorbing difficulty that it was able to "distract me from the pain that I was living through." A "monumental puzzle," translating became "a source of inexhaustible pleasure, at a time when life seemed nothing but a vale of tears." Instead of feeling empathetic identification with members of the House of Atreus, Shapiro says it was "the historical remoteness of the story"

9. Alan Shapiro, "Some Questions concerning Art and Suffering," *Tikkun* 19.1 (January–February 2004): 28–32.
10. Brian Wilkie, ed., *Literature of the Western World* (Upper Saddle River, N.J.: Prentice Hall, 1997), 1:607.
11. Shapiro, "Some Questions concerning Art," 28.

that allowed him to detach himself from his own pain as he was "learning all about a family more dysfunctional than mine." He thus associates the "pleasure" of translation with "the distance between the world of the play and the messy particulars of everyday existence."[12]

There are of course differences between Shapiro's relationship to Greek literature and what we see in Glück's poetry. For one, Shapiro did not try to enter his own experiences (of divorce, a demented landlady, and a dying brother) into language through the Greek personae. For Shapiro, the technical problems of connecting Aeschylus to our own time had to do with finding an appropriate idiom to bring the play to life for a new audience. For Glück, the challenge was more one of solving a narrative problem—how to create a dynamic and believable sequence of lyric poems that are meant to be read as if they were in dialogue with each other. For Shapiro, the act of translation became a momentary distraction from immediate suffering. For Glück, the narrative line of a prior text becomes a format, a performance space, through which to give shape, meaning, and amplified significance to her own suffering. For both Shapiro and Glück, however, the fact of distance that is involved in recasting experiences of great hardship into a work of art is part of what makes possible "the transformation of suffering into aesthetic pleasure."[13]

In this study, we have seen Glück embracing what she calls "the fact of distance" (between representation and lived reality) as a way to make her experience available to readers as art, but also as a way to write her autobiography that would not otherwise have been possible through the confessional mode. It is as if Glück could not recall her experience as meaningful, and therefore as available for representation, without placing elements of her life story into a remote language through a variety of myths and masks.

Shapiro believes that the pleasure we receive in reading "poems about the darker aspects of existence" has to do with "the form giving imagination of the artist." Form, he says, is the visible sign that a transformation, a turning, has taken place between lived experience in its blooming and buzzing confusion and the shaped and ordered simulations of art that allow us to bring meaning to bear on what is otherwise the nonsensical flow of real life. For Shapiro, art—both the act of translating Aeschylus and the more overtly autobiographical book of poems *Song and Dance* that he wrote about his brother's dying—became a form of "avoidance of grief. . . . I was transforming an intractable sorrow into an aesthetic problem that the writing of the

12. Ibid.
13. Ibid., 30.

poems was a way to solve." The act of writing made Shapiro happy, if only for the time being, and even if his problems did not resolve themselves through writing. Writing becomes a form of deferral of suffering, even if, in the end, the act of writing may not bring long-lasting comfort. "The division between art and suffering is absolute," Shapiro writes, "even as we still try helplessly to bridge it."[14]

In the end, Shapiro argues against the instinct to monumentalize suffering in art (he gives Yeats's "Easter, 1916" as an example). He counsels poets to privilege a kind of writing that self-consciously addresses the situation of the artist who "wants to raise the dead" with his art, but who also "recognizes the impossibility of what it nonetheless is helpless not to try to do":

> The epitaph, the work of art, the good poem, heals paradoxically: the distance necessary for memorialization, the distance that enables one to use one's tenderness as skill, the distance needed to create the space for artistic exercise, for forging a social response out of private grief, acknowledges in and through its pleasure and beauty the unredeemable loss and bodily anguish for which no artifact can compensate.

Shapiro thus has come to feel that he wants "the kind of beauty that acknowledges the insufficiency of beauty," that "there is no good substitute for the precious flesh."[15]

In an interview with Ann Douglas after the publication of *Descending Figure,* Glück states her own version of Shapiro's dilemma—that art, however meaningful and satisfying, is an inadequate substitute for flesh:

> I've . . . felt the temptation of the Absolute as a danger; the mysticism, the spirituality out of which I suppose, my best poems will come, has in some ways to be fought. I tried—try—to introduce and reintroduce the earthly, the temporal, because my orientation is always toward the eternal. . . . I do some corrective reading. I often read poets like [Alan] Dugan and [David] Ignatow, poets who make poems out of tables and coffeepots to *remind* myself of that material, literal world I keep trying to escape: the world of particular fact, not paradigm. . . . I realize I have a craving for that which is immutable. The physical world is mutable. So, you cast about for those situations, or myths, that will answer the craving.[16]

14. Ibid., 30–31.
15. Ibid., 32.
16. Douglas, "Descending Figure," 25.

The emphasis Glück does place in *Meadowlands* on the realm, if not exclusively of Dugan's and Ignatow's "table and coffeepots" then of an aging woman as she confronts the dissolution of her family, the diminishment of her creative range, the personal losses entailed in a devotion to the solitary life, as well the fear of being undesirable to a philandering husband, all may represent a necessary and even welcome leveling device for a poet. Glück admits to the "powerful hold over me" of "the absolute, the eternal, the immutable—that condition which does not exist in the physical world" but which has driven her to amplify and to shield her autobiography through the Homeric parallel. "Parable of the Dove" (M) describes a speaker, much like the author as she portrays herself in the interview, who "wanted to walk among them, / to experience the violence of human feeling, / in part for its song's sake" (M 31). In "Moonless Night," the speaker denigrates her typical attempt to contain life's rich ongoingness with the mastery of form as a sign of illumination: "Such a mistake to want / clarity above all things," when "On the other side, there could be anything, / all the joy in the world, the stars fading, / the streetlight becoming a bus stop" (M 9).

In such poems that disregard the epic comparison, as Melissa Brown argues, "the range of common experiences . . . teaches the speakers of *Meadowlands* about loss, the kind of daily loss which constitutes our discontinuous lives."[17] However much Glück in *Meadowlands* may try to embrace "the range of common experiences," by suturing together Greek epic personae and scenes from a broken marriage in contemporary middle-class suburbia, the allusions to Homer do intrude upon the local, deflated environment—in a way that makes the quotidian seem, by contrast, even more bathetic. Glück still has a long way to go to become one of Altieri's poets of "immanence," regardless of how many volumes of Dugan and Ignatow she may have read. At the same time, her expression in both interviews and poetry of a deep misgiving—about her desire for "clarity above all things" and her contrary desire, in poems from *Vita Nova* and *The Seven Ages,* to embrace life—connects her ambivalence toward "translating" Greek literature into a current idiom with Shapiro's awareness that no artistic skill, no amount of the "distance needed to create," can compensate for the "unredeemable loss" and "bodily anguish" that propel so many artists. Glück is driven incessantly to try on and then put away various masks and myths through which, however provisionally and insecurely, she confronts her life as an example of the hard facts of human experience.

17. Brown, "Love of Form," 157.

Works Cited

Abrams, M. H. "Structure and Style in the Greater Romantic Lyric." In *Romanticism and Consciousness: Essays in Criticism,* ed. Harold Bloom, 201–29. New York: Norton, 1970.

Abrams, M. H., et al., eds. *Norton Anthology of English Literature.* Vol. 2. 7th ed. New York: Norton, 2000.

Alighieri, Dante. *Vita Nuova.* Translated by Mark Musa. Bloomington: Indiana University Press, 1973.

Alter, Robert. "The Achievement of Gershom Scholem." In *Gershom Scholem: Modern Critical Views,* ed. Harold Bloom. New York: Chelsea House, 1987.

———. *Canon and Creativity: Modern Writing and the Authority of Scripture.* New Haven: Yale University Press, 2000.

Atlas, James. *My Life in the Middle Ages: A Survivor's Tale.* New York: HarperCollins, 2005.

Auden, W. H. "The Shield of Achilles." In *The Norton Anthology of English Literature: The Twentieth Century,* ed. Jon Stallworthy and David Daiches, 2511–12. New York: Norton, 2000.

Auerbach, Erich. *Mimesis: The Representation of Reality in Western Literature.* Translated from German by Willard R. Trask. Princeton, N.J.: Princeton University Press, 2003.

Baigell, Matthew. *Jewish Artists in New York: The Holocaust Years.* New Brunswick, N.J.: Rutgers University Press, 2002.

Barron, Jonathan. "At Home in the Margins: The Jewish American Voice Poem in the 1990s." *College Literature* 24.3 (October 1997): 104–23.

———. "Commentary in Contemporary Jewish American Poetry." In Barron and Selinger, *Jewish American Poetry,* 233–49.

Barron, Jonathan N., and Eric Murphy Selinger, eds. *Jewish American Poetry: Poems, Commentary, and Reflections.* Hanover, N.H.: Brandeis University Press, 2000.

Barry, Peter. *Beginning Theory: An Introduction to Literary and Cultural Theory.* Manchester, England: Manchester University Press, 1995.

Baumlin, James S. "Reading Bloom, or Lessons concerning the 'Reformation' of the Western Literary Canon." *College Literature* 27.3 (Fall 2000): 22–47.

Bedient, Calvin. "'Man Is Altogether Desire'?" *Salmagundi* 90-91 (1991): 212–30.

Behlman, Lee. "The Escapist: Fantasy, Folklore, and the Pleasures of the Comic Book in Recent Jewish American Holocaust Fiction." *Shofar* 22.3 (Spring 2004): 56–71.

Berger, Charles. "Poetry Chronicle: Amy Clampitt, Louise Glück, Mark Strand." *Raritan* 10.3 (Winter 1999): 119–33.

Bernstein, Charles. "Solidarity Is the Name We Give to What We Cannot Hold." In *My Way: Speeches and Poems.* Chicago: University of Chicago Press, 1999.

Bettelheim, Bruno. *The Uses of Enchantment: The Meaning and Importance of Fairy Tales.* New York: Vintage, 1976.

Biale, David. *Eros and the Jews: From Biblical Israel to Contemporary America.* Berkeley and Los Angeles: University of California Press, 1997.

Birnbaum, Philip. *Encyclopedia of Jewish Concepts.* New York: Sanhedrin Press, 1979.

Bleich, David. "Learning, Learning, Learning: Jewish Poetry in America." In Barron and Selinger, *Jewish American Poetry,* 177–93.

Bloom, Harold. *The American Religion: The Emergence of the Post-Christian Nation.* New York: Simon and Schuster, 1992.

———. *The Anxiety of Influence: A Theory of Poetry.* 1973. 2nd ed. New York: Oxford University Press, 1997.

———. *Kabbalah and Criticism.* New York: Seabury, 1975.

———. *Omens of Millennium: The Gnosis of Angels, Dreams, and Resurrection.* New York: Riverhead, 1996.

Bogen, Don. "Review of 'The Triumph of Achilles.'" *The Nation* 2 (1986): 53–54.

Bonds, Diane S. "Entering Language in Louise Glück's 'The House on Marshland': A Feminist Reading." *Contemporary Literature* 31.1 (1990): 58–75.

Brown, Melissa Lee. "The Love of Form Is a Love of Endings: Poetic Hunger and the Aesthetic Body in Louise Glück." Ph.D. diss., University of Iowa, 1997.

Burt, Stephen. "'The Dark Garage with the Garbage': Louise Glück's Structures." In Diehl, *On Louise Glück,* 74–89.

Butler, Judith. "Contingent Foundations." In *Feminists Theorize the Political,* ed. Judith Butler and Joan W. Scott. New York: Routledge, 1992.

———. *Inside/Out: Lesbian Theories, Gay Theories.* Edited by Diana Fuss. New York: Routledge, 1992.

Camus, Albert. *The Plague.* Translated by Stuart Gilbert. New York: Vintage, 1991.

Caruth, Cathy. *Unclaimed Experience.* Baltimore: Johns Hopkins University Press, 1996.

Chandler, James. *Wordsworth's Second Nature: A Study of the Poetry and Politics.* Chicago: University of Chicago Press, 1984.

Chodorow, Nancy. *The Reproduction of Mothering: Psychoanalysis and the Sociology of Gender.* Berkeley and Los Angeles: University of California Press, 1978.

Costello, Bonnie. "*Meadowlands:* Trustworthy Speakers." *Pn Review* 25.6.128 (July–August 1999): 14–19.

Daly, Mary. *Beyond God the Father: Toward a Philosophy of Women's Liberation.* Boston: Beacon Press, 1973.

DeMeester, Karen. "Trauma and Recovery in Virginia Woolf's *Mrs. Dalloway.*" *Modern Fiction Studies* 44.3 (Fall 1998): 649–74.

Dickinson, Emily. "The Brain—Is Wider than the Sky." In Ramazani et al., *Norton Anthology.*

Diehl, Joanne Feit, ed. *On Louise Glück: Change What You See.* Ann Arbor: University of Michigan Press, 2005.

Diggory, Terence. "Louise Glück's Lyric Journey." *Salmagundi* 124–25 (Fall 1999–Winter 2000): 303–18.

Dimock, George E., Jr. "The Name of Odysseus." In *Homer: A Collection of Critical Essays,* ed. George Steiner and Robert Fagles, 106–21. Englewood Cliffs, N.J.: Prentice Hall, 1962.

Dodd, Elizabeth. *The Veiled Mirror and the Woman Poet: H.D., Louise Bogan, Elizabeth Bishop, and Louise Glück.* Columbia: University of Missouri Press, 1992.

Doreski, William. *The Modern Voice in American Poetry.* Gainesville: University Press of Florida, 1995.

Douglas, Ann. "Descending Figure: An Interview with Louise Glück." *Columbia Magazine* (1980): 116–25.

Drury, John. *Creating Poetry.* Cincinnati: Writer's Digest Books, 1991.

Duncan, Erika. "The Hungry Jewish Mother." In Heschel, *Jewish Feminist,* 27–39.

Eliot, T. S. "Journey of the Magi." In *The Longman Anthology of British Literature,* ed. David Damrosch. Compact edition. New York: Longman,

2000.

———. "The Love Song of J. Alfred Prufrock." In Ramazani et al., *Norton Anthology.*

Felman, Shoshana, and Dori Laub. *Testimony: Crises of Witnessing in Literature, Psychoanalysis, and History.* New York: Routledge, 1992.

Finkelstein, Norman. *The Ritual of New Creation.* New York: State University of New York Press, 1992.

Fischer, Michael. "Memory: Experimental Sondages in the (Post)modern World." In *Autobiography and Postmodernism,* ed. Kathleen Ashley, Leigh Gilmore, and Gerald Peters. Amherst: University of Massachusetts, 1994.

Fishbane, Michael. "Inner Biblical Exegesis: Types and Strategies of Interpretation in Ancient Israel." In Hartman and Budick, *Midrash and Literature,* 19–40.

Flory, Wendy Stallard. Handout on *The Wild Iris.* Course on American Women Poets, Purdue University, Fall 2003.

Fox, Everett. *The Five Books of Moses.* New York: Schocken Books, 2000.

Frankel, Ellen. *The Five Books of Miriam: A Woman's Commentary on the Torah.* New York: Putnam, 1996.

———. *The Illustrated Hebrew Bible: Seventy-Five Selected Stories.* New York: Stewart, Tabori and Chang, 1999.

Fredman, Stephen. *A Menorah for Athena: Charles Reznikoff and the Jewish Dilemmas of Objectivist Poetry.* Chicago: University of Chicago Press, 2001.

Freud, Sigmund, and Josef Breur. *Studies on Hysteria.* Translated from the German and edited by James Strachey, in collaboration with Anna Freud, assisted by Alix Strachey and Alan Tyson. New York: Basic Books, 1957.

Frost, Robert. "Provide, Provide." In Ramazani et al., *Norton Anthology.*

Fukuyama, Francis. *The End of History and the Last Man.* New York: Free Press, 1993.

Ginzberg, Louis. *Legends of the Jews.* New York: Jewish Publication Society, 1901.

Girard, René. *Job: The Victim of His People.* Translated by Yvonne Freccero. London: Athlone Press, 1987.

Glück, Louise. "Afterword: The Restorative Power of Art." In Diehl, *On Louise Glück,* 190.

———. *Ararat.* New York: Ecco Press, 1990.

———. *Averno.* New York: Farrar, Straus and Giroux, 2006.

———. *The First Four Books of Poems: Firstborn, The House on Marshland,*

Descending Figure, The Triumph of Achilles. New York: Ecco, 1995.

———. *Meadowlands.* New York: Ecco Press, 1996.

———. *October.* Louisville, Ky.: Sarabande Books, 2004.

———. *Proofs & Theories: Essays on Poetry.* New York: Ecco, 1994.

———. *The Seven Ages.* New York: HarperCollins, 2001.

———. *Vita Nova.* New York: Ecco Press, 1999.

———. *The Wild Iris.* New York: Ecco Press, 1992.

Goodhart, Sandor. *Sacrificing Commentary: Reading the End of Literature.* Baltimore: Johns Hopkins University Press, 1996.

Gordon, Margaret Ann. "Reconceiving the Sacred: Louise Glück and Postmodern Spirituality." Ph.D. diss., University of Mississippi, 2000.

Greenblatt, Stephen. *Renaissance Self-Fashioning from Moore to Shakespeare.* Chicago: University of Chicago Press, 1980.

Gregerson, Linda. "The Sower against Gardens." *Kenyon Review* 23.1 (Winter 2001): 115–33. Reprinted in Diehl, *On Louise Glück,* 28–47.

Grossman, Allen. *The Long Schoolroom: Lessons in the Bitter Logic of the Poetic Principle.* Ann Arbor: University of Michigan Press, 1997.

———. *The Sighted Singer: Two Works on Poetry for Readers and Writers.* Baltimore: Johns Hopkins University Press, 1992.

Gubar, Susan. "Eating the Bread of Affliction: Judaism and Gender." In *Critical Condition: Feminism at the Turn of the Century,* 69–90. New York: Columbia University Press, 2000.

Hass, Robert. Dust jacket commentary. *Vita Nova.* New York: Ecco Press, 1999.

Hartman, Geoffrey. *The Longest Shadow: In the Aftermath of the Holocaust.* New York: Palgrave Macmillan, 2002.

———. "The Struggle for the Text." In Hartman and Budick, *Midrash and Literature.*

Hartman, Geoffrey H., and Sanford Budick, eds. *Midrash and Literature.* New Haven: Yale University Press, 1986.

Herman, Judith. *Trauma and Recovery.* New York: Basic Books, 1992.

Heschel, Abraham Joshua. *God in Search of Man: A Philosophy of Judaism.* New York: Farrar, Straus, and Giroux, 1976.

———. *Moral Grandeur and Spiritual Audacity.* Edited by Susannah Heschel. New York: Noonday, 1996.

ng a Jewish Feminist: A Reader. New York: Schocken Books, 1983.

Holtz, Barry, ed. *Back to the Sources: Reading the Classic Jewish Texts.* New York: Summit Books, 1984.

Homans, Margaret. *Bearing the Word: Language and Female Experience in Nineteenth-Century Women's Writing.* Chicago: University of Chicago

Press, 1986.

Howe, Florence, ed. *No More Masks: An Anthology of Twentieth-Century American Women Poets.* New York: HarperCollins, 1993.

Keats, John. "To Autumn." In *The Premier Book of Major Poets,* ed. Anita Dore, 36. New York: Ballantine Books, 1991.

Keller, Lynn. "'Free/of Blossom and Subterfuge': Louise Glück and the Language of Renunciation." In *World, Self, Poem: Essays on Contemporary Poetry from the "Jubilation of Poets,"* ed. Leonard M. Trawick, 120–29. Kent: Kent State University Press, 1980.

Kojève, Alexandre. *Introduction to the Reading of Hegel.* Translated by James H. Nichols, Jr. Ithaca: Cornell University Press, 1969.

Kramer, Michael P., and Hana Wirth-Nesher, eds. *The Cambridge Companion to Jewish American Literature.* Cambridge, England: Cambridge University Press, 2003.

Lesser, Wendy. "Poetic Sense and Sensibility." In *Contemporary Literary Criticism,* vol. 44, ed. Sharon K. Hall. Detroit: Gale Research, 1986.

Levinas, Emmanuel. *Totality and Infinity: An Essay on Exteriority.* Translated by Alphonso Lingis. Pittsburgh, Pa.: Duquesne University Press, 1969.

Levitt, Laura. *Jews and Feminism: The Ambivalent Search for Home.* New York: Routledge, 1997.

Longenbach, James. "Letter to the Editor." *PMLA* 115.7 (December 2000): 2058.

———. "Poetry in Review." *Yale Review* 84.4 (October 1996): 158–69.

Lowell, Robert. "Epilogue." In *The Longman Anthology of Poetry,* ed. Lynne McMahon and Averill Curdy. New York: Pearson Longman, 2006.

———. "Interviewed by Frederick Seidel." A 1961 *Paris Review* interview reprinted in *Robert Lowell: A Collection of Critical Essays,* 12–35. Englewood, N.J.: Prentice Hall, 1968.

———. "Skunk Hour." In *Twentieth-Century American Poetry,* ed. Dana Gioia, David Mason, and Meg Schoerke. Boston: McGraw-Hill, 2004.

Lyotard, Jean-François. *The Postmodern Condition: A Report on Knowledge.* Translated by Geoff Bennington and Brian Massumi. Minneapolis: University of Minnesota Press, 1984.

Matson, Suzanne. "Without Relation: Family and Freedom in the Poetry of Louise Glück." *Mid-American Review* 14.2 (1994): 88–109.

Mellor, Anne K. *Romanticism and Gender.* New York: Routledge, 1993.

Miklitsch, Robert. "Assembling a Landscape: The Poetry of Louise Glück." *Hollins Critic* 19.4 (Oct. 1982): 1–13.

Mitchell, Stephen, trans. *The Book of Job.* New York: HarperCollins, 1992.

Molnar, Michael R. *The Star of Bethlehem: The Legacy of the Magi.* New

Brunswick, N.J.: Rutgers University Press, 1999.

Morris, Daniel, ed. *Poetry's Poet: Essays on the Poetry, Pedagogy, and Poetics of Allen Grossman.* Orono, Me.: National Poetry Foundation, 2004.

Munich, Adrienne. "Notorious Signs, Feminist Criticism, and Literary Tradition." In *Making a Difference: Feminist Literary Criticism,* ed. Gayle Greene and Coppelia Kahn, 238–60. London: Methuen, 1985.

Muske, Carol. "The Wild Iris." *American Poetry Review* 22.1 (January–February 1993): 52–54.

Osherow, Jacqueline. *Dead Men's Praise.* New York: Grove Atlantic, 1999.

Ozick, Cynthia. "Notes toward Finding the Right Question (A Vindication of the Rights of Jewish Women)." *Forum 35* (Spring–Summer 1979): 37–60.

Payne, Michael. *Reading Theory: An Introduction to Lacan, Derrida, and Kristeva.* Oxford: Blackwell, 1993.

Peskowitz, Miriam, and Laura Levitt, eds. *Judaism since Gender.* New York: Routledge, 1997.

Petuchowsky, Jakob J. *Understanding Jewish Prayer.* New York: Ktav Publishing, 1972.

Phillips, Adam. *Promises, Promises: Essays on Literature and Psychoanalysis.* New York: Basic Books, 2001.

Pinsky, Robert, ed. *Americans' Favorite Poems: The Favorite Poem Project Anthology.* New York: Norton, 2000.

———. *The Life of David.* New York: Schocken Books, 2005.

Plaskow, Judith. *Standing Again at Sinai: Judaism from a Feminist Perspective.* San Francisco: Harper, 1990.

Pope, Justin. "Poet Laureate Glück Will Do It Her Way." *Capital Times: Web Edition.* November 19, 2003.

Ramazani, Jahan, Richard Ellmann, and Robert O'Clair, eds. *The Norton Anthology of Modern and Contemporary Poetry.* Vol. 1. 3rd ed. New York: Norton, 2003.

Rich, Adrienne. "Diving into the Wreck." In *Norton Anthology of Modern and Contemporary Poetry.* Vol. 2, *Contemporary Poetry.* 3rd ed. New York: Norton, 2003.

———. "Split at the Root: An Essay on Jewish Identity." In *Adrienne Rich's Poetry and Prose,* ed. Barbara Charlesworth Gelpi and Arthur Gelpi, 224–38. New York: Norton, 1993.

Robinson, James. "Louise Glück." In *Contemporary Poets,* 6th ed., 394–96. New York: St. James Press, 1996.

Robinson, Lilian S. "Treason Our Text: Feminist Challenges to the Literary Canon." In *The New Feminist Criticism: Essays on Women, Literature,*

Theory, ed. Elaine Showalter, 105–22. New York: Pantheon, 1985.

Rosen, Norma. "Midrash, Bible, and Women's Voices." *Judaism* 180.45.4 (Fall 1996): 442–45.

Rosenberg, Liz. "Geckos, Porch Lights, and Sighing Gardens." *New York Times Book Review,* December 22, 1985, 22–23. Reprinted in *Contemporary Literary Criticism Yearbook–1986,* ed. Sharon K. Hall, 215. Detroit: Gale Publications, 1986.

Rosenthal, M. L. *Running to Paradise: Yeats's Poetic Art.* New York: Oxford University Press, 1994.

Rubin, Steven J., ed. *Telling and Remembering: A Century of American Jewish Poetry.* Boston: Beacon, 1997.

Satlof, Claire. "History, Fiction, and the Tradition: Creating a Jewish Feminist Poetic." In Heschel, *Jewish Feminist.*

Scarry, Elaine. *Dreaming the Body.* New York: Farrar, Straus and Giroux, 1999.

Schwartz, Delmore. "In Dreams Begin Responsibilities." In *Jewish American Literature: A Norton Anthology,* ed. Hilene Flanzbaum et al., 540–45. New York: Norton, 2001.

Schwarz, Daniel R. *Imagining the Holocaust.* New York: St. Martin's Press, 1999.

Sedgwick, Eve Kosofsky. *Between Men: English Literature and Male Homosocial Desire.* New York: Columbia University Press, 1985.

Selinger, Eric. "'It Meant I Loved': Louise Glück's *Ararat.*" *Postmodern Culture* 3.3 (May 1993): 1–29.

———. "Shekhinah in America." In Barron and Selinger, *Jewish American Poetry,* 250–71.

Shakespeare, William. *King Lear.* New York: Signet, 1963.

Shapiro, Alan. "Some Questions concerning Art and Suffering." *Tikkun* 19.1 (January–February 2004): 28–32.

Shaw, Robert B. "Review of *The Triumph of Achilles.*" *Poetry* 148.1 (April 1986): 42–44.

Shreiber, Maerra. "A Flair for Deviation: The Troublesome Potential of Jewish Poetics." In Barron and Selinger, *Jewish American Poetry,* 272–83.

———. "Jewish American Poetry." In Kramer and Wirth-Nesher, *Jewish American Literature,* 149–69.

———. "'Spiritual Warfare': Allen Grossman on the Relation between Poetry and the Institutions of Holiness, with Special Reference to Reznikoff's *Testimony.*" In Morris, *Poetry's Poet.*

Smith, Anne-Marie. *Julia Kristeva: Speaking the Unspeakable.* London: Pluto Press, 1998.

Sollors, Werner. *Beyond Ethnicity: Consent and Descent in American Literature.* New York: Oxford University Press, 1986.

Stallworthy, Jon, and David Daiches, eds. *The Norton Anthology of English Literature: The Twentieth Century.* New York: Norton, 2000.

Stern, David. *Midrash and Theory.* Evanston, Ill.: Northwestern University Press, 1996.

Stevens, Wallace. *Letters of Wallace Stevens.* Edited by Holly Stevens. New York: Knopf, 1966.

———. "Notes toward a Supreme Fiction." In *Stevens: Poems,* selected by Helen Vendler. New York: Knopf, 1993.

———. *The Palm at the End of the Mind: Selected Poems and a Play.* Edited by Holly Stevens. New York: Vintage, 1990.

———. "Sunday Morning." In Ramazani et al., *Norton Anthology.*

Stitt, Peter. "Contemporary American Poems: Exclusive and Inclusive." In *Contemporary Literary Criticism Yearbook–1986,* ed. Sharon K. Hall, 214–15. Detroit: Gale Publications, 1986.

Strand, Mark. *October.* New York: Sarabande Books, 2004.

Telushkin, Joseph. *Biblical Literacy: The Most Important People, Events, and Ideas of the Hebrew Bible.* New York: William Morrow, 1997.

Townsend, Ann. "The Problem of Sincerity: The Lyric Plain Style of George Herbert and Louise Glück." *Shenandoah* 46.4 (Winter 1996): 43–61.

Trakas, Deno. "Louise Glück." In *American Poets since World War II, Part 1 (A–K). Dictionary of Literary Biography,* 290–95. Detroit: Gale Publications, 1980.

Unterecker, John. *A Reader's Guide to William Butler Yeats.* New York: Noonday, 1959.

Vendler, Helen. "In the Zoo of the New." *New York Times Book Review,* October 23, 1986, 47–52.

———. "Louise Glück." In *A Part of Nature, Part of Us: Modern American Poets,* 303–11. Cambridge, Mass.: Harvard University Press, 1980.

———. *The Music of What Happens: Poems, Poets, Critics.* Cambridge, Mass.: Harvard University Press, 1988.

———. *Poems, Poets, Poetry: An Introduction and Anthology.* New York: St. Martin's Press, 1997.

———. "Review of *The House on Marshland.*" *New York Times Book Review,* April 6, 1975, 37–38.

———. "Sociable Comets." *New York Review of Books,* July 16, 1981, 24–26.

———. *Soul Says: On Recent Poetry.* Cambridge, Mass.: Harvard University Press, 1995.

Wilkie, Brian, ed. *Literature of the Western World: Volume 1.* Upper Saddle River, N.J.: Prentice Hall, 1997.

Williamson, Alan. *Contemporary Poetry and Introspection.* Cambridge, Mass.: Harvard University Press, 1984.

Wolosky, Shira. "On Contemporary Literary Theory and Jewish American Poetics." In Kramer and Wirth-Nesher, *Jewish American Literature,* 250–68.

Wooten, Anna. "Louise Glück's *The House on Marshland.*" *American Poetry Review* 4 (July–August 1975): 5–6.

Wordsworth, William. "Lines Composed a Few Miles above Tintern Abbey, on Revisiting the Banks of the Wye During a Tour, July 13, 1798." In Abrams et al., *Norton Anthology of English Literature,* 236.

Yeats, William Butler. "Among School Children." In Ramazani et al., *Norton Anthology.*

———. "The Magi." In Ramazani et al., *Norton Anthology.*

———. *Selected Poems and Two Plays of William Butler Yeats.* Edited by M. L. Rosenthal. New York: Collier, 1962.

Yezierska, Anzia. *Bread Givers: A Struggle between a Father of the Old World and a Daughter of the New.* 1925. New York: Persea Books, 1975.

Žižek, Slavoj. *Looking Awry: An Introduction to Jacques Lacan through Popular Culture.* Cambridge, Mass.: MIT Press, 1991.

Index

About the Author

Daniel Morris is Professor of English at Purdue University. He is author of *The Writings of William Carlos Williams: Publicity for the Self* (University of Missouri Press, 1995), *Remarkable Modernisms: Contemporary American Authors on Modern Art* (2002), *After Weegee: Essays on Contemporary Jewish American Photographers* (2011), *Lyric Encounters* (2013), *Not Born Digital: Poetics, Print Literacy, New Media* (2016), and *Kenneth Goldsmith's Recent Work on Paper* (2019). He has also published four volumes of poetry, including *Hit Play* (2015) and *Blue Poles* (2019).